Renaissance Public Participation

Construction [of the Duomo in Florence, Italy] was frequently delayed during the fourteenth century by the diversion of resources to other projects, by disagreements over building plans, and by public indifference and inertia. The construction of the cathedral was primarily a civic, not an ecclesiastical enterprise; the commune provided most of the money for the project, and delegated responsibility for the building to the Lana guild, the corporation of cloth manufacturers. The guild appointed four of its members as *operi,* with six-month terms of office, to supervise the work. These *operi* frequently requested advice from citizens with specialized knowledge—builders, sculptors, painters, goldsmiths—and on a few occasions organized a referendum on building plans in which "every person in the city of whatever status or condition" was invited to participate.

—Gene A. Brucker, *Renaissance Florence*

THE PUBLIC PARTICIPATION HANDBOOK

THE PUBLIC PARTICIPATION HANDBOOK

Making Better Decisions Through Citizen Involvement

James L. Creighton

JOSSEY-BASS
A Wiley Imprint
www.josseybass.com

Published by Jossey-Bass
A Wiley Imprint
989 Market Street, San Francisco, CA 94103-1741   www.josseybass.com

Jossey-Bass books and products are available through most bookstores. To contact Jossey-Bass directly
call our Customer Care Department within the U.S. at 800-956-7739, outside the U.S. at 317-572-3993
or fax 317-572-4002.

Jossey-Bass also publishes its books in a variety of electronic formats. Some content that appears in print
may not be available in electronic books.

Readers should be aware that Internet Web sites listed in this work may have changed or disappeared
between when this work was written and when it is read.

Library of Congress Cataloging-in-Publication Data

Creighton, James L.
  The public participation handbook : making better decisions through citizen involvement / James L.
Creighton.—1st ed.
    p. cm.
  Includes bibliographical references and index.
  ISBN 0-7879-7307-6 (alk. paper)
  1. Political participation—United States—Handbooks, manuals, etc. I. Title.
  JK1764.C733 2005
  352.3'7—dc22

                                                                        2005000732

Printed in the United States of America
FIRST EDITION
HB Printing   10 9 8 7 6 5 4 3 2 1

CONTENTS

TABLES, FIGURES, EXHIBITS, AND WORKSHEETS

Tables

Figures

Exhibits

Worksheets

PREFACE

I've been conducting public participation programs since 1972 when a representative from a government agency called me and said, "There's a new law that's been passed that requires us to hold public meetings to discuss our proposed timber sales. We're spending all our time in our planning meetings discussing how many police we have to have to prevent a riot. Can you do any better?"

Fortunately I was able to do somewhat better, and since then I've been involved in designing and conducting more than three hundred public participation programs on topics as diverse as forest management, water development and water quality, nuclear waste cleanup, prescribed burning, community planning, electric power rates, transportation planning, siting of electric and gas transmission lines and substations, health effects of electric and magnetic fields, welfare reform, low-income housing, and many more.

This book draws on my own experience and the experience of numerous other practitioners in the field. Those of us who have been involved from the early days in the field did not find the answers on how to design an effective public participation program in any one discipline. We borrowed heavily from techniques and skills developed in the group dynamics field, from people like Thomas Gordon, particularly valuable insights on interpersonal communication skills and facilitative meeting leadership. We traded techniques back and forth with people in the organization development field on how to design and conduct interactive meetings. From the field of sociology, we borrowed insights on values research, interviewing, survey research, and identification of those in the community who are influential. Because public participation always includes a component of communicating information to the public, we used the best we could find in communications theory, as well as the practical insights and skills of people working with the media. For supporting rationale, we turned to the participatory management literature, such as the works of Douglas MacGregor (1960), and later to a new generation of political theorists, such as Carole Pateman (1970) and Benjamin Barber (1984). More recently, the field has been informed by insights from the literature on deliberative democracy, which emphasizes both participation and the creation of mechanisms for informed dialogue (Rawls, 1993; Habermas, 1996; Dryzec, 2000; Macedo, 1999), as well as the field of risk communication (Slovic, 2000; Flynn, Slovic, and Kunreuther, 2001).

The benefit of this eclectic approach was that we were not constrained by any particular discipline that imposed its rules about how things should be done. But this also meant that public participation did not fit comfortably in any one academic discipline. Previous books I've written on public participation have been used in university courses in urban planning, forestry, public relations, political science, civil engineering, and architecture.

The field has been developed largely by people with the bias of the craftsman, not the theorist or academic scientist. As we tried things out, the question was always, "Does this idea or technique help me solve the problem?" If in our own experience it worked, particularly if it worked several times, we added it to our personal tool kit, and others in the field quickly emulated it.

Those who seek rigorous empirical studies to verify all the counsel I offer in this book could be disappointed. Efforts to study public participation empirically have been sporadic and sometimes unconvincing to those actually conducting everyday programs. Some recent works by Beierle and Cayford (2002), Burby (2003), and others hold out hope that this gap is being filled. An extensive literature is developing in Europe, as well as a number of studies related to the use of participation in international development projects.

While this base of empirical research grows, I have presented what I believe is the best available advice based on the actual experience of practitioners. It has worked for me, and I hope it will also work for you.

My thinking has been influenced and informed by working with many other practitioners in the field. I particularly acknowledge colleagues such as Jerome Delli Priscoli, Lorenz Aggens, Martha Rozelle, and others too numerous to mention. There have also been many clients along the way who have contributed with their support and the opportunity to try out new ideas.

My wife, Maggie Creighton, has worked with me in the field off and on since the first client asked for public participation training more than thirty years ago.

Precisely because she approaches things differently than I do, she has taught me how to work with people in ways that would not have occurred to me. She has played a crucial role in my life and in my work.

My thanks to the team at Jossey-Bass—Dorothy Hearst and Allison Brunner—for their enthusiasm and support in making this book possible.

Los Gatos, California   James L. Creighton
January 2005

References

Barber, B. *Strong Democracy: Participatory Politics for a New Age.* Berkeley: University of California Press, 1984.

Beierle, T., and Cayford, J. *Democracy in Practice: Public Participation in Environmental Decisions.* Washington, D.C.: Resources for the Future, 2002.

Burby, R. J. "Making Plans that Matter: Citizen Involvement and Government Action." *Journal of the American Planning Association*, 2003, *46*(1), 33–49.

Dryzek, J. S. *Deliberative Democracy and Beyond: Liberals, Critics, Contestations.* New York: Oxford University Press, 2000.

Flynn, J., Slovic, P., and Kunreuther, H. *Risk, Media and Stigma.* London: Earthscan, 2001.

Gordon, T. *Leader Effectiveness Training: The Proven People Skills for Today's Leaders Tomorrow.* New York: Berkley Publishing Group, 2001. (Originally published 1977.)

Habermas, J. *Between Facts and Norms: Contributions to a Discourse Theory of Law and Democracy.* Cambridge, Mass: MIT Press, 1996.

Macedo, S. *Deliberative Politics: Essays on Democracy and Disagreement.* New York: Oxford University Press, 1999.

MacGregor, D. *The Human Side of Enterprise.* New York: McGraw-Hill/Irwin, 1985. (Originally published 1960.)

Pateman, C. *Participation and Democratic Theory.* Cambridge: Cambridge University Press, 1970.

Rawls, J. *Political Liberalism.* New York: Columbia University Press, 1993.

Slovic, P. *The Perception of Risk.* London: Earthscan, 2000.

THE AUTHOR

James L. Creighton, Ph.D., is the president of Creighton & Creighton in Los Gatos, California. He has been an independent consultant in the public participation field since 1972 and has designed or conducted more than three hundred public participation programs. He is the founding president of the International Association for Public Participation, an international organization of professionals and people interested in the public participation field. He is the author of *The Public Participation Manual* (Abt Books, 1981) and *Involving Citizens in Community Decision Making* (National Civic League, 1992), and author or coauthor of four other books, including *Getting Well Again*, an international best seller. He has written more than thirty guides on public participation and related topics for government agencies and trade associations. His client list includes more than fifty federal or state agencies and many companies in the United States and Canada, and he has also been involved in public participation or dispute resolution projects or training in Russia, the Republic of Georgia, Egypt, Brazil, Japan, and Thailand.

THE PUBLIC
PARTICIPATION
HANDBOOK

INTRODUCTION

Democracy is a work in progress. Our understanding of what democracy means has evolved over time. There is no one single form of democracy, as the variety in forms of governance in democratic countries illustrates. The challenge is always to realize democracy in practice.

Another experiment in democracy is underway today. Increasingly, public participation in governmental decision making is considered part of the very definition of democracy. Public participation is now a legal requirement or prerequisite for governmental decision making in most of the Western world. Public participation requirements have been embedded in virtually every important piece of environmental legislation in the United States and Canada since the 1970s. More than thirty-five European countries are signatories to the 1998 Aarhus Convention, formally known as the United Nations Economic Commission for Europe Convention on Access to Information, Public Participation in Decision Making, and Access to Justice in Environmental Matters, which took effect in 2001. Those signatory governments commit to take steps to ensure public participation and access to information in all environmental decision making. Public participation is also a prerequisite for international economic development project funding by the World Bank and the various regional banks. Many companies have also conducted public participation programs as part of decisions about management of natural resources, siting of facilities, and environmental cleanup or remediation.

The example of public participation in Renaissance Florence shown on the frontispiece of this book clearly illustrates that public participation is not a new discovery. What is new is that public participation in agency decision making is increasingly considered standard practice. Many recent political theorists argue that it is a defining characteristic of modern democracy. As two British theorists recently put it, "Democracy without citizen deliberation and participation is ultimately an empty and meaningless concept" (Pimbert and Wakeford, 2001, p. 23).

It is one thing to make a commitment to public participation in the abstract. It is quite another to do it. There have always been and continue to be challenges translating the ideals of democracy into practical institutions. There are many challenges translating the concept of public participation into the sometimes harsh reality of everyday interaction between agencies or companies and the public. There are the realities of budgets and legal constraints. There is a need to make expeditious decisions. There is a need to base decisions on the best available scientific and technical information, even if at times large segments of the public are badly informed or ignorant of the basic premises of the scientific method. There are external political realities.

This book is written for the thousands of people in federal, state, or local agencies, community organizations, or corporations who see the value of involving the public in decisions made by their organizations but seek practical guidance on how to do this effectively. As the word *handbook* in the title suggests, this is essentially a how-to book, written from the perspective of a practitioner for people who will be designing and conducting public participation programs.

The primary focus of this book is the pragmatics of designing and conducting public participation programs. But some theory is needed, particularly for those new to the field. In Part One, I provide a brief overview of what public participation is, the characteristics of effective public participation, and the benefits that can be derived from its use.

There is no such thing as a one-size-fits-all public participation (and beware of people who think there is). But there are critical issues that can make the difference between a successful and an unsuccessful program. Part Two provides a thought process for how to design a public participation program. The thought process has three stages—decision analysis, process planning, and implementation planning—with each stage becoming more specific as you move through the thought process. At the end of this thought process, you could arrive at a different solution from someone else addressing the same issues. But you will have a clear rationale for why you are doing what you have decided to do and reasonable confidence that there are not major gaps in your thinking.

Part Three provides an overview of public participation techniques—both techniques for getting information to the public and techniques for getting information from or interacting with the public. If you are new to the field, you will probably find it helpful to read both chapters in this part in detail, so that you have a good sense of how and when to use the various techniques set out in this book. If you are already experienced in the field, you may want to skim these chapters, stopping on those techniques with which you are less familiar, or using these chapters as a checklist to remind you of techniques that you could be using.

No matter what kind of public participation program you develop, you will usually end up conducting some kind of meetings. Part Four specifically addresses public meetings, describing different kinds of meeting formats, the thought process for selecting a particular meeting format, designing and conducting interactive meetings, meeting leadership, and meeting logistics.

Part Five contains a series of chapters on the use of general-purpose public participation tools. It contains chapters on working with advisory groups, conducting interviews, working with the media, analyzing public comment, evaluating public comment, and use of consultants.

Part Six contains a single chapter that presents three cases illustrating three very different participation strategies and the reasons for choosing those strategies.

The book ends with a brief coda—a summary of basic themes from throughout the book.

Reference

Pimbert, M., and Wakeford, T. "Overview: Deliberative Democracy and Citizen Empowerment." *PLA Notes,* 2001, *40*, 23–28. [www.iied.org/docs/pla/pla_fs_5.pdf].

PART ONE

OVERVIEW OF PUBLIC PARTICIPATION

This book shows how to design and conduct a public participation from beginning to end. But before discussing the mechanics of public participation, the theory of public participation needs to be addressed.

Chapter One provides a definition of public participation. Then it addresses two challenging questions. The first question is, What does *participation* mean? It's fine to say that participation is a virtuous thing. But does that mean only that citizens have a chance to comment before decisions are made, or does it mean that agencies can make decisions only when the public agrees with the agency's proposed action?

The second question is, Why do agencies retain decision-making authority? Many agencies are willing to open up their decision-making processes to the public, but in most circumstances, they stress that they retain the ultimate decision-making authority. Is this undemocratic, or is it necessary to provide accountability in a democratic system?

Chapter Two examines the rationale for public participation. No discussion of public participation is complete without looking at the role of expertise and technical knowledge in decision making. Many technical people, and many of those in agencies, do not perceive the need for public participation in decisions they view as technical in nature. But many decisions agencies view as technical in nature are, in fact, values choices about what is good or important, informed by expert technical information. What is the public's role in making these fundamental values choices?

Public participation requires extra effort, an expenditure of staff time and energy that agencies do not have to make when they make top-down decisions. What are the benefits that agencies can hope to receive in return for this additional effort?

Some kinds of public participation programs are more likely to achieve these benefits than others. What are the characteristics—in my experience, at least—of public participation programs that are effective in achieving these benefits?

CHAPTER ONE

DEFINING WHAT PUBLIC PARTICIPATION IS (AND IS NOT)

Public participation is the process by which public concerns, needs, and values are incorporated into governmental and corporate decision making. It is two-way communication and interaction, with the overall goal of better decisions that are supported by the public.

I have surveyed other definitions of public participation and find that most include at least these elements:

- Public participation applies to administrative decisions—that is, those typically made by agencies (and sometimes by private organizations), not elected officials or judges.
- Public participation is not just providing information to the public. There is interaction between the organization making the decision and people who want to participate.
- There is an organized process for involving the public. It is not something that happens accidentally or coincidentally.
- The participants have some level of impact or influence on the decision being made.

The International Association for Public Participation (IAP2) approaches the definition of public participation by defining core values of public participation, as shown in Exhibit 1.1. But the same critical elements emerge.

EXHIBIT 1.1. INTERNATIONAL ASSOCIATION FOR PUBLIC PARTICIPATION CORE VALUES FOR THE PRACTICE OF PUBLIC PARTICIPATION.

- The public should have a say in decisions about actions that affect their lives.
- Public participation includes the promise that the public's contribution will influence the decision.
- The public participation process communicates the interests and meets the process needs of all participants.
- The public participation process seeks out and facilitates the involvement of those potentially affected.
- The public participation process involves participants in defining how they participate.
- The public participation process provides participants with the information they need to participate in a meaningful way.
- The public participation process communicates to participants how their input affected the decision.

Source: International Association for Public Participation. Copyright © 2000 International Association for Public Participation. All rights reserved. [http://iap2.org/practitionertools/index.shtml]. Reproduced with permission.

These definitions of public participation also exclude some kinds of participation that are legitimate components of democratic society: the electoral process, lawsuits, and strikes and extralegal protests. These forms of participation are important to citizen activism, but they are not the kind of participation discussed here.

What Does *Participation* Mean?

The word *participation* has many different meanings. Some people use it as if it were synonymous with public information programs—getting the word out to the public. It is frequently used to describe public hearings at which the public comments on what an agency proposes to do. It has also been used to imply that an agreement is reached with the public that will be affected by it.

No one can design a public participation program without being clear on which interpretation applies in their particular program.

Participation is best understood as a continuum. Since it is a continuum, there are really an infinite number of points along the scale, but for our purposes there are the four major categories shown in Figure 1.1:

FIGURE 1.1. CONTINUUM OF PARTICIPATION.

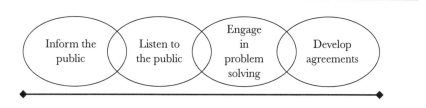

Note: For a more detailed portrayal of such a continuum, see the International Association for Public Participation's Public Participation Spectrum, downloadable at http://iap2.org/practitionertools/index.shtml.

1. Inform the public.
2. Listen to the public.
3. Engage in problem solving.
4. Develop agreements.

Public Information and Public Relations

Public information programs are essentially one-way communication to the public. They are an integral part of the paternalistic decide-announce-defend so often derided in the public participation literature. But although public information by itself does not constitute public participation, it remains an essential component of an effective public participation program. People cannot participate unless they receive complete and objective information on which to base their judgments.

Procedural Public Participation

Many agencies have initiated two mechanisms for improved participation: public hearings, at which the public can comment on proposed actions, and increased access to information, by issuing reports (for example, environmental impact statements) or establishing information repositories, locations where the public has access to all relevant studies and documents. These mechanisms can be referred to as "procedural" public participation or even "checklist" public participation. They serve an important function—in the absence of other kinds of public participation—because they force a certain degree of openness and create a legal record on which decisions can be based (and challenged in court). But they can become simply a procedural hoop through which the agency must jump, without having much impact on the decision and no chance for collaborative problem solving.

Consultation and Collaborative Problem Solving

Government agencies have had considerably greater success working collaboratively with the public to find a solution that will enjoy broad support. This approach does not always result in agreements. Sometimes all that occurs is that the positions are clarified through interaction and everybody understands the reasoning behind the decision. Sometimes sufficient agreement is built that the agency is able to proceed with sufficient legitimacy that there is tacit acceptance even by those who do not support the action.

Hans and Annamarie Bleiker (1994) have used the term *informed consent* to describe this level of participation. They write, "We define 'informed consent' as: the grudging willingness of opponents to (grudgingly) 'go along' with a course of action that they—actually—are opposed to" (p. I-7). In my experience, there is often a small base of opposition that continues to fight on, but there is a sufficient level of consensus so that political opposition is marginalized and overcome easily.

I have described this collaborative approach elsewhere as consensus seeking (Creighton, 1992). That is, the agency seeks as high a level of consensus as possible, but it doesn't always get a consensus and it reserves the right to make a final decision if consensus is not reached. But there is a degree of power sharing in that the agency engages in collaborative problem solving in an effort to get as high a level of acceptance as possible.

When the process is over, the public has usually influenced the decision even if there is no final agreement and the agency retains the ultimate authority to act. The public's influence may have helped to determine how the problem was defined, the range of alternatives that were considered, the evaluation criteria that were applied, and the process by which the decision was made, even if there is not agreement on the final result.

Getting Agreement and Consensus Building

One problem with the use of the term *consensus seeking* is that it is readily confused with the term *consensus building*, which increasingly is used for processes that have the goal of reaching full agreement. As Lawrence Susskind (1999, p. 6), one of the leading advocates of the consensus-building approach, states: "Consensus building is a process of seeking unanimous agreement. It involves a good-faith effort to meet the interests of all stakeholders. Consensus has been reached when everyone agrees they can live with whatever is proposed after every effort had been made to meet the interests of all stakeholding parties." Then he hedges this somewhat: "Most dispute resolution professionals believe that groups or assemblies should seek unanimity, but settle for overwhelming agreement that goes as far as possible toward meeting the interests of all stakeholders" (p. 7).

The clear advantage of the "agreement" approach is that if there is genuine agreement, the agency can proceed with reasonable confidence that implementation is ensured. This assumes, of course, that the agency itself concurs with the decision being made and has the legal and budgetary authority to implement the consensus decision. It also assumes that those who signed on to the agreement in fact represent the constituencies they claim to represent and can deliver the support of these constituencies for the agreement. If these preconditions are not met, the agreement-seeking approach can create expectations that, if unfulfilled, may sour the relationship with citizens even more.

What Level of Participation Is Right?

An experienced practitioner of public participation will answer the question, "What level of participation is right?" with an authoritative, "It depends." From the perspective of a practitioner, the question that must be answered is very practical: What kind of participation is required for the decision to have the legitimacy it needs so that once the agency reaches a decision, it is able to implement that decision? How much participation is required for a decision to actually count?

I have seen circumstances where it has been appropriate to be at each of the four points along the continuum. If an agency is, by virtue of legislation or executive decision, precommitted to a single course of action, it is far better that this agency simply inform the public (or at most go through the mechanics of a public hearing) than employ a bogus process of participation that has no chance of having an impact on the outcome. This doesn't mean that the public will see the process as legitimate (although this depends on the extent to which the public sees the action as addressing a significant problem that requires immediate action). But even if the process of making this one decision is not perceived as legitimate, at least it will be seen as honest. A bogus participatory process destroys the credibility of all future attempts to provide genuine participation on other issues.

At the other end of the continuum, the conditions under which an agency decides to enter into direct negotiations with stakeholders to achieve an agreement are very restrictive. But they do occur, and techniques to get agreement, such as negotiations, should be employed when those conditions prevail.

If a decision has the potential to be controversial, the decision is more likely to be perceived as legitimate if there has been a genuine effort to engage in problem solving rather than a pro forma public hearing. But even that choice can be constrained by schedule, budget, and political realities.

The question is not, "What can we get away with?" but, "What does it take for the decision to count?" You may be able to get away with a lesser level of participation during the decision-making process, only to discover that you are unable to implement your decision due to public opposition and the lack of legitimacy for your decision-making process.

Why Do Agencies Retain Decision-Making Authority?

In public participation, the agency retains the ultimate decision-making authority, although it may choose to share that decision making in return for a higher level of public acceptance. For some people, this makes public participation seem something less than true democracy, a failure to grant power to the people. But there are compelling reasons that agencies retain ultimate decision-making power even if they find it in their enlightened self-interest to share some portion of that power:

• Agencies are constrained by mandates and authorities that limit what they can do. As frustrating as these mandates and authorities can be, there must be an orderly process for addressing them, or soon agencies would do whatever they wanted, and without any accountability to the public. Although the line of accountability back to elected officials is often long and tenuous, it must always be there. Otherwise, any claim by the bureaucracy to democratic legitimacy is false.

• In many cases, agencies are implementing laws. If the public brings sufficient pressure to bear on elected officials, these laws can be changed. But otherwise, the agency must operate within the constraints imposed by the law.

• Agencies often have contractual obligations they must meet. If they abrogate contracts and other legal obligations whenever public sentiment wants them to, they will soon be unable to enter into any binding contract, and all existing actions will be stalled by litigation.

• The public that achieves consensus may do so because it isn't paying the costs. A public participation program that gets a consensus that everybody else should pay for the special benefit of a few has to be balanced by some intervening authority that can require attention to the needs of everybody who is paying for the project.

• Controversies over the actions of government agencies are most frequently the result of genuine disagreements within the public about what should be done.

• In the final analysis, those who choose to participate in a public participation program are self-selecting. Their only job is to represent their self-interest, not discern the public interest. Because they do not, and cannot, claim to be "the public" in the same way that an election speaks for "the public," their contribution can be influential but cannot dictate the final decision.

Just as participation is an essential ingredient of democracy, so is accountability. Public participation programs may influence agency decisions, but they cannot be substituted for them.

References

Bleiker, H., and Bleiker, A. *Citizen Participation Handbook for Public Officials and Other Professionals Serving the Public.* (8th ed.) Monterey, Calif.: Institute for Participatory Management and Planning, 1994.

Creighton, J. L. *Involving Citizens in Community Decision Making.* Washington, D.C.: Program for Community Problem Solving, National League of Cities, 1992.

Susskind, L. "An Alternative to Robert's Rules of Order for Groups, Organizations, and Ad Hoc Assemblies That Want to Operate by Consensus." In L. Susskind, S. McKearnan, and J. Thomas-Larmer (eds.), *The Consensus Building Handbook.* Thousand Oaks, Calif.: Sage Publications, 1999.

CHAPTER TWO

THE RATIONALE FOR PUBLIC PARTICIPATION

Why is public participation beginning to be viewed as an integral part of democracy itself? Traditionally, the defining characteristic of democracy is the right to elect the leaders of the government. The theory is that elected officials make the important decisions and then hold the bureaucracies accountable for implementing these decisions. But today the executive branches of governments make numerous decisions on an everyday basis—administrative decisions—that have the gravest import for the societies these bureaucracies serve. Since the 1930s, the size and scope of all levels of government have expanded rapidly in the United States and all other industrial nations. In addition, the scope of the decisions being made has expanded greatly, touching more and more aspects of people's lives.

As the size and scope of government have grown, decisions previously made by elected officials in a political process were delegated to technical experts in large bureaucracies. An extensive management literature grew up describing methodologies for "scientific decision making" and techniques for "maximizing benefits." Decisions could capture "the public interest," it was alleged, by scientifically analyzing "the greatest good for the greatest number."

In an age when even elected representatives bemoan their inability to control the bureaucracies, the role of the bureaucracy in decision making is a major challenge to democratic theory. When major decisions are delegated to unelected bureaucrats, how do we ensure that the will of the people is expressed in those decisions? To what extent do the interests of the bureaucracy itself distort or conflict with the public interest?

The question of the authority of expertise in administrative decision making is fundamental to democracy. The hidden premise of leaving it to the experts is that experts are somehow superior in discerning what is right for society. A corollary is that if an issue is complicated, the public cannot deal with it. As a result, in most government agencies, the question is framed as, "Why should the public be involved in technical decisions?" The answer is that the public does not need to take part in technical decisions—but agencies make many decisions they believe are technical that in fact are not.

Experts cannot make decisions without assigning a weight or priority to competing values that society believes are good. When decisions are made about what level of health or safety risk is "acceptable," how much it is "reasonable" to pay to protect an environmental resource, or how costs should be distributed among various classes of people, these are not technical decisions even if they involve a great deal of technical information. These are decisions about values or philosophy.

The hard choices that agency managers make are decisions between competing benefits that society views as "good," such as affordability, equity, environmental protection, or safety. Agency managers have to decide the reasonable balance point given the present state of knowledge.

Imagine for a minute that a community is bisected by a river. There is serious pollution in the river—so much that nobody dares swim or fish in it. The pollution comes from a number of sources: an upstream manufacturing plant, return flows from upstream agriculture, runoff from city streets.

Who is better qualified to make decisions about what should be done to clean up the river: the public or technical experts? Most people would agree that technical experts are best qualified if the decision is:

- How much pollution is in the river, and what kind
- How the pollution could be cleaned up
- What the costs of each cleanup alternative would be
- What levels of exposure are associated with health risk

Assuming that the technical experts have made all these judgments without perceptual blinders and other technical experts reviewing their work agree that the work was done well and meets recognized professional standards, a decision must still be made about how much cleanup should occur. Suddenly everything gets harder, because cleaning up the river to the point it is clean enough so people can swim in it safely or eat fish caught in it may require shutting down the upstream factory, necessitate expensive changes to irrigation practices, or require additional treatment of discharges from community sewers. At a minimum, the project will use up funds that could otherwise be allocated to education, housing, health care, or filling potholes.

As long as they are considering only one values dimension at a time, whether it is cost, health risk, or feasibility, technical experts are the best-qualified people to make the call. But the minute a technical expert has to choose between two values, the issue is no longer simply technical: it is a decision about what is more important, jobs or clean water, individual freedom or environmental protection, human health concerns or the needs of other species. By their very nature, these decisions are values choices. Most hard decisions—what are normally called policy decisions—are essentially this kind of values choice, informed with technical information.

Values choices involve assigning a weight or priority to one thing society thinks is good compared to another thing society thinks is good. In Figure 2.1, someone who supports Policy A believes that the social good on the left side of the scale is more than twice as important as the social good on the right side. Policy B strives to give them equal weight. Policy C reverses the priority.

There is nothing about technical training that makes technical experts more qualified than others to make values choices—even when technical experts hold management positions that require they make such decisions. This is not to say that technical experts don't have opinions about such matters; in fact, one of the criticisms of engineers is that they often assume that the cheapest workable solution is—virtually by definition—also the best. But that simply means that engineering training teaches people to place a very high value on cost. Someone whose primary interest is worker safety or environmental protection might believe the engineer's approach was biased and shortsighted.

FIGURE 2.1. VALUES UNDERLYING A POLICY DECISION.

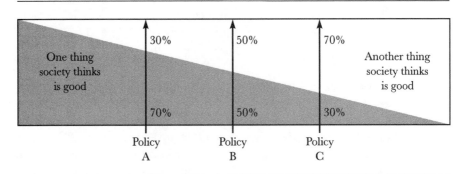

Expertise and scientific study may inform these choices, but ultimately there is nothing about expertise that provides a basis for making these fundamental values choices. Democracy is intended precisely to give the people power over choices about the ultimate aims and goals of government action.

Public participation creates a new direct link between the public and the decision makers in the bureaucracy. At its most basic level, public participation is a way of ensuring that those who make decisions that affect people's lives have a dialogue with that public before making those decisions. From the perspective of the public, public participation increases their influence on the decisions that affect their lives. From the perspective of government officials, public participation provides a means by which contentious issues can be resolved. Public participation is a way of channeling these differences into genuine dialogue among people with different points of view. It is a way of ensuring genuine interaction and a way of reassuring the public that all viewpoints are being considered.

Public participation provides decision makers with information about the relative importance the public assigns to the values choices that underlie a particular decision. That doesn't mean that knowing the public's values provides a simple answer. The "public" in public involvement is almost never the entire electorate. Furthermore, segments of the public are often in strong disagreement with each other. Just because a decision maker understands the values that each of these segments of the public has—and that is useful information—this information alone doesn't dictate what the decision should be. It is not unusual for people in a local area to agree on values that are different from those held by the national public. For example, the public in any community typically wants very high levels of protection regarding health risk, often more than that for which the government (which presumably represents national sentiment) is willing to pay. Conversely, when cleaning up the environment costs local jobs, the local community might be quite willing to settle for a lower standard than has been set nationally. Meeting the needs of all the individual communities along a river could result in poor management policy for the river as a whole. So although public participation informs the decision-making process, it doesn't necessarily make the decision for the agency.

Public participation is not limited to government agencies. In market economies, many of the resources of the society are in the hands of private institutions. Some of these institutions are quasi-public institutions, such as regulated utilities. Others are corporations whose ownership of vast resources means they too are making important decisions about how resources are allocated. Many of these organizations are now involving the public in decisions such as siting of facilities as the result of governmental regulation or enlightened self-interest.

Benefits of Public Participation

In my experience, public participation has these benefits:

   • *Improved quality of decisions.* The process of consulting with the public often helps to clarify the objectives and requirements of a project or policy. The public can force rethinking of hidden assumptions that might prevent seeing the most effective solution. Public participation often results in considering new alternatives, beyond the time-honored, and possibly time-worn, approaches that have been used in the past. The public often possesses crucial information about existing conditions or about how a decision should be implemented, making the difference between a successful or an unsuccessful program.

   • *Minimizing cost and delay.* Public participation does take more time, as Figure 2.2 shows (although if the participation is an integral part of the decision-making process, not as much time as some people may think). Unilateral decisions are always the quickest to make but often very expensive to implement. Frequently there is so much resistance that they are never implemented at all.

   The efficiency of making a decision cannot be measured merely in terms of time and costs, but also must take into account any delays or costs created by how the decision was made. If decision making is quick but alienates interested individuals and groups, it may have been very expensive in the long run. Unilateral decisions may become tied up in controversy, delays, or litigation. Even if the decision is somehow implemented, the next time the agency needs something in that community, the process will start out with ill will and animosity.

FIGURE 2.2. COMPARISON OF LENGTH OF TIME: UNILATERAL DECISION VERSUS PUBLIC PARTICIPATION.

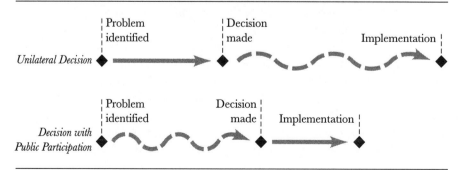

• *Consensus building.* A public participation program may build a solid, long-term agreement and commitment between otherwise divergent parties. This builds understanding between the parties, reduces political controversy, and gives legitimacy to government decisions.

• *Increased ease of implementation.* Participating in a decision gives people a sense of ownership for that decision, and once that decision has been made, they want to see it work. Not only is there political support for implementation, but groups and individuals may even enthusiastically assist in the effort.

• *Avoiding worst-case confrontations.* Once a controversy becomes bitter and adversarial, it is much harder to resolve the issue. Public participation provides opportunities for the parties to express their needs and concerns without having to be adversarial. Early public participation can help reduce the probability that the community will face painful confrontations. Nevertheless, public participation is not magic; it will not reduce or eliminate all conflicts.

• *Maintaining credibility and legitimacy.* The way to achieve and maintain legitimacy, particularly when controversial decisions must be made, is to follow a decision-making process that is visible and credible with the public and involves the public. Public participation programs will also leave the public more informed of the reasoning behind decisions.

• *Anticipating public concerns and attitudes.* As the agency's staff works with the public in public participation programs, they will become increasingly sensitized to the public's concerns and how the public views the agency's operations. These views are often internalized, so that staff is more aware of the probable public response to the agency's procedures and decisions even when the issue is not large enough to justify a formal public participation program.

• *Developing civil society.* One of the benefits of public participation is a better-educated public. Participants not only learn about the subject matter, but they also learn how decisions are made by their government and why. Public participation trains future leaders as well. As citizens become involved in public participation programs, they learn how to influence others and how to build coalitions. Public participation is training in working together effectively. Today, individuals may represent only groups or interests. Tomorrow, they form the pool from which regional and national leadership can be drawn. Through public participation, future leaders learn the skills of pulling together to solve problems.

This list is based on my own experiences with approximately three hundred public participation cases. If you asked me for proof of these claims, I would, like most other practitioners, give you anecdotes. The empirical research on the benefits of public participation has been limited until recently, when studies have begun to build a firm empirical base for these claimed benefits.

As one example, Thomas Beierle and Jerry Cayford (2002) recently conducted an analysis of 239 public participation cases over the past thirty years. They evaluated public participation based on five social goals (quite similar to the ones above):

Goal 1: Incorporating public values into decisions

Goal 2: Improving the substantive quality of decisions

Goal 3: Resolving conflict among competing interests

Goal 4: Building trust in institutions

Goal 5: Educating and informing the public

Beierle and Cayford concluded: "The case study record of the past 30 years paints an encouraging picture of public participation. Involving the public not only frequently produces decisions that are responsive to public values and substantively robust, but it also helps to resolve conflict, build trust, and educate and inform the public about the environment" (p. 74).

The World Bank has been evaluating participation in international development projects. In a major report on lessons learned from bank experience in participatory development, the authors concluded:

A statistical analysis of evaluations of 121 rural water supply projects throughout Asia, Africa and Latin America supported by 18 international agencies including the Bank, revealed "beneficiary participation" as the single most important factor in determining overall quality of implementation. . . . The analysis also demonstrated that beneficiary participation was the single most important factor to contributing to increased access and control over water resources. It also resulted in community members acquiring new water-related and organizational skills, and strengthened community organizations which went on to undertake other development activities [World Bank, 1994, p. 23].

These two studies are examples of a growing body of empirical research verifying that the claims made for public participation are indeed real.

Characteristics of Effective Public Participation

Over the years, I have endeavored to identify the characteristics of public participation programs that are perceived as legitimate or effective by both the organization conducting the process and the public participating in the process. The following sections identify those characteristics.

Public Participation Is Viewed as the Way Decision Makers Get the Mandate They Need to Act

In many areas of decision making, such as in the environmental arena or reproductive health, there is no general societal consensus or broader context of agreement that can guide administrative decision making. This makes each individual decision a battleground for the larger debate. Under these conditions, a program or project manager cannot make implementable decisions by simply completing administrative procedures and applying technical expertise.

Effective managers use public participation as a way of getting a mandate on the individual decision or project on which they are working. Peter Johnson, who served as the administrator (the equivalent of a CEO) at the Bonneville Power Administration during an extremely controversial period, was a skilled practitioner of this approach. He noted:

> I am more convinced than ever that public involvement is a tool that today's managers in both public and private institutions must understand. With external stakeholders now exerting substantial influence on organizations in every sector, conflict is inevitable. The only choice is whether to dodge the controversy or learn to harness it.
>
> Those who harness it by including third parties rather than trying to vanquish them will have the opportunity to consider new possibilities and to test out new ideas in the heat of dialogue. While others are mired in disputes and litigation, astute practitioners of public involvement will have hammered out an agreement and gotten on with the project. In short, they will have made better decisions and found a new source of competitive advantage [Johnson, 1993, p. 12].

This implies, however, an important rethinking of the manager's role. No longer is the manager simply making a technically feasible, fiscally responsible decision. This may produce a decision that is so controversial that it cannot be implemented. Instead, the manager is also responsible for creating a process that results in sufficient acceptance so the decision can be implemented successfully.

The Public Participation Process Is Well Integrated into the Decision-Making Process

Every time you go to the public, you should know why you are interacting with them at this particular point in the decision-making process, what issues need to be discussed with the public, and what decisions the public's comments could have an impact on. In other words, public participation should be fully integrated with the decision-making process. If it is not, you'll find yourself going to the public too early or too late to discuss important decisions. You'll be vague on exactly what it is you want from the public. The public will get the sense that its participation affects nothing. Your organization will get tired of spending money doing something that brings no value.

The Interested Public Is Involved in Every Step of Decision Making

Most important decisions don't occur in just one moment of time. Instead, numerous smaller decisions are made along the way. For example, decisions are made about how the problem is defined, what alternatives are considered, what evaluation criteria are applied, and what mitigation measures will be utilized.

People concerned about the decision being made are wise enough to know that these incremental decisions matter. Some ways of defining a problem exclude consideration of particular alternative solutions. For example, if the problem is defined as where to locate a transmission line, the alternatives will be much more limited than if you define the problem as how to provide adequate power to this community. The second problem definition opens up the possibility of decentralized energy solutions that would not be considered if the problem is viewed solely in terms of siting a transmission line.

Interested parties want and need to participate in these incremental decisions for the final decision to be legitimate. In some cases, these stakeholders are not totally satisfied with the final decision, yet they are willing to go along with it because of the satisfaction derived from being included in the earlier decisions that led up to the final decision.

This doesn't mean that all stakeholders will participate at each stage in the process. The closer you get to a final decision, the more people are likely to be involved. But the opportunity to participate at each stage is essential to success.

Programs Are Targeted to Ensure the Involvement of All Stakeholders Who Perceive Themselves to Be Affected

The public is different from issue to issue. Public participation programs are always involving a subset of the public, just as the number of people who participate in elections is always a subset of the total population, albeit a dramatically larger number of people. But the subset changes with the issue.

For example, the people interested in the location of an electric power transmission line are usually those who will be visually affected by the line. If there is a clear and demonstrable benefit in terms of the availability or reliability of power, there may also be people who are motivated by the benefits of that transmission line. But in very broad terms, the public for a twenty-mile transmission line is twenty miles long and about half a mile wide, the approximate limit of its visual impact.

The public for a health care issue often does not have this geographical definition. Although there may be pockets of people in certain areas who are more affected by health care decisions (for example, areas with heavy concentrations of low-income people or the elderly), the issues underlying health care involve economic interests and political philosophies that are not distributed geographically. In other words, there is no single public but a seemingly endless multitude of interests and groups.

The reality is that people participate when they perceive themselves to have a significant stake in the decision being made. That stake may be rooted in economics, use, or other direct impacts, or it may be rooted in values or philosophy. But people don't participate unless they perceive their interests or values to be affected.

People in the public participation field have tried various ways to describe these constantly shifting definitions of the public. We've tried *publics, audiences,* and various other phrases to describe the particular combination of interests that choose to participate in a particular issue. People now use the term *stakeholders* to describe those who choose to involve themselves in a particular issue. This is, at best, an inelegant term, but it is winning the battle of common use. The term is workable so long as you remember that the stakeholders are not a special class of people and do not necessarily represent constituencies beyond themselves. In a good public participation process, anyone can decide he or she is a stakeholder. Membership in the stakeholder class is self-defined.

But because public participation programs inevitably deal with a subset of the larger problems, there are certain basic obligations to the larger public. The first is that the larger public must be kept informed of the possible impacts of a decision, so that they can decide whether they wish to become involved in the public participation process. Thus, there is an obligation to establish and maintain an effective public information program as a precondition for the public participation program. Second, there must be visible points of access into the public participation program. If citizens decide they want to participate, they must be given a clear understanding of how and where they can participate.

From my experience, the two most frequent problems with ensuring that the people participating in a public participation program are in fact representative of the public are a failure to include the full range of opinion, and a failure to include interests for whom there is no obvious mechanism for representation.

Most agencies consider alternative solutions. But most also have built-in perceptual blinders. Agencies that have solved water supply problems in the past by building new storage dams will almost always start out addressing a new problem by looking for alternative dam sites, not considering the full range of institutional and nonstructural alternatives available. The result is that the alternatives they consider are all variations on a central theme.

Similarly, most agencies have developed communication with numerous stakeholders, but typically the range of stakeholders with whom they communicate encompasses people who share a concern and priority for the mission of that agency. If a public participation process includes only those people in the mainstream of opinion, those whose opinions fall outside that mainstream will feel unrepresented and left out of the process. As a result, they are likely to see the public participation process as fundamentally flawed. They will have no stake in accepting the outcome of that process and will seek other ways to influence the decision, such as turning to the courts or elected officials.

My experience is that it is less crucial to have a cast of thousands participate in a public participation program than it is to have the full range of opinion represented. If people choose not to participate, that's unfortunate but rarely a source of political controversy. But if people feel left out, that's a prescription for significant controversy.

Multiple Techniques Are Used, Aimed at Different Audiences

Normally a public participation program does not consist of a single activity. It is a succession of activities, each appropriate for the task being completed and the audience of interested parties.

In major public participation programs, there may be a number of activities going on at the same time, each reaching a slightly different audience. For example, one of the more successful projects in which I was involved had these activities:

- A policy committee representing all the key governmental organizations that oversaw the process
- A technical committee with technically qualified representatives of both agencies and organized groups who worked to get agreement on study methodologies
- A citizen advisory committee appointed by the governor
- Public workshops for the general public
- Periodic newsletters to inform anybody who expressed an interest (the mailing list held about five thousand names before we were through)

Not every issue requires this massive an effort, and some require more. Nevertheless, typically there are multiple activities, each designed to accomplish a specific task with a specific audience.

◆ ◆ ◆

With this overview of public participation theory completed, we turn now to the pragmatics of designing a public participation program.

References

Beierle, T., and Cayford, J. *Democracy in Practice: Public Participation in Environmental Decisions.* Washington, D.C.: Resources for the Future, 2002.

Johnson, P. T. "How I Turned a Critical Public into Useful Consultants." *Harvard Business Review,* Jan.–Feb. 1993, Reprint No. 93103.

World Bank. "Section V. Lessons Learned from Bank Experience in Participatory Development." *The World Bank and Participation: Operations Policy Development.* Washington, D.C.: World Bank, Sept. 1994, pp. 21–32. [www.worldbank.org/participation/pathhistory.pdf].

PART TWO

DESIGNING A PUBLIC PARTICIPATION PROGRAM

Public participation that isn't an integrated part of the decision-making process is a waste of time for both the organization and the public. Before we ask anyone to spend their time participating in our decision-making processes, we owe it to them to ensure that we are offering them the opportunity to participate in a manner and at a time that gives them the greatest opportunity to have a useful influence on the decisions being made.

There is no such thing as a one-size-fits-all public participation plan. But there is a systematic way of thinking through the issues that will help produce a successful plan that fits the unique requirements of a particular decision or issue. This part lays out such an approach. Chapters Three through Five provide detail on each of the three stages of that thought process.

There are three stages in developing a public participation plan (Figure P2.1).

The first stage consists of an analysis of the decision-making context in which the public participation program will be conducted. During this stage, the tasks are to clarify the decision-making process, consider whether there are issues about the process itself that could affect the credibility of the public participation process, and make a decision about whether public participation is needed for this decision. Although much of this stage is about the decision-making context and not public participation itself, it is a necessary precursor for public participation that is fully integrated into the decision-making process.

FIGURE P2.1. STAGES OF PUBLIC PARTICIPATION PLANNING.

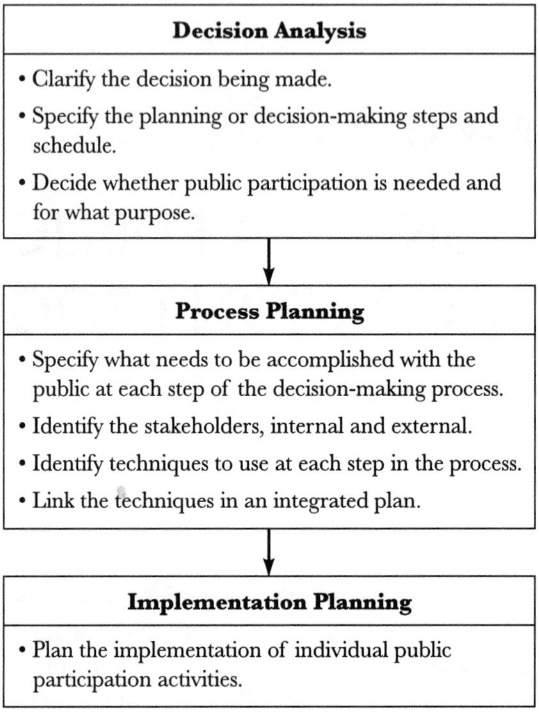

Decision Analysis

- Clarify the decision being made.
- Specify the planning or decision-making steps and schedule.
- Decide whether public participation is needed and for what purpose.

↓

Process Planning

- Specify what needs to be accomplished with the public at each step of the decision-making process.
- Identify the stakeholders, internal and external.
- Identify techniques to use at each step in the process.
- Link the techniques in an integrated plan.

↓

Implementation Planning

- Plan the implementation of individual public participation activities.

The second stage involves the kind of planning people normally think of when they talk about developing a public participation plan: identifying the public participation activities and how they fit into the sequence of the decision making process. This stage of planning, which I call process planning, involves the careful analysis of what you are trying to accomplish with the public at each stage in the decision-making process and identifying the techniques that best meet those objectives.

The third level of planning is implementation planning. If, for example, you know you are going to have a series of public workshops to evaluate alternatives, implementation planning would involve important details such as: How many workshops do you need to hold? Where will you hold them? How will you publicize the workshops? Who is going to facilitate the meetings? Who is going to prepare the printed material to hand out? Who will take care of setting up the chairs?

CHAPTER THREE

DECISION ANALYSIS

Decision analysis, the first of the three stages in designing a public participation program, is designed to do four things:

- Get everybody within your own organization starting from a common understanding of the decision being made and the need for public participation.
- Clarify the steps and timing of the planning or decision-making process for the issue on which you are working.
- Identify any characteristics of the decision-making process that could undermine the credibility of the public participation process, so you can address them in advance (before it happens in front of the public).
- Make a decision about whether public participation is needed, and if it is, what level of participation is required.

Decision analysis has six steps (Figure 3.1):

1. Decide who needs to be involved in decision analysis.
2. Clarify who the decision maker will be.
3. Clarify the problem being solved or the nature of the decision being made.
4. Specify the stages in the decision-making process and the schedule for those stages.

FIGURE 3.1. STEPS IN DECISION ANALYSIS.

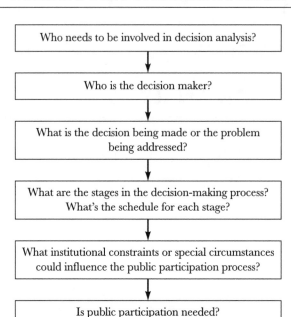

Who needs to be involved in decision analysis?

Who is the decision maker?

What is the decision being made or the problem being addressed?

What are the stages in the decision-making process? What's the schedule for each stage?

What institutional constraints or special circumstances could influence the public participation process?

Is public participation needed? If so, what level of participation is needed?

5. Identify institutional constraints and special circumstances that could influence a public participation process.
6. Decide whether public participation is needed and, if so, what level or kind of participation is required.

The following sections look at these steps in detail.

Step 1: Decide Who Needs to Be Involved in Decision Analysis

The first step in decision analysis is to consider who needs to be involved in planning for the public participation process and get them involved early in the process.

Typically, one person in an organization has the responsibility to prepare a public participation plan. Normally this should be the person responsible for the overall decision-making or planning process. The responsibility should not be put off on a public affairs office or public involvement specialist. The ideal situation is one in which the project manager (whatever title this person has) feels respon-

sible for the plan and sees the public participation program as an integral part of
the decision-making process for which he or she is responsible. People with public
participation experience may be called on to help develop the plan and may do
the actual writing of the plan. But the general elements of the plan need to be
agreed on first, with the concurrence of the project manager and other key people in the organization.

In large organizations, public participation plans can rarely be implemented
by a single part of the organization. The project manager may reside in a planning or other functional organization but will need to call on the skills of public
affairs, governmental affairs, graphics and layout people, publications, contracting, local office managers, and others. If you were developing a participation program for siting a dam, for instance, some or all of the following departments might
need to be involved: planning, engineering/geophysical, lands acquisition or right-
of-way, governmental affairs, construction, graphics, publications, public affairs,
media relations or corporate communications, and possibly others.

If these other organizations don't buy into the plan or don't understand their
responsibilities to make the plan happen, implementation is weakened. Rarely can
one part of the organization order another part of an organization to do something on the exact schedule and in the exact manner desired by the part of the
organization doing the ordering. But when different parts of the organization have
agreed as a team on a plan and their roles in implementing the plan, then performance is seen as voluntary and the turf battles are reduced dramatically.

A number of people may need to be included in planning during decision
analysis—for example:

- Those who have program or functional responsibility for the issue or decision,
such as program managers
- Those who understand how this decision links to other decisions, such as a senior manager or those who oversee multiple projects
- People or organizational units that will be affected by the decision or will be expected to implement the overall decision once it is made, such as other programs
or functional units (for example, construction or operations and maintenance)
- People or organizational units that will be called on to support the public participation effort, such as public affairs, people who prepare environmental reports, or legal counsel
- Those whose participation is needed for credibility, such as those in other agencies, particularly regulatory agencies, and sometimes members of citizen advisory committees or key stakeholders
- Those with special expertise who will be needed to implement the public participation program, such as facilitators, writers, graphic artists, and media relations

Get all these people together and lead them through the subsequent steps in decision analysis. By the time you are through, it will be the whole team's plan, not just your plan.

Step 2: Clarify Who the Decision Maker Will Be

In smaller organizations, asking who the decision maker will be may seem like an odd question because it may be obvious. But in large bureaucracies, it is not always obvious. Is it the regional director? The assistant secretary? The secretary (minister)? People at lower levels in a bureaucracy often see themselves as simply making recommendations that are passed on up the line. People at higher levels sometimes say, "By the time things get to me, most of the decisions have already been made."

Why does it matter who makes the decision? This question has been built into the decision analysis because of the following kinds of experiences:

You've worked hard to conduct a public participation program that includes all the significant interests, and you've ensured that there were genuine opportunities for these groups to discuss their differences. To your delight, this led to a creative solution that could resolve a major controversial issue. You were in the fortunate position of being able to recommend a solution that enjoyed as much of a consensus as you can ever hope for in the real world. Then to your horror, a senior official in your organization announces that the proposed solution is unacceptable. Nobody knows why. You feel so undercut that you don't feel as if you can ever again face the public and look them in the eye.

Maybe that official knows something you don't know and there's a good reason for the decision. It just hasn't been communicated to you. But maybe not. There's no sure-fire guarantee that a senior manager will appreciate the value of a decision that enjoys broad public support.

It is possible to reduce the risks. The best way to reduce the risk is to identify the decision maker and get him or her as involved as possible in the design of the public participation program. If possible, ask this person the following questions:

- What are the issues that you believe will be most controversial?
- Which stakeholder groups are most likely to exert influence at the level of senior management?
- Whose participation in the process is essential for credibility?
- At what points do you want to be briefed on the interim results of the public participation process?

- What boundaries or constraints do you believe need to be placed on the process?
- Do you as the decision maker want to review the public participation plan?

In other words, do whatever you can to find out what influences the decision from the perspective of the decision maker, and do whatever you can to engage the decision maker from the start in the design of the public participation process. This reduces (but cannot eliminate) the possibility that the decision maker will ignore the public process and impose his or her own personal preferences.

Normally it is unrealistic to think that senior management of large agencies will be involved in designing individual public participation programs. The person who is most crucial may not be the one who finally signs off on the decision but rather is the person who recommends what the decision should be.

Decision makers often get their information about what the public feels on a second-hand basis, that is, they depend on you to provide briefings or summaries. One of the problems with this is that decision makers don't always get the intensity of the message—that is, how strongly people feel about it. If possible, have decision makers participate in the process from time to time, even if only as an observer, so they experience the intensity of public concerns firsthand.

There is another reason for defining who the decision maker will be. In some cases, decision making is shared between your organization and another organization. The most likely other organizations will be regulatory agencies. If they can veto your decision, view them a partner in the decision making. Consider this experience with a client organization:

A federal agency assumed that it would go through the entire decision-making process, decide what to do, and then submit the regulatory reports necessary to get approval from the federal environmental regulator and the state environmental regulator. The regulators were not invited to participate at any time during the decision-making process. They showed up at the agency's public meetings but were given no role. They weren't even introduced at the public meetings.

By the time the agency submitted draft environmental documents, the regulators were so angry at being excluded that they "got even" by finding fault with anything they could. They even decided to hold their own public participation meetings, with the intimation to the public that the agency couldn't be trusted to do an honest job.

In reality, the regulators didn't have that much trouble with the decision being made. They simply felt they had a legitimate place at the table, and when ignored, they got even by throwing up organizational barricades.

If there are co-decision makers, such as regulatory agencies, the wisest thing to do is get them involved as much and as early as possible in the public participation program. Let them help design it, and give them a role in the meetings if they want it. It's in your interest to have them feel like an equal partner. They'll be confident that the public participation was adequate because they were there at the table with you.

Regulators may not want to be involved. Many believe that an arms-length approach is essential to regulation. Although this attitude is often outdated, there are circumstances where regulators need to keep a distance in order to be credible. There are also regulatory agencies that do not want to be involved early on because they like the power that comes from saying they had nothing to do with the decision. But even agencies that do not want to be seen as playing a role of the substantive part of the decision may still be willing to be involved in the public participation process. To the extent they are willing, it is in your interest to include them, even if planning becomes more challenging.

Step 3: Clarify the Decision Being Made or the Problem Being Answered

Once you have the public participation planning team put together, ask each person on the team to write a one- to two-sentence description of the problem that is being solved or the question that is being answered. The responses are often very revealing. Many times different parts of the same organization have fundamentally different understandings of the problem being addressed. Here's an example:

One of the U.S. national laboratories had been working on a process to remove sodium from nuclear waste. This waste was produced originally by an experimental nuclear power plant (a process intended to be much safer than existing nuclear power plants).

Sodium is reactive: it will burn if it gets wet or is exposed to certain elements. As a result, it needs to be removed before the waste can be stored in a long-term nuclear waste repository. The program to develop a sodium-removal technology was substantial and had an annual cost of some $10 million.

The laboratory had developed a technology it believed was workable, and the next step was to build an operating facility to employ the technology. This facility would cost at least $100 million. Before that decision could be made, the agency had to prepare an environmental impact statement.

When I conducted interviews at several levels of the organization and with key external stakeholders, I found that people had very different perspectives on what decision was being made. From the perspective of the national laboratory, the decision was whether to build a full-sized plant. This required an assessment of the science and an understanding of the uncertainties in extrapolating the results of a bench-test experiment to full production.

But the national laboratory was part of a larger federal agency. Within that federal agency was an organization that was responsible for ensuring the agency complied with all environmental laws and regulations. One of the requirements of preparing an environmental impact statement is to consider alternatives. From the perspective of the environmental compliance organization, the questions were: What are the alternative technologies for removing sodium? How do they compare? Have the standards been set at the long-term nuclear waste repository so that we know whether the waste—once it goes through the sodium-removal process—can be stored with other waste? The environmental compliance part of the organization worried that an environmental impact statement written with the national laboratory's very limited definition of the issue would not comply with the law.

When I interviewed external stakeholders, located in Washington, D.C., their primary concern was whether this technology would contribute to nuclear proliferation. One of the by-products of sodium removal was weapons-grade plutonium. They feared this technology was transportable and could be used to produce plutonium that could be used in nuclear weapons. From their perspective, the issue was whether the United States was going to take a step that contributed to nuclear proliferation.

For this issue, there were two audiences. First, there was a very concerned audience living around the national laboratory, facing the possibility of the program's being shut down entirely or gaining substantial new money to proceed with the program. Elected officials in the state where the national laboratory was located were also very concerned. There was another audience in Washington, D.C., where those in the agency headquarters were in dialogue with external stakeholders and elected representatives who were concerned with potential nuclear proliferation.

Although this case was complex, it was not that different from numerous other cases I've seen. It's not at all unusual for different parts of the organization to have very different definitions of the problem. But it is extremely embarrassing to go out to the public with one problem, only to find out during the public meeting that another part of your organization thinks you should be working on a different problem. That's why it is important to identify these internal differences before going to the public.

These differences also need to be resolved before designing a public participation program. You could design a public participation program to discuss whether the sodium-removal facility should be built. You could design a program to discuss which technologies are best for sodium removal. You could design a program to discuss whether this technology could contribute to nuclear proliferation. But you can't design a program that does all three simultaneously. For one thing, the affected stakeholders are substantially different for the three different problem definitions.

One of the outcomes you hope for from discussing the problem definition is that you will clarify the need for the project. Someone or some part of your organization thinks there's a problem that needs to be solved or a project that is needed. But go back and take a hard look at project need.

The public's first questions are almost invariably about need. This is human nature. If someone asks you, "Which color rug do you want?" or "Which make of car do you want to buy?" your instinctive reaction is to talk about whether you need a new rug or a new car before you're willing to talk about what kind. The public reacts the same way. When you ask, "Which site do you prefer, site A or site B?" their response is likely to be, "Why do we need the project at all?"

The public not only asks questions about project need; they ask questions that are penetrating and potentially embarrassing. Every experienced public participation practitioner has a story of a public meeting in which the public asked such good questions that by the end of the meeting, the agency was reconsidering whether the project was necessary. This is legitimate public participation, but it is less embarrassing to ask the hard questions before you go to the public.

Remember that part of the reason for discussing project need is to help everybody on the internal team get up to the same level of understanding. Questions are not necessarily challenges; they're simply people's way of getting comfortable and informed. By carefully considering how you have defined the problem, you can satisfy yourself that you have framed the question appropriately. It is also a chance to obtain internal agreement.

Even when there is agreement on the problem definition, you may still not have stated the decision or framed it in a way the public can understand or relate to. For example, decisions can be defined so narrowly that the agency poses a question that isn't of great interest to the public instead of a larger question of great interest—for example, "Where should irrigation canals be located?" rather than the much more interesting question, "Is this an appropriate area for irrigated agriculture?" As another example, decisions are set out in such a way that the public is asked to react to technical options rather than values choices—for example, stakeholders are asked to comment on alternative dam designs rather than larger questions such as, "Which is more important, the most economically efficient dam or a dam that provides protection for environmental resources?"

The public thinks in terms of values and priorities—the larger questions of political philosophy—rather than technical options. If you appear to be asking the public to choose between technical options, they may decide not to participate or question why technical staff aren't making the decision. If this is happening, you have several choices: (1) restate the decision at a higher level so that the values choices are obvious, (2) clarify the values decisions that underlie the technical options, or (3) decide that this is not a decision that requires a public participation program.

Because both the organization and the public have time and resource constraints, you can go to the same public with only a limited number of issues. Be sure that the issues you take to the public are those the public wants to address and, once decisions are made, give you the most leverage for your technical programs; that is, once decided, the decisions allow you to make a large number of technical decisions without the need for additional major public participation programs.

Another reason for getting different perspectives on the problem being addressed is to ensure that you don't define the problem so narrowly that you rule out options the public believes need to be discussed. Here's an example of how that can happen:

An electric utility company was aware that the transmission line that carried power from a generating plant in an urban area to a small timber mill community would soon reach its capacity. This timber mill community was at the end of a peninsula. Most of the peninsula, except the area nearest the water, was a national park. This small community was continuing to grow through tourism and new residents who were people wanting to move away from urban areas.

The electric company had identified alternative routes, but it was concerned whether any of them would be acceptable to the public. Some routes came very close to expensive homes built along the waterfront. Others came close to the national park in the heart of the peninsula. Some people objected to being able to see a power line from a national park.

When we met with the community, the residents made an important statement: "We don't have a power line problem; we have a power supply problem. Why can't we build a small generating plant here in town next to the timber mill and produce the power that would have come from the power line?"

It turns out they were right. A small generating facility in town, built in conjunction with the timber mill, made a lot more sense than building a power line.

Almost all organizations have a propensity to use the same solutions that worked in the past: power companies think about power lines, transportation agencies think about freeways, regulatory agencies think about new regulations, and so on. But as the example shows, how the problem is defined either creates or rules out alternatives.

The general rule is that the definition of the problem should be at least as broad as the definition you are going to hear from stakeholders. Otherwise, some stakeholders may see your program as illegitimate because it isn't addressing the right questions.

It isn't always possible to define the decision broadly. Your organization may have a limited mandate that doesn't allow you to consider all the alternatives that stakeholders would like to consider. Sometimes stakeholders play a shell game of telling you that whatever alternatives you are considering aren't good enough; there's always another one over here, they say, that you haven't considered. When you consider those, they'll find others.

Certainly there may be organizational constraints that limit the alternatives, but don't limit alternatives just because you just haven't thought about the problem enough. That's why one of the first steps in decision analysis is to reach agreement on what the problem is that you are trying to solve.

Step 4: Specify the Stages in the Decision-Making Process and the Schedule for Those Stages

Step 4 is to identify the basic stages to follow in reaching a decision. Then put these stages on a time line that will permit completion by the target date and meet any intermediate milestones.

The reason for this step is relatively simple: you need to define the decision process and schedule so that you can define the points in the process where you need to consult with the public and when they will occur. You need to be certain the stages of the decision-making process are well defined so it is possible to identify what role the public can or should play in each stage.

In some cases, the decision-making process has already been well defined when you begin public participation planning. If it is not well defined, this is the time to do it.

By defining the decision-making process, you start to answer the public's most basic question: "How will you make the decision?" You certainly won't be able to explain to people how their participation matters if you can't explain the process by which the decision will be made.

A decision-making process is simply the sequence of stages to arrive at a decision. The simplest and most generic decision-making process has these steps:

1. Define the problem.
2. Establish evaluation criteria.
3. Identify alternatives.
4. Evaluate alternatives.
5. Select a preferred alternative.

This sequence doesn't explain how a decision gets made at each stage. It just specifies what the stage will be.

You've probably been in meetings where you completed these stages in thirty minutes. But for major decisions, each stage of the process may take months.

Some decisions, such as construction or planning projects, have well-defined decision processes. These processes are sometimes displayed using a project management tool such as a PERT chart, Gantt chart, or Critical Path Analysis, show-ing a seemingly infinite number of activities. When a lot of steps are shown, the problem is to highlight the major stages, and not all the subactivities, so the pub-lic can understand the process.

But the process for other decisions may be ill defined. Policy decisions in par-ticular may not have well-defined decision-making processes. When you design public participation for an issue and the decision-making process is poorly defined, you need to stop and get clarity on the decision-making process before proceed-ing with the design of a public participation program.

Exhibit 3.1 shows the decision-making process for a major technology deci-sion. It basically follows the five generic stages, but some of the generic stages have been broken up into substages. Whether it takes only five stages to accomplish these tasks or fifty, the basic progression usually remains the same.

Once you have defined the stages in your decision-making process, you can attach schedule estimates as well. Often this is driven by the end date. For exam-ple, you may know that in twelve months, you must file an application for federal funding for whatever the plan will be. This defines the target. Work backward from there to define reasonable time periods for each of the stages you needed to reach that target.

EXHIBIT 3.1. DECISION-MAKING PROCESS FOR A MAJOR TECHNOLOGY DECISION.

1. Develop a problem statement and solution criteria.	May 2005
2. Identify the values sets to be portrayed in alternatives.	July 2005
3. Formulate conceptual alternatives.	September 2005
4. Evaluate conceptual alternatives.	December 2005
5. Present a comparison of conceptual alternatives.	January 2006
6. Select alternatives that should be considered in greater detail. [This stage may include combining alternatives or modifying alternatives to reduce unacceptable impacts.]	April 2006
7. Refine the criteria to be used in evaluating the detailed alternatives.	May 2006
8. Refine the remaining alternatives.	August 2006
9. Evaluate the refined alternatives.	December 2006
10. Present a comparison of the refined alternatives.	January 2007
11. Select a course of action.	April 2007

One reason for starting at the end point is that it helps you identify the drivers for the schedule. Examples of schedule drivers include these:

- There's a legal or regulatory requirement to complete an action by a certain time.
- The head of your organization has publicly announced that a product will be completed by a certain date.
- If a decision isn't made by a certain date, you'll miss the budget cycle, and the program will be halted.
- Your boss says it had better be done by a certain date!

Some of these drivers are within the power of the organization to change, but some are not.

Why does schedule matter for public participation programs? Unless public participation is well planned, it can cause delays in the decision-making process. When this happens, all the planning stops while the participation process goes on.

To avoid this, integrate the technical studies and the public participation program. For example, let's assume you know you want to make a decision (such as which alternatives will be studied to a higher level of detail) by a certain time. You also know you would like (or need) to have public participation in that decision. But there are technical studies that need to be completed before decisions can be made, and if the public is to participate effectively, the information from these studies needs to be communicated to the public before you ask them to participate in the decision. To avoid delays, you need to be alert to the sequence and timing of both the technical and public participation activities. To keep everything on track, consider the stages in the public participation program and the technical work that has to be done as part of one integrated process (see Figure 3.2).

The schedule can have impacts beyond the challenge of integrating the decision-making process and the public participation process. For example, if

FIGURE 3.2. SEQUENCE OF TECHNICAL STUDIES AND PUBLIC PARTICIPATION ACTIVITIES.

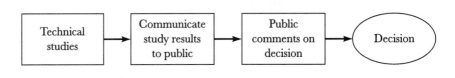

the time frame is too short, the public may get the message that the agency is not serious about allowing genuine participation. This can undermine the credibility of the public participation process. The schedule may also influence which public participation techniques are used, as there may be techniques that can't be completed in the time available. In this situation, it may be necessary to switch to techniques that will not be as effective but can be completed more quickly.

Step 5: Identify Institutional Constraints and Special Circumstances That Could Influence the Public Participation Process

The next step is to identify institutional constraints or special circumstances that may affect the decision whether to conduct a public participation program, or the nature of the public participation program—for example:

• *The agency is already committed to a particular decision or outcome.* If the agency has already made a decision, public participation is a sham. Save public participation for times when the agency really wants it, needs it, and is willing to respond to the public's ideas.

• *There is opposition from within the organization to conducting public participation on this issue.* Sometimes there is enough internal resistance to conducting a public participation program that the planning team may need to make a considered judgment about the risks of committing to a major program. If the opposition is too strong, the team could find itself undercut midway through the process.

• *There are schedule or resource constraints.* Schedule or resource constraints may limit the use of certain kinds of techniques or make it impossible to conduct effective public participation.

• *There are constraints on the release of information.* Occasionally the public needs certain information in order to participate intelligently but that information has not yet been released due to security considerations or the need to protect intellectual property.

The credibility of the organization and particularly the credibility of the public participation staff and program will suffer from conducting public participation that is a sham. If you identify these kinds of constraints, decide how you can work around them and still have an effective program, or decide that under the circumstances, it is inappropriate to attempt any public participation program at all.

Step 6: Decide Whether Public Participation Is Needed, and, If So, What Level of Participation Is Required

Having completed steps 1 through 5, you now have the information you need to make a decision about whether a public participation program is needed. Many minor actions do not require participation. Some major actions obviously require participation if there is to be any hope of implementation. The challenge is to decide the ones in the middle—the judgment calls. Here are a few considerations:

• *Does the decision fall within the jurisdiction of rules or regulations that require public or stakeholder participation?* Decisions that come under federal or state environmental laws, for example, are subject to the public participation requirements in those laws. This does not mean, though, that these requirements should not be exceeded, or that a number of similar decisions covered under such laws could not be combined into a single large public participation process.

• *Will the decision be controversial?* It's always hard to predict controversy. There are some indicators, though. Issues are more likely to be controversial when:

• The decision will have significant impacts.
• The decision affects some people much more than others (there could be claims of inequity).
• The decision will have an impact on an existing vested interest or use (people will have to give up something they think of as a right).
• The decision ties into something else that is already controversial (for example, anything related to nuclear power or abortion).

• *Does the decision involve trade-offs or weighing of one value (for example, environmental protection or health) in comparison with another (for example, cost or security)?* The public is usually happy to let agencies make purely technical decisions. But some decisions that are called technical are actually decisions about the relative weight or importance that should be given to one consideration or value over another. It is precisely these decisions about the relative weight or importance of various values that are the prime candidates for public participation.

There would be no need to ask, "Is public participation needed?" if there were not times when the appropriate answer is no. Sometimes the level of public interest is just too low, particularly when compared to other issues on which your agency may be offering opportunities for participation. Sometimes the agency is already locked in to a particular outcome, and providing opportunities for participation is a charade or fraud. There are times when the agency simply doesn't have the resources, and it is better to accept the potential for controversy and re-action from a decision made without consultation than begin a public participation program that creates expectations that cannot be fulfilled.

If you do determine that some form of public participation is needed, the next question is, "What is the goal of the public participation program?" As dis-cussed in Chapter One, the term *public participation* is used to describe very differ-ent kinds of involvement:

- Informing the public
- Procedural public participation (for example, public hearings)
- Collaborative problem solving
- Developing agreements

Each of these kinds of public participation may be appropriate in certain cir-cumstances. Start by being clear on why you want to conduct a public participa-tion program—for example:

- You are required to conduct public participation to fulfill regulatory requirements.
- You want to maintain or improve a positive working relationship with public parties.
- Public parties possess information that is important to making good decisions.
- High levels of controversy could threaten implementation.
- The public must be involved in implementation, so commitment to the deci-sion by the public is essential.

Your purpose in conducting public participation drives the selection of what type of program you need:

• If the goal is to have a better-informed public (but public comment is not likely to influence the decision), it may be more appropriate to conduct a public information program. Remember, however, that a better-informed public is not automatically a more supportive public.

• If the goal is strictly to fulfill requirements, then you may implement a min-imal program. If the issue is controversial, this kind of public participation will not buy much credibility. The public can tell when you are just going through the motions.

• If the goal is to give the public the opportunity to be heard before a final decision is made but you are not expecting interaction among stakeholders, it may be appropriate to conduct the kind of public participation programs that simply satisfy procedural requirements, such as a public hearing.

• If you need support or informed consent for a decision, it is usually necessary to use a collaborative problem-solving approach to public participation, with the public having genuine influence on the decision (although the agency or organization retains final decision-making authority).

• If no decision can be made until the parties actually buy in to the entire substance of the decision, then the situation requires that you get agreement. Full agreement usually requires a defined negotiation process, a manageable number of parties, well-defined parties, and parties able to make binding commitments or some external mechanism for binding the parties.

Above all, it is essential to establish clear expectations within your organization and with the public about what kind of participation is being provided. The biggest problems arise when the public expects a higher level of involvement than the organization is willing to consider. The most important remedy is for the organization to be clear with the public about what level of involvement it is actually seeking.

If you are not sure whether public participation is needed or what kind is appropriate, here is a suggestion. Make a list of those stakeholders who are most likely to be interested. Make sure the list includes a cross-section of viewpoints. Contact individuals representing those parties, and lay out the issue for them, asking whether they are likely to want to participate and how strong their interest would be. Don't worry that they will automatically tell you that participation is required; they're busy too and have other issues that may be more important to them.

If you decide that public participation is needed, you're ready to move on to process planning. If you decide it is not needed, the decision analysis you've done should still have value as you proceed with the decision-making process.

CHAPTER FOUR

PROCESS PLANNING

The second stage in designing a public participation program is *process planning*. By the end of this stage of planning, you will identify the specific public participation activities for each stage in the decision-making process and put them on a time line. These activities and the schedule are then documented in a public participation plan.

Process planning encompasses these steps:

- Decide who needs to be on the planning team.
- Identify stakeholders and identify potential issues and concerns.
- Assess the probable level of controversy.
- Define public participation objectives.
- Analyze the exchange of information that must take place to achieve the public participation objectives.
- Identify special considerations that could affect selection of techniques.
- Select public participation techniques.
- Prepare a public participation plan.

Figure 4.1 shows these steps in the form of questions to be answered. This chapter includes a series of worksheets that will be helpful in leading a planning team through this planning effort. Feel free to duplicate and use them.

FIGURE 4.1. THE PROCESS PLANNING STEPS.

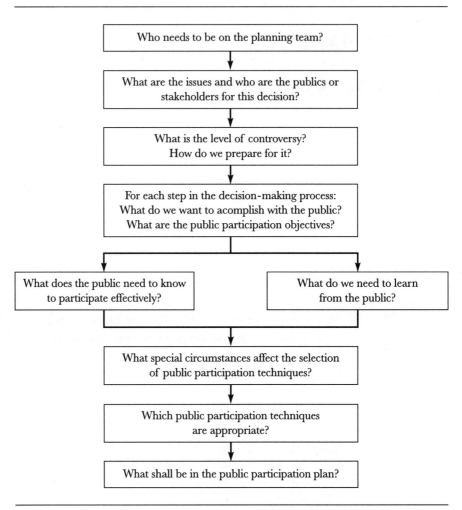

Decide Who Needs to Be on the Planning Team

This step is a reprise of the first step in decision analysis. The goal is to identify the people who need to be involved in developing the public participation plan. You need either their expertise to develop the plan or their commitment to the plan to ensure its effective implementation.

Some people who were involved in planning during decision analysis may drop off the team, some new members will be added to the planning team, and a core group will remain. For example, senior managers who were needed for decision analysis may not need to be involved in process planning. Process planning is more likely to require the involvement of people with expertise at implementing public participation programs, such as meeting facilitators, writers, or media relations specialists.

You may need to include:

- People from parts of the organization who could be affected by the decision, such as those from the program offices that will be involved in implementing the decision
- People or organizational units that will be called on to assist with the public participation effort, such as public affairs, legal, publications, and media relations
- People with special expertise who will be needed to carry out the public participation plan, such as writers, graphic artists, and facilitators
- People whose participation is needed for credibility

Worksheet 4.1 can be used for this activity.

Identify Stakeholders, and Identify Potential Issues or Concerns

The next step is actually two steps, which are completed simultaneously: (1) identify the people and organizations likely to see themselves as having an interest or stake in the decision (*stakeholders* or *interested parties*), and (2) identify the issues and concerns that are likely to arise during the decision-making process.

The reason these steps are done side by side rather than sequentially is that when you think of potential stakeholders, you'll immediately think of issues you know these stakeholders will raise. As you think of potential issues, you will automatically think of stakeholders who will be concerned about those issues. Experience shows it is just easier to do them side by side than attempt to do them one after the other.

Identify Stakeholders

The public for each issue or decision consists of those who see themselves as having a stake in the decision. As a result, the public is different for each issue.

There are several reasons to identify stakeholders:

- To ensure that key stakeholders are not left out
- To target the public participation program to reach the parties interested in the specific decision
- To assess the potential level of controversy

WORKSHEET 4.1. IDENTIFYING WHO
NEEDS TO BE INCLUDED IN PROCESS PLANNING.

People from organizational units who will be affected by the decision	
People or organizational units who will be called on to assist with the public participation effort	
People with special expertise that will be needed, such as writers or graphic artists	
People whose participation is needed for credibility	

There are many different approaches for identifying stakeholders. The approach I use most frequently is to analyze the different interests people could have in the decision, such as:

- Economics (for example, people could receive some economic benefit or loss as a result of the decision being made)
- Use (for example, the decision could threaten an existing use of a valuable resource or could make that resource available)

- Mandate (for example, agencies having regulatory authority over environmental impacts, health standards, or zoning)
- Proximity (for example, people who could experience air, soil, or water pollution or could be affected by dirty air, excess noise, or increased traffic during construction)
- Values or philosophy (for example, people with strong beliefs about the way resources should be managed)

Another approach is to ask questions such as these:

- Who might be affected?
- Who are the representatives of those likely affected?
- Who are the voiceless?
- Who is responsible for what is intended?
- Who will be actively opposed?
- Who can contribute resources?
- Whose behavior would have to change if this decision were made?

There are other possible typologies for identifying stakeholders:

By Probable Interest

- Directly affected
- Indirectly affected
- Possible interest
- General interest

By Sector

- Public sector
- Private sector
- Interest groups
- Individuals

By Location

- Local
- Regional
- National
- Neighboring countries
- International

One of the values of doing planning in a team is that the planning team will be able to identify a much more comprehensive and specific list of stakeholders than any one individual could develop.

You may also want to do some homework to ensure you identify all the key stakeholders. There are other sources of information about potential stakeholders—for example:

- Get people to self-identify. Send out information, and let people who are interested identify themselves.
- Analyze prior decision-making documents. Review past decision-making documents, such as environmental documents or reports, and see who has participated in similar past decisions.
- Ask other people, and seek local help. Ask others you know are knowledgeable or have an interest to tell you who else may need to be involved by virtue of position (role in an influential organization), reputation (power behind the scenes), or influence on past decisions of a similar nature.
- Identify based on staff knowledge. Use the knowledge of other staff in your organization who are knowledgeable about the issues and community to help you identify likely stakeholders.
- Identify based on past participation on similar issues. Go through recent local newspapers, and identify the people or groups that have been active on similar issues within the community.

Worksheet 4.2 provides a simple way to go about identifying stakeholders. Start by listing issues that are likely to emerge during this decision-making process. Think about who is likely to see themselves as affected by those issues. As you identify stakeholders, you will identify other issues that will emerge if those stakeholders are involved. So you'll go back and forth between the columns.

Worksheet 4.2 provides columns for both external and internal stakeholders (people or organizational units inside the organization). In fact, internal stakeholders often have as much or more impact on decisions as external stakeholders. Internal stakeholders might include senior decision makers, other program offices, those in procurement, people responsible for preparing environmental reports, legal counsel, public affairs—anybody whose responsibilities (policy, staffing, budget, compliance) could be affected by the decision. It's not important to draw a fine line dividing people who are internal and those who are external. What is important is to remember the need to provide participation opportunities for stakeholders within the organization.

Once stakeholders have been identified, determine the level of participation they will want. One useful way to do this is to think of the public as being

WORKSHEET 4.2. MATCHING ISSUES AND STAKEHOLDERS.

Issues	Internal Stakeholders	External Stakeholders

organized in orbits of influence and interest. Lorenz Aggens, one of the most experienced practitioners in the field, is the developer of the orbits analogy and terminology. Aggens views the orbits as comparable to the structure of the atom. As he describes it, "Think of each level as an 'orbit' of activity around the project nucleus—the decision-making process. The closer an orbit of activity is to this decision making center, the greater the opportunity there is for public influence in that decision" (1983, p. 193). The price for being near the center—having more influence on the decision—is greater expenditure of time, resources, and energy. Aggens portrays the public as consisting of six orbits: decision makers, creators, advisers, reviewers, observers, and unsurprised apathetics.

This concept of orbits of participation is valuable. I particularly appreciate the idea that people can move from an outer orbit to a more active orbit, but it requires an investment of their time and energy. I see people doing this frequently during the course of a public participation program, either because we have made their participation inviting or their level of concern has risen.

I have modified Aggens's categories somewhat. Aggens's emphasis is entirely on the public external to the organization. My experience is that it is useful to extend the concept of orbits into the myriad regulators or other governmental entities that interact during agency decision making.

Here's a more detailed description of the orbits, combining Aggens's original categories with changes I've found helpful when designing a public participation program (Figure 4.2):

• Unsurprised apathetics: These are people who choose not to participate. They may be too busy at work or very active in some other aspect of community life, but have little interest in the subject of your public participation program. They may not be apathetic people (they may be actively involved in schools, church, or other organizations), but they are apathetic to your issue. The qualifier *unsurprised* means that you have made efforts to provide them with information (through the media, for example) so that they are unsurprised (or uninterested) when a decision is made. But they have had the opportunity to make a choice whether to participate.

• Observers: These people read newspaper articles about the process or read your public information documents, but unless they become very concerned with what they see going on, your organization will not hear from them. They are nevertheless an important part of public opinion generally, because they make comments to other units of government, public interest groups, and special interest organizations. They may choose to become active participants if they grow concerned about the direction things are going or if a project loses its transparency.

FIGURE 4.2. MODIFIED ORBITS OF PARTICIPATION.

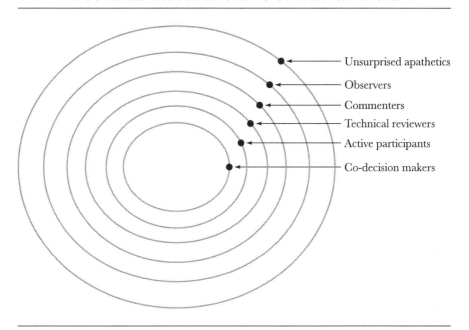

- Unsurprised apathetics
- Observers
- Commenters
- Technical reviewers
- Active participants
- Co-decision makers

• Commenters: These individuals or groups are very interested in the issue, but also have to deal with all the other things going on in their lives. They might comment by speaking at a meeting or by sending a letter, but wouldn't make the time commitment to participate in an advisory group.

• Technical reviewers: My experience is that many agencies interact in arriving at an agency decision. Some agencies may not share in arriving at the substantive decision, but do share decision making authority (and sometimes are the sole decision makers) when it comes to the methodologies used to evaluate the impacts of projects. A federal agency whose mission is to protect wildlife habitat will, for example, issue guidelines on how to evaluate the impact of an action on wildlife habitat. In the United States, the Office of Management and Budget has issued numerous guidelines on how economic impacts will be assessed.

• Active participants: These are people who will commit the time and energy to be sure they have an influence on the decisions. They will participate in an advisory group, attend workshops or meetings, organize the community, and engage in other ways. They care about this issue, and it is in your organization's interest to channel their energy and commitment into your public participation program. Examples are state or local officials, environmental groups, civic groups, industry groups, home owners or landowners, leaders or members of interest groups, and people concerned about planning or development decisions in a community.

Try very hard to avoid leaving any active participants out of the public participation process. If they are not included, they may show up late in the process and undercut what you've done, or they may make themselves heard in some other forum, such as through a political channel or in a courtroom.

• Co-decision makers: I use the term *decision makers* to include the people in your organization who will make the final decision, plus those people or organizations that effectively have veto power over your organization's decision. Increasingly decisions are made not just by one agency, but by several agencies acting in concert. A co-decision maker might be a regulatory agency, a local government with permitting authority, key customers, or a partner in a joint venture.

The biggest problem with co-decision makers comes when you pretend they are not genuine co-decision makers, and they are given only the opportunity to comment on the decision. This can be insulting, and it starts the process off on the wrong foot. Co-decision makers should be provided a seat at the table. You should try to include them, for example, in designing and conducting the public participation process. The more they are drawn into the process from the start, the less danger there is that you will go through the entire process only to have them announce you guessed wrong and overrule the decision.

Systematically think through who is in these orbits for the issue on which you are working. In particular, concentrate on the membership of the inner orbits. A team best accomplishes this task so that people can share their knowledge of who has an interest in the issue. Use Worksheet 4.3 as a simple summary sheet to record your thoughts as to which individuals or groups are in which orbits. This worksheet also includes a column for internal stakeholders. Just like the external public, they too are in orbits of participation, with different levels of ability and willingness to expend time and energy to participate in the decision.

Be particularly alert for key interests that may not yet be organized to represent themselves but have a significant stake in the outcome of the decision and are likely to move into one of the inner orbits as the decision-making process moves forward. For example, who represents electric utility rate payers in an issue regarding siting of a transmission line? Who represents recreation users at a lake where thousands spend time each summer? Who represents beneficiaries of community health services? Even when you think you have found people or organizations that represent these interests, how do you make sure they are truly representative or are just claiming to represent a whole class of people while arguing for a limited point of view?

WORKSHEET 4.3. STAKEHOLDERS' LEVELS OF INVOLVEMENT.

	External Stakeholders	Internal Stakeholders
Co-decision makers (agree to the decision)		
Technical reviewer (influence the methodology)		
Active participant (influence the decision)		
Commenter (heard before the decision)		

If you're working on a project where some people are proposing an expensive solution and no one seems to be representing a concern for cost, you do not want your organization to be the fiscal watchdog. This puts you in an advocacy role. Instead, try to have all concerns and interests represented so that they talk to each other and address each other's interests.

A major reason for identifying orbits of potential involvement is that you may need to use different public participation techniques to involve different orbits. This is illustrated in Exhibit 4.1.

Not only are the stakeholders different for each issue, but which stakeholders participate changes over time. For example, the number of stakeholders increases with controversy. This is a "by definition" statement, since the word *controversy* means that a comparatively large number of people feel strongly about the issue. The public for a particular issue may always be a relatively small percentage of the population, but that percentage increases as controversy grows.

In addition, because groups become active for very different reasons, they will choose to be involved at different stages of the decision-making process. For example, people in the community who are aware of the need for water conservation may participate in the early stages of developing a community's water conservation policy; other groups and interests will get involved only after they see how the proposals might affect them. Neighborhood groups may be involved only after potential sites for a facility have been identified. They may be very active as long as a site in that neighborhood is under discussion and stop participating the minute that site is dropped from consideration.

Groups that raise concerns about health risks often do so as a tactic; they may be primarily concerned with preventing a facility from being located in their neighborhood, but they will raise the question of health risks in an effort to gain political support. But new people will get interested in health risks as a result, and while the people who initially raised questions about health risks may be using the issue as a tactic, the people whose interest is attracted by the health issue are genuinely concerned about health risks. The key point is that the list of stakeholders is constantly evolving, with different people getting involved at different stages as they see their interest being affected.

EXHIBIT 4.1. MATCHING PARTICIPATION MECHANISMS TO ORBITS OF PARTICIPATION.

Orbit of Participation	Possible Participation Mechanisms
Co-decision makers	Interagency teams, partnering, negotiation
Active participants	Interactive workshops, advisory groups, or task forces
Technical reviewers	Peer review processes, technical advisory committees
Commenters	Public meetings, comment periods
Observers	Newsletters, information bulletins, Web pages
Unsurprised apathetics	Press releases, news stories

People will also participate more in some stages of the decision-making process than others. Some steps are relatively technical in nature. Typically only the well-organized groups with technical expertise will be of significant influence during these stages. However, these stages are usually followed by stages when social choices must be made. This is normally when a broader public can and will participate. So the public may expand and contract several times during the course of the decision-making process.

More people will participate as the decision moves closer. Although the public may expand and contract several times during the course of the decision-making process, there is still a general trend: as a decision comes closer and closer, more people choose to participate. This is because the potential benefits and costs become more visible and more people see themselves affected by the decision.

One significant problem in designing public participation programs is that many people assume that the program started the first day they participated and want to reexamine all assumptions, alternatives, and decisions that have been made over the months. As a result, it's important to document all stages of public participation and show how public comment influenced previous decisions.

One conclusion to be drawn from the observation that the list of stakeholders changes during the course of a decision-making process is that there are different levels of participation at each stage in that process. It is possible, for example, to attempt too much public participation at a particular step, just as it is possible to provide too little. Too much early enthusiasm, for example, can be dampened when the decision-making process extends over several years. Public participation programs need to balance early involvement for people who have a continuing interest in a problem, coupled with opportunities for involvement of a broader public at those points where their participation will be most effective.

Identify Potential Issues and Concerns

As you identify stakeholders, you'll find yourself simultaneously identifying potential issues—for example:

Aesthetics	Air quality
Cultural resources	Economic benefit and return
Economic development	Employment
Health	Housing affordability
Land use	Natural resources and ecology
Noise	Other related projects
Political control	Population

Property values	Resource recycling
Jobs	Growth
Secondary uses	Safety
Service reliability	Services
Solid and hazardous waste	Tax revenues
Traffic and roads	

The major reason for identifying potential issues and concerns up front is that it provides time to address these issues effectively. This preparation might take the form of developing studies, revisiting organizational policies, or gathering information. Without this kind of advance work, stakeholders will raise issues, and the organization will be unable to respond in a timely manner. When this happens, not only does the organization look uninformed, unresponsive, or unprepared, but advocacy groups can make claims about these issues that go unanswered because the organization is not ready to respond. The result is that these groups own the issue for a period of time, often dictating the tone of the discussion in the media or even in public forums. The best way to avoid this is by anticipating the issue and being ready to respond with solid information or a well-thought-out position.

I encourage organizations to develop an issues management plan that spells out what preparatory work the organization must do for each major issue. In particular, consider these points:

- Studies that must be completed before this issue can be resolved
- Policy decisions that must be made before this issue can be resolved
- Informational materials that must be developed before this issue can be addressed

You may need months to complete the research or obtain the expert advice you need, particularly since you must allow time to procure those services. Major policy decisions can also take months. Preparing publications is time-consuming, particularly given all the reviews that publications usually go through. If you start thinking about the need for research, a new policy, or a publication a few weeks before you need them, they probably will not be available on time. If at all possible, begin identifying issue management activities far enough in advance so you will have the information, policy, or publication ready when you need it.

Worksheet 4.4 is a summary sheet concentrating on the issues management topics that emerge most often, but with space for other issues that occur less frequently.

WORKSHEET 4.4. DEVELOPING AN ISSUE MANAGEMENT PLAN.

Issue	Responsibility	Completion
Studies that must be completed before this issue can be resolved		
Policy decisions that must be made before this issue can be resolved		
Informational materials that need to be developed to address this issue		
Other actions needed		

Assess the Probable Level of Controversy

Just as there are little cars and big cars to meet different needs, there are small, modest public participation programs and massive programs costing millions. The goal is to match the number and kind of public participation activities to the probable level of controversy.

Even people who are highly experienced in public participation get taken by surprise when estimating controversy. Sometimes an issue that seems as if it should be highly controversial doesn't generate much interest, while something that seems quite bland may become a battleground.

There is no magic way to predict controversy, but there are indicators of probable controversy:

- The impacts are significant.
- There has been prior controversy on the same issue (for example, controversy over prior actions).
- The issue ties in to another major issue over which there is continuing controversy or a power struggle (such as nuclear power or weapons production).
- The issue touches on local political topics, such as land use or economic development, that are the basis for political debate within the community.
- The issue is the total reason for the very existence of stakeholder groups, which will see themselves in a life-or-death struggle.

Worksheet 4.5 is a simple tool for making such an assessment. Record the issues that were identified previously in the left column, and then determine whether each issue will have a low, medium, or high level of controversy. Looking at the level of controversy of the issues you've identified, make a judgment as to the overall level of controversy associated with the process as a whole.

Sometimes people within the public participation planning team know the stakeholders well enough to make an informed judgment as to how intense their interest will be. On occasion, though, the only way to assess the potential for controversy is to meet with stakeholders and discuss their interest in the issue and their suggestions for what kind of participation they think is appropriate. These interviews or small group meetings can play an important role in developing a successful public participation plan.

There is no mathematical formula that results in a precise assessment of potential controversy. Your organization needs to know or learn about the community and the groups with which it will be working. Keep in mind that the level of controversy may be influenced by other issues affecting the community. If there are questions about how groups feel, the best approach is to ask them.

WORKSHEET 4.5. ASSESSING THE LEVEL OF CONTROVERSY.

Issue	Prior Controversy on Same Issue		Tie-In to Another Major Issue or Power Struggle		Significance to Major Stakeholders			Probable Level of Controversy		
	Yes	No	Yes	No	Low	Medium	High	Low	Medium	High
Probable Level of Controversy for Entire Process:										

Define Public Participation Objectives

The next step in the planning process is to answer the question: "What do we need to accomplish with the public by the end of each stage in the decision making process?"

During decision analysis, you defined the stages in your decision-making process. Revisit these stages now to be certain they are still appropriate; if they are, develop one or more public participation objectives for each stage.

To develop public participation objectives, ask, "What do we have to have accomplished with the public by the end of this stage?" Then write an objective that describes the completion of that task. For example, if the decision-making process followed the five generic decision-making stages discussed in Chapter Three, then the public participation objectives might look like Exhibit 4.2.

Objectives often specify what level of participation is required. For example, if you were evaluating alternatives and needed participation by the public, you could write the objective in various ways:

- Determine the acceptability of each of the alternatives to the various stakeholders.
- Identify the issues and concerns associated with each alternative.

EXHIBIT 4.2. GENERIC PUBLIC PARTICIPATION OBJECTIVES.

Stage in the Process	Objective
Define the problem	Obtain a complete identification and understanding of how the problem is viewed by all significant interests.
	Identify the level of public interest in the issue.
Establish evaluation criteria	Identify a complete list of possible criteria for evaluating alternatives.
	Agree on evaluation criteria.
Identify alternatives	Develop a complete list of all possible alternative actions.
Evaluate alternatives	Develop a complete understanding of the impacts of the various alternatives as viewed by the public.
	Assess the relative merit assigned to alternatives by various interests.
Select a course of action	Determine which alternative would be the most acceptable.

- Identify changes in plans or mitigation activities that could improve the acceptability of each alternative.
- Get agreement on a preferred alternative.

Of the four options, the objective of getting agreement implies a much higher level of involvement and might require an entirely different public participation approach than simply learning about stakeholder attitudes. Use Worksheet 4.6 to summarize the public participation objectives associated with each step in the decision-making process.

Analyze the Information Exchange

In order to accomplish each of your public participation objectives there is information you will need to provide to the public and information you need to get from the public. In other words, there is an exchange of information that must take place. At this step, determine for each stage in the decision-making process the two following questions:

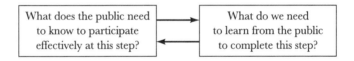

Exhibit 4.3 provides an example of what this analysis might look like for the problem definition stage of decision making.

My own experience is that this kind of analysis gets tedious when done in a team. So, unlike the previous steps, it's a lot easier for one person to do this step individually, and then have the team review it (see Worksheet 4.7).

Identify Special Considerations That Could Affect Selection of Techniques

Often there are special circumstances or considerations that could determine or influence which public participation techniques you will use. These circumstances or conditions have to do with characteristics of the issue, characteristics of the public, or characteristics of your organization. Here are a few of the special circumstances or considerations that could affect which public participation techniques you select.

WORKSHEET 4.6. SETTING PUBLIC PARTICIPATION OBJECTIVES.

Stage in Decision-Making Process	Public Participation Objectives

EXHIBIT 4.3. DEFINING THE INFORMATION EXCHANGE.

Stage One: Define the problem.

Public Participation Objective 1: Obtain a complete identification and understanding of how the problem is viewed by all significant interests.

Information exchange

To stakeholders	From stakeholders
• The nature of the study and decision-making process	• How different groups see the problem
• What the organization knows about the problem or issue	• How the problem affects them
• Opportunities for public participation	• The intensity of the impacts
	• Which parts of the public see themselves as affected

Public Participation Objective 2: Identify the level of public interest in the issue.

Information exchange

To stakeholders	From stakeholders
• The nature of the study and decision-making process	• Which groups or interests want to participate
• The kinds of public participation possible	• How intensely the groups want to participate
	• Which techniques are most acceptable or suitable

Characteristics of the Issue

The nature of the issue itself can impact the design of your public participation program. Examples include:

Duration of the Decision-Making Process. Some decisions can be made within a few months. Others may take several years. It's very difficult to sustain public interest for long periods of time. Lengthy planning processes often have periods during which technical studies are being conducted and little decision making is occurring. These are then followed by a short period during which a number of important decisions are made. The challenge is to hold public interest during the inactive times so that people will get involved at the decision points. It's also important to sustain credibility when the process seems to disappear. Techniques that might be used include periodic newsletters to describe study progress, an advisory group to oversee technical studies, or publication of summaries or interim reports (Worksheet 4.8).

WORKSHEET 4.7. IDENTIFYING THE INFORMATION EXCHANGE.

Stage in the Decision-Making Process:	Information *to* the Public	Information *from* the Public
1.		
2.		
3.		
4.		
5.		

WORKSHEET 4.8. IDENTIFYING SPECIAL CIRCUMSTANCES.

Special Circumstances	Yes	No	Impact on Program
Cultural/ethnic sensitivities (for example, most people who will be affected are from a single cultural or ethnic minority).			
National interest (for example, most interested stakeholders are in another city, not near the site)			
Distance (interested stakeholders are scattered over a large area geographically)			
Issue connected politically to other issues—difficult to keep this issue distinct			
Level of interest—outrage versus apathy			
Political sensitivities—key political figures have positions or reputations to defend related to this issue			

Technical Complexity. Some issues are relatively easy for the public to understand, and others are extremely difficult. Technically complex issues require an effective public information program before the public can be expected to participate. You may need to employ writers and graphics specialists to develop synopses of the technical information in language or images that the public can grasp. Or you may need to use a technical task force to review the studies and, in effect, vouch for the adequacy of the technical work performed.

Existing Level of Interest. Some issues generate the active involvement of hundreds of people. Others can be resolved by assembling all the key actors in a single room. If hundreds of people are going to participate, you'll need to use different techniques than you will if only a few will be taking part. A cast of hundreds or thousands not only means the methods must be different, it also means that your mailing list is huge, the quantity of newsletters or reports needed is considerable, and analysis of public comment will be a significant effort. Staff and budget need to reflect the challenge.

Importance of Issue to Groups. One group may oppose or support a proposed action, but not consider it so essential that it fights to the death. To another group, the issue may seem life or death. A group representing local merchants, for example, faces many issues over the years, and although it may have positions on those issues, it will make a major expenditure of effort on only a few. A single-issue group formed specifically to support or oppose a single decision or action has no other reason for its existence than to fight to the bitter end. If a group cannot afford to lose—politically, economically, or whatever else—it will fight to the end, no matter what kind of public participation program is designed. Such a group is also more willing to manipulate or abridge the process if there is a tactical advantage in doing so. Although it may be that no public participation program can satisfy such groups, it is important that the forums give ample opportunity for these groups to express their concerns so they don't feel they have to go outside the process to be heard.

Characteristics of the Public

The characteristics of the stakeholders interested in the decision can impact the design of your public participation program. Examples include:

A Public Informed or Uninformed on the Issue. Some issues have been a battleground for a number of years, so the public is relatively well informed. On other issues, you'll have to do a public information program just to convince people that the issue is important enough to bother to become involved. If the public has been involved for some time, it may have been exposed to a great deal of information and still not be accurately informed. On some issues, the public may be so polarized into opposing sides that the sides will only trust information that comes from sources that support a predetermined position. If this is the case, you may need to design your program so that information is communicated through media that these groups trust, or you may need to arrange for a third party who is credible to the group to review the material and verify its accuracy.

Hostile or Apathetic Public. Public hostility or apathy may be a reaction to a single issue or the result of a generalized perception of your organization. If the public is hostile, opportunities must be provided for people to express this anger before they can work together cooperatively. In my experience, a hostile public will insist on large public meetings: they want everybody to hear their anger, and they want the power that comes with numbers. You'll need to design any such meeting as a venting session (and you may need more than one of them). Don't try to do any sort of problem solving or try to break the audience into smaller discussion groups until people have had their opportunity to vent.

If the public is apathetic, you may need to design a public information program to stimulate their interest or at least permit an informed choice not to participate.

Divided or United Public. If the community is clearly united, then public participation can be relatively straightforward. But if the public is bitterly divided, it may take a number of conflict resolution forums and the passage of time to arrive at a clear sense of direction from the public. In those circumstances, it is difficult to come out of public participation with a clear sense of direction.

Geographical Compactness or Dispersion. The location of a facility, such as an electric power substation, is likely to be of concern primarily to immediate neighbors. Concern about the increased cost of water or electricity, in contrast, is usually not limited to a specific geographical area. Clearly a public participation program will be different if you need to consult only with people who live within a few blocks rather than residents dispersed over a large area. But if everyone in the wider area is involved, you'll have to plan a much larger program.

Outside Interest. Some issues generate such intense national interest that people from outside the area directly affected by a facility or issue will take an active role in the decision. Fortunately, most issues are not that extreme. But in some instances, issues may have regional significance. In these cases, you may need to provide information to an audience that extends far beyond the immediate community, and you may not be able to resolve the issue without consulting with regional, state, or national groups.

Maturity of the Issue. Some issues cannot be resolved until the time is ripe. Usually that time occurs when both sides realize that continued conflict is getting them nowhere and that they will have to compromise in order to obtain what they want. Sometimes this discovery is made only after the opposing parties have battled with each other for years. Decisions about whether to try to resolve such issues should be made only after an assessment of the parties' willingness to resolve the issue.

Existing Institutions. Sometimes existing institutions in the area, such as home owner associations, can provide a mechanism for participation. Some communities use cable television as a tool for two-way communication.

Characteristics of the Organization

The characteristics of the organization making the decision can impact the design of your public participation program. Examples include:

Organizational Credibility. If your organization's credibility is low, you will need to address the unpleasant reality that it is not a credible source of information and not trusted to perform objective studies. When this is the case, use information from credible third parties as much as possible. Have third parties review all draft publications, or ask an advisory group to review them before you release them to the public. Consult with affected stakeholders during the design of the public participation process, possibly even including a few stakeholders in the public participation design team. Issue contracts to outside experts to do needed studies or provide peer review of your work. Above all, think of ways to maintain visibility for everything that happens in the decision-making process. If you are not credible, people will be suspicious. If credibility is high, you may be able to eliminate some of these credibility-building activities.

Political Sensitivity. Sometimes an issue will be of great concern to senior managers. It may affect a particularly important constituency, set a precedent, or be of particular concern philosophically. In these cases, you may need to involve these internal people who are sensitive about the issue in the planning of the public participation program.

Precommitment to a Single Alternative. In some cases, an organization is committed to a single alternative, even though there is public pressure to consider a range of options. This position may result from legal requirements, a decision by elected officials, or the project's past history. This situation is not promising for public participation, because you may find yourself constantly resisting the public. This can lead to escalation of the issue.

Don't pretend to be interested in what the public has to say if your organization is willing to consider only one alternative. The public will quickly notice the difference between your words and your actions. It will destroy your credibility for this issue and make future public participation programs less credible.

Resources. Sometimes limited resources reflect a lack of management commitment. But sometimes resources are indeed limited, and that's a fact of life. In these cases, concentrate the public participation activities at the key decision point, which is after alternatives have been identified but before you become committed to a preferred alternative.

Worksheet 4.8 lists some of the special circumstances from the paragraphs above that occur frequently. Use the worksheet to remind you of special circumstances in your case that could affect selection of public participation techniques.

Select Public Participation Techniques

All the previous steps are designed to ensure that you know exactly what it is you want to accomplish with the public, who the stakeholders are, and by when the decision must be made. Now the task is to select the techniques for public participation. In order to do this, you need to know about the available techniques and the strengths and weaknesses of each. The techniques are covered in detail in Chapters Six and Seven. Here we examine the logic to selecting techniques.

In the process of defining the decision-making process and schedule in decision analysis, you will have identified the key decision points and the schedule for those decisions (Figure 4.3). The key decision-making stages and the schedule for completing each stage form the structure around which you design the public participation activities.

Public participation activities are planned for each stage in the decision-making process (Figure 4.4). Each stage typically requires a technique for getting information to the public to initiate that stage. Often this includes a summary of what occurred in the prior stage, what was said by the public during that stage, and how those comments influenced decision making. Frequently used techniques are newsletters, reports, briefings, and media releases.

When a process has been out of sight and out of mind for a few months (particularly for six months or more), suspicions are likely to grow among the

FIGURE 4.3. DECISION POINTS ON A GENERIC TIME LINE.

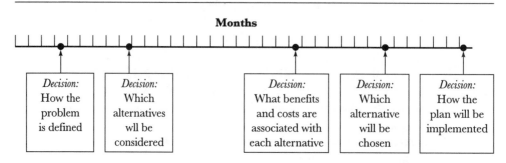

public. Under these conditions, some public participation activities will need to be conducted to maintain visibility and credibility for the process. This might be a newsletter to report on what is happening or meetings of an advisory committee or task force during this time.

The most critical point for active participation by the public is in the weeks immediately prior to a major decision. That's when people can have the most impact. But in order for them to participate, they must first be given information about the results of technical studies and impacts associated with the options being considered. The techniques for informing the public might include reports, newsletters, briefings, advertisements, open houses, and Web page postings. The techniques for participation usually involve one or a series of workshops, public meetings, open houses, mail-in or e-mail comments, or reports by advisory groups or task forces.

A similar round of activities is repeated for each stage in the decision-making process. The techniques chosen need to take into account the probable level of interest and involvement. For example, the stage during which there is likely to be the greatest amount of participation is just before a final decision is made, so the techniques that are chosen need to accommodate this high level of interest. Earlier stages may generate considerable interest from highly organized groups, but may not involve the numbers of people that would be involved in later stages.

To illustrate how this all fits together, Figure 4.5 is an example of a public participation process, this one involving selection of the route for an electric transmission line. This process uses three types of meetings—open houses, workshops, and then public comment meetings—reflecting increased public interest as the process moves closer to a decision. One of the principal techniques for evaluating alternative routes is the establishment of a neighborhood advisory committee. A series of three newsletters keeps the public connected with the process.

FIGURE 4.4. TYPICAL POINTS AT WHICH
PUBLIC PARTICIPATION TECHNIQUES MAY BE REQUIRED.

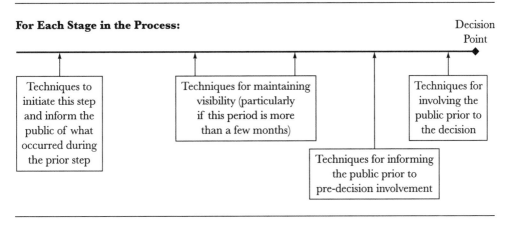

FIGURE 4.5. PLANNING STAGES AND
PUBLIC PARTICIPATION ACTIVITIES ON A TIME LINE.

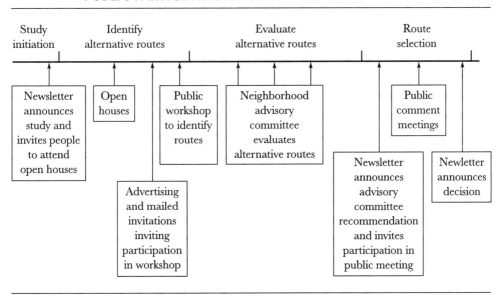

Worksheet 4.9 can be useful as you begin to identify and organize the public participation activities at each stage of the decision-making process.

Prepare a Public Participation Plan

There are important reasons for preparing a written public participation plan:

- Preparing a plan ensures a careful analysis of the ways that public participation fits into the decision-making process, so there are clear connections between the public participation activities and key decisions.
- Preparing a plan and sending it to key parts of the organization for review and comments is a way of verifying there is buy-in and commitment to the approach.
- The plan provides an opportunity for management review of the proposed public participation program. This informs management about the issue and alerts them to political implications of which it might otherwise be unaware.
- The public participation plan can be reviewed by interested stakeholders to obtain their commitment to the process and communicate with them about their opportunities to participate.
- If there are challenges to the adequacy of the program, the existence of a documented plan helps show the rationale for the kind of public participation chosen.

Public participation is usually a team effort. As with many other activities that involve multiple components of an organization, the potential is also there for things to be held up due to internal disagreements or plain old turf battles. By working together to develop a team plan, you are also accomplishing something else: you are getting commitment to implement the plan. When only one part of the organization feels a sense of responsibility for a strategy, that department often has difficulty persuading the other parts of the organization to carry out their portion of the plan in a timely manner. But if the whole team feels it is "our" plan, you have gone a long way toward getting implementation. Often the person in the group with the most public participation experience will be responsible for writing up the plan, based on the decisions made by the team. But the team should feel that it is the team's plan, not the author's.

Some guidelines for preparing public participation plans follow.

What Should Be in a Public Participation Plan

The heart of the plan is a description of the public participation activities that will take place, showing the sequence of activities and how they are interrelated. But if you were a manager or a citizen reviewing the adequacy of a plan, you also

WORKSHEET 4.9. PUBLIC PARTICIPATION ACTIVITIES.

Stage in the Decision-Making Process:	Public Participation Activities	Responsibility	Completion
1.			
2.			
3.			
4.			
5.			
6.			

need to know something about its political context and why this plan is appropriate in these specific circumstances. Thus, a public participation plan should include as a minimum:

- A description of any consultation with outside groups or individuals who contributed to development of the plan
- A description of the key issues raised by the proposed decision and how controversial they are likely to be
- Key individuals, groups, and interests likely to be affected by the issue and whether they will see this decision as significant or controversial
- An assessment of public interest in the decision
- The decision-making process that will be followed to arrive at a decision (on a time line)
- The planned public participation activities
- A review of points at which the planning team will be assembled to reassess whether the plan is on target
- The budget and staff resources that will be needed to implement the plan

How Long the Plan Should Be

There is no set length for public participation plans. The key requirement is that the information be sufficient to permit management to assess the adequacy of the program, allow development of budgets and estimates of staff time, and clearly communicate to the public what it can expect.

Who Should Be Responsible for Developing the Plan

In most decision-making processes, one person is designated as the program or project manager, who is responsible for seeing that the technical studies are done, reports are prepared, and recommendations are developed for organization officials or managers. This person should also be responsible for taking the lead in convening the team that will help prepare the plan, even if he or she draws on the assistance of a public participation specialist to do it. The project manager is held responsible because he or she is the person who can ensure that public participation is an integral part of the way that the decision is made.

◆ ◆ ◆

At the end of this book is an example of a public participation plan for involving citizens in a decision about a municipal solid waste landfill. It is written so that people who were not involved in preparing the plan can understand why public participation was needed and the logic that went into selecting the activities that were used.

Once you have developed your plan, you have the overall strategy for your program in place. But there are still many details to be filled in, so the next stage is implementation planning.

Reference

Aggens, L. "Identifying Different Levels of Public Interest in Participation." In J. L. Creighton, J. D. Priscoli, and C. M. Dunning (eds.), *Public Involvement and Dispute Resolution*. Fort Belvoir, Va.: U.S. Army Institute for Water Resources, 1983.

CHAPTER FIVE

IMPLEMENTATION PLANNING

This chapter discusses the third stage of the public participation thought process, implementation planning. As the name implies, you address the myriad specific details of implementation during implementation planning. For example, if you were planning a public meeting, you would address such questions as these:

- How many meetings do we need? In what cities?
- What meeting facilities will be used?
- What's the agenda for the meeting?
- How will we publicize public participation activities?
- Who will write the newsletters, meeting announcements, feature stories, and other materials?
- Who will lead the meeting? Who will make the organization's presentation during the meeting?
- Who is responsible for setting up the rooms?

The answers to these questions (and the hundreds of similar questions you have to address to implement a program) are very specific to the decision under consideration, your organization, and the stakeholders with whom you'll be working.

Most of my advice regarding implementation is contained in subsequent chapters dealing with the most commonly used public participation techniques.

There are a few comments I need to make, though, about getting organized to conduct a public participation program and the challenges of implementation.

Organizing for Implementation

Implementing a public participation program involves many people, often from different parts of an organization. The challenge is to manage the program in such a way that it is an effective team effort. As we've discussed in previous chapters, one of the most effective ways to create that sense of teamwork is to involve other people—the key people, at a minimum—in jointly developing the public participation plan. Go to other parts of the organization before you form a strong conception of the specific approach that should be used in your public participation program. If you decide how it should be done and then go to them, you will have to sell your plan. In addition, others may not have much sense of commitment or responsibility toward your plan. Invite others in from the beginning, and go through the process of developing the plan together.

Once there's buy-in to your plan, a number of skills or roles are involved in making a public participation program work. One person on the team may be able to provide more than one of these skills. Not everyone who possesses a skill you need will have to be included in planning the overall program; for example, the person who knows how to do mailings may need to be included only when the discussion has to do with the mailing. But you do need to consider all of the following skills and account for them in some way.

Spokesperson

Someone within the group needs to be effective at public speaking, presenting information before groups during briefings or public meetings, and communicating with the media. Generally this should not be a consultant. The person representing your organization should be from your organization, particularly when you are describing policy decisions. A consultant can describe the participation process or give technical information about the alternatives, but should not be explaining substantive decisions made by the organization.

Technical Experts

Normally you'll need one or more people on your team who are expert on the issue being considered. If the decision being discussed raises other issues (for example, if the new low-income housing is proposed for property where there may have been storage of hazardous wastes or people are afraid that the proposed new substation will create electromagnetic fields that may contribute to cancer), you'll also need expertise in these related areas of concern.

Meeting Facilitation

Another key skill is effective meeting leadership. Sometimes this skill is obtained by hiring a professional facilitator. People within your organization may have received facilitation training and can play this role. But be sure to keep the spokesperson and facilitator roles separate and distinct. When anybody who has been the organizational spokesperson tries to act as the facilitator, she or he will no longer be seen as neutral on the content of the meeting and may be viewed as manipulating the structure of the meeting to produce a predetermined outcome. (See Chapter Ten for further discussion of the role of the internal facilitator versus external facilitator.)

Graphic Artist

You may need graphics for printed materials, slide show presentations, or displays. Although you don't want the material to look slick, generally the more visually attractive materials are, the more attention they'll get paid.

Publications—Writing and Production

You may be preparing meeting handouts, reports, or even newsletters and therefore need someone who is good at writing materials in terms that the public readily grasps. Someone may need to prepare a script for a slide show. You'll also need someone to oversee printing and distribution. Sometimes you will need to translate materials into several languages.

Publicity and Media Relations

You'll need someone who knows how to get publicity about the issue and can work with the media to explain the issue in terms that are meaningful to the public.

Mailing List Preparation and Database Maintenance

You may need to send a direct mailing to a neighborhood or to some other targeted audience. You'll need someone who knows how to identify appropriate mailing lists to pinpoint that audience. You'll also be storing public comments, preferable in a form where you can go to the database to help you analyze information. Therefore, you'll need someone who is competent in setting up and maintaining a database.

Logistics

Someone needs to take responsibility for coordinating all the details—for example, arranging for the rooms, getting chairs set up, loading the cars, bringing materials, and making sure you have an extension cord.

Some Hard-Learned Lessons

I have learned a few hard realities about implementing public participation programs.

Never Take a Local Elected Official by Surprise

The first rule of governmental affairs is never to take an elected official by surprise. Few people like surprises, particularly unpleasant ones. But a local elected official who is taken by surprise in front of a constituent is particularly upset and embarrassed as well. Once you've embarrassed an elected official, you'll have trouble influencing that person in the future. When embarrassed, elected officials often make public statements that lock them into positions from which it is difficult for them to retreat later.

So if you are going to begin a public participation program on an issue that is controversial for people within an elected official's constituency or announce a decision that may upset his or her constituents, be sure to inform the elected official before you make the information public. This notice might be a telephone call or a personal briefing. Your governmental affairs staff may want to drop off a newsletter on a potentially controversial topic a day or two before it reaches constituents. Often the timing is critical. Whoever is making the contact has to understand that contact must be made before the newsletter reaches constituents or before the story appears in the newsletter, or the consequences could be substantial.

The Most Time-Consuming Activity Is Getting a Publication Approved

Getting an organization to commit to the language in a publication always takes considerably longer than you expect and often slows the whole process or gets the publications out of sync with the other public participation activities. Inevitably people who care very little what you say in presentations during meetings will want to personally approve every word in a newsletter. Someone will insist that the organization's lawyers review it. It will come back from the lawyers with all sorts of corrections that have nothing to do with legal issues, and you may not be able to tell which corrections matter from a legal perspective and which simply reflect the lawyer's personal writing style.

It's also human nature that reviewers do not come to grips with the material in the same way in a draft document that they will with a final document. So just because someone had few comments on a draft doesn't mean that person won't have many comments as soon as he or she realizes the document has to be taken seriously.

There is no sure way to circumvent these problems. The best you can do is allow more time in the schedule for publications than you think you'll need. You'll end up needing all the extra time you can get.

Always Visit the Meeting Room in Advance

I have developed a personal rule to visit all meeting rooms in advance of the meeting time, but occasionally I get lax. Everything will go fine for awhile, and then I'll show up prepared to run an interactive workshops with participants divided into small groups only to find that the meeting room is an auditorium with fixed chairs in rows. So stick with the rule: always check out the meeting room in advance. Find out what kind of chairs are there. Find out who has a key if the meeting is at 7:00 P.M. and the building closes at 5:00 P.M. Find out how to get into the storage room for chairs and tables. Never assume the room will be set up the way you requested.

Always Have a Technology Backup Plan

You've prepared a marvelous presentation for your public meeting using a computer and a digital projector. But what's your backup plan in case the computer freezes up, the bulb on the projector burns out, there are no electric plugs a reasonable distance from where the projector has to be set up, there is no screen or place to show the slides, or the power goes out? All of these catastrophes have happened to me. I've also had the opening speaker not show up. I've had the meeting room locked up and no way to get in the room.

Although I'm in awe of what can be done with technology, heavy dependence on technology leaves you particularly vulnerable if anything goes wrong. So after you've planned how you want things to work, do a little planning on what to do if they don't work as expected, particularly what happens if the technology doesn't work. You may need to duplicate handouts just in case the PowerPoint presentation can't be shown. You may need to be sure you have flip charts in case the brainstorming list you were going to display on a screen using your laptop can't be shown. Always take power cords and extra lamp bulbs for the digital or overhead projector and any other supplies you need to survive in case of technological crises.

Make Sure You Don't Outnumber the Public

Earlier I listed the skills you need to implement a public participation process. The list is considerable. Often that means that if you have a meeting, lots of people feel involved in making the program work and they all want to be at the meeting. But there's no surer way to make a community feel either overwhelmed or upset at how many resources are being expended than to have more people from your organization show up at public meetings than people from the community. You may have to send very clear messages to your staff to ensure that your own people don't outnumber the public.

◆ ◆ ◆

With these general words of caution based on occasionally painful experience, we turn now to the specifics of using a variety of public participation activities.

PART THREE

PUBLIC PARTICIPATION TOOL KIT

The previous chapters have described the thought process necessary to identify the tasks and audiences for which you need to use techniques. The following two chapters contain an overview of what I believe are the most frequently used public participation techniques. Think of them as a tool kit from which you can draw the tools appropriate to the specific circumstances of your public participation program. Every technique has value, but only if appropriately used for the task for which it was intended.

This does not mean that I have included every technique that exists. In addition, elements from one technique can be combined with elements of another to produce something sufficiently different that the new approach can be given a different name. Different consultants may call the same techniques by different names. Consultants often distinguish themselves by developing or employing a specific technique, sometimes identifying these techniques in a way that will make their own technique distinctive.

This list provides a sense of the possibilities. I hope it will be sufficiently broad that it will give you permission to create your own techniques. Much of the innovation in the field occurs when someone faces a challenge and develops a new approach to address it. Typically people build on techniques they already know, adapting those techniques or combining techniques in ways that produce something new. There is value in knowing about the existing range of techniques as a starting point. But this list should not be seen as a constraint.

I have divided these chapters into two categories, public information techniques and public participation techniques, as a reminder that while getting information to the public is an integral part of public participation, getting information to the public is not by itself public participation. Public participation requires two-way communication and genuine interaction with the public.

The participation techniques could also be divided into two categories. Some techniques solicit information from the public but do not provide for a significant exchange of information and are not designed to result in genuine deliberation between affected citizens. The descriptions of the techniques in Chapter Six, on information to the public, are less detailed than the descriptions in Chapter Seven, on the information from the public. The reason is that many organizations are already knowledgeable about public information techniques and are likely to have public information professionals on staff. If you do need more information about public information techniques, a good place to start is the *Communicators Guide for Federal, State, Regional and Local Communicators*, developed by the Federal Communicators Network [http://govinfo.library.unt.edu/npr/library/papers/bkgrd/communicators.pdf].

If you are relatively new to the field of public participation, you may want to read through the entire list of techniques carefully to understand the range of possibilities. If you are an experienced practitioner, you may want to scan the list, pausing on those techniques that are less familiar. Whenever you are in the process of designing a public participation program, you can use these chapters as a checklist to remind you of possible techniques to consider.

Some public participation techniques are general-purpose tools that you are likely to use in a number of public participation programs. Virtually every public participation program includes some kind of public meeting. Chapters Eight through Eleven provide a much more detailed look at how to design and conduct a variety of different kinds of public meetings and workshops. Other techniques covered in more depth in subsequent chapters include:

Chapter Twelve	Working with Advisory Groups
Chapter Thirteen	Conducting Interviews
Chapter Fourteen	Working with the Media
Chapter Fifteen	Analyzing Public Comment
Chapter Sixteen	Evaluating Public Participation
Chapter Seventeen	Using Public Participation Consultants

At the end of Chapter Seven are references to resource materials with detailed descriptions of techniques and instructions for using them. There are more references for the participatory techniques than for the public information techniques because most organizations are already familiar with most of the public information techniques.

There is also a wealth of information on almost all of these techniques on the Internet. Go to a major search engine, and type in the name of the technique. You'll be astonished at the range of the materials available, much of which can be downloaded immediately.

CHAPTER SIX

TECHNIQUES FOR GETTING INFORMATION *TO* THE PUBLIC

This chapter provides an overview of techniques for getting information to the public. Inside every public participation program is a good public information program. Before people can participate, they need information so they can participate in an informed manner. In particular, they need information about how a decision could affect them and their interests.

Participants need complete, unbiased information. They need the same kind of information (although perhaps written more simply) that you would provide decision makers within your own organization. And like your decision makers, if the public senses you are biasing the information to produce a particular outcome or omitting information that might change the outcome, they will stop trusting you as the source of information and start looking to others. In fact, if your organization is seen as an advocate for a particular outcome, the public will assume that you are manipulating information to produce the outcome you desire.

The media will always write stories that maximize controversy. This is their idea of newsworthiness. Interest groups will provide information that is slanted or given spin to support their particular position. They assume you will do this too.

This leaves the organization sponsoring the public participation program in a difficult position. You are usually the only potential source of complete and unbiased information. But you are also likely to be viewed with suspicion, particularly by groups advocating a particular outcome.

You must make exceptional efforts to ensure the information you give to the public is as objective as possible. You may want to have your materials reviewed by other agencies, such as regulatory agencies or an existing citizen advisory group or peer review panel. In some cases, organizations have contracted with outside groups, such as the League of Women Voters (a nonpartisan organization committed to the informed involvement of the public) to write documents.

You may never convince advocacy groups that your material is objective. They have a stake in being critical. The target is the middle. The goal is to ensure that people who do not have a predetermined position perceive the information they receive from you as useful and trustworthy.

Be aware that your efforts to achieve objectivity may not be supported by people in your own organization who are more used to a public relations orientation. They may define their job as making the organization look good, even if it means spinning the story by leaving out certain facts or controlling the emphasis. One of the reasons it takes so much time to get documents reviewed inside organizations is that there can be struggles between people with a public participation orientation and people with a public relations orientation.

I've consulted to several government agencies for a number of years, some as many as thirty years. Based on that experience, my judgment is that in the long run, any organization comes out ahead if it is perceived as a source of complete and unbiased information. There are times this will cause temporary embarrassment. But credibility, once lost, is very hard to regain.

Here we look at some of the most frequently used techniques for providing information *to* the public.

Briefings

Briefings consist of a personal visit, a small group meeting, or a telephone call to inform people of progress being made or an action about to be taken. They are a way of keeping key elected officials, agencies, or key interest groups informed. They often lead to two-way communication: you may receive valuable information back in response to your announcement.

Briefings may be particularly important if your actions could result in political controversy that could affect elected officials or agencies. If you are taking an action that could affect an elected official or manager of an agency, never let that official find out about it by reading the newspaper or, worse, having a constituent phone and ask her what she's going to do about it. As much as possible, you should provide the information first even if people don't like what you're telling them.

That way there's no added resentment from being taken by surprise and embarrassed in front of constituents.

When possible, take along a document or publication that provides the same information you are presenting in the briefing. This gives elected officials or senior managers something they can pass on to their staff. This is important, because what gets passed on otherwise is not predictable.

Although valuable, briefings require considerable staff time. Typically they are targeted at particularly important groups or important groups that could have a negative reaction if they don't feel consulted before a decision is made or an action taken.

Exhibits and Displays

One way to inform the public and stimulate people to participate in your public participation program is to set up exhibits or displays in public places that get lots of foot traffic, such as in a major shopping mall, or at major community events such as county fairs, street fairs, or sporting events. Although preparing an exhibit or display can be costly, it can often be designed so that it can be used at other events or locations. An exhibit is always more effective if it is also staffed by a knowledgeable person who can answer questions.

Feature Stories

A feature story is a news story that is written or narrated by a reporter rather than just an announcement based on your news release.

One way to get the media interested in doing a story is to send a news release to a newspaper or radio and television stations. This is particularly likely to get their attention if the issue is already newsworthy or controversial. But you're more likely to get someone interested if you make a personal contact with an editor or reporter who has an interest in this kind of issue. Start by identifying who at the newspaper has been covering stories about your organization. If there's no one you know, look for a reporter who specializes in the kind of issues in which your organization is involved. Typically reporters, at least on larger newspapers, have an area of emphasis, such as environmental stories, health stories, or political stories. You can also contact an editor (such as the city editor, if your issue is local).

Once you've identified someone to contact, be prepared to give a short, pithy explanation of why this issue is newsworthy; this is your pitch. You may also need to offer a hook to the story that increases the story's human interest value. For example, if you are trying to get a story on cleaning up unexploded ordnance and explosives on a military base that has been closed, pitch the story with some strong human interest angle, such as a cleanup worker and how his family feels about his going out every day and handling dangerous explosives. Or (after consulting with your safety officer) take a reporter out to watch workers dig up and detonate dangerous items.

If you are dealing with television reporters, remember that television is a visual medium. Part of your pitch should be identifying interesting visual material that could be included in the story. Television reporters are always looking for a way of making the story go beyond talking heads (pictures of people being interviewed). Remember that the visual image will stick with people. If your message is to tell people that something is safe but the visual image is of something that is frightening or dangerous, the image is what people will remember.

When you talk with reporters, establish and maintain your credibility. Make an effort to provide full and complete information. Let the reporter know how to verify what you are saying by providing suggestions for credible third parties or documents he or she can check out. Expect the reporter to ask you what people who oppose your organization's actions say. Avoid characterizing what others say (they should speak for themselves), but provide the reporter with names of people who have a different point of view.

Provide the reporter with backup publications. This gives the reporter something to rely on if he or she needs to clarify an issue. Also, the reporter will put this material in a file and will draw on them when stories come up in the future.

If your project becomes highly controversial, the problem is no longer getting the news media interested. It is being sure that you provide information that is timely, factual, and objective.

Information Repositories

Many state or federal environmental laws require the organization proposing an action to give the public access to the studies and background documentation used during the decision-making process. This usually requires setting up an information repository in public places (such as public libraries) where documents can be stored and are available for public viewing.

As Internet access becomes universal, information repositories at physical locations will be replaced entirely by virtual repositories or open-access Web pages. Organizations that have established Web pages report that people who have access to the Web much prefer the Web-based repositories, and visits to physical repositories have dropped dramatically. The advantage of the virtual repository is that people can go on the Web in their own home or office at any hour of the day or night, access all the relevant documents, download them, and print them out.

For the moment, not everyone has access to the Internet. However, most public libraries offer free or inexpensive computer access, and these are often more conveniently located than a few physical repositories.

Some people feel uncomfortable using a computer. This group often includes older people or people from minority communities who have not been exposed to computer use as part of their daily lives. The number of these people is rapidly shrinking, however. Recent data show that once seniors master the Internet, they access it more frequently and for longer periods of time than the rest of the population. Internet use by minority communities is beginning to equal use by the general population. In fact, some minorities, particularly Asians, use the Internet more than the general population. So although it may be necessary to maintain a few physical repositories, the need for them will soon vanish.

Internet

The potential for using the Internet as a medium for public participation is substantial. Based on how the Internet has been used so far, it is clear that it can serve in a number of ways:

- An information repository or library, providing access to all documents and reports that are used during the decision-making process
- A way to quickly broadcast information about meetings or events to large numbers of people who have expressed an interest in the issue or decision being made
- A hotline that people can contact to get up-to-the-minute information about an emergency (such as a forest fire or water deliveries during drought conditions), a construction schedule, or updates on legislative deliberations
- A chatroom where people interested in the issue can post messages or documents for others to read or carry on a continuing discussion of the issue
- A way people can submit e-mail comments on alternatives under consideration or comment on study progress
- A place to post photos (or even videos) that show the alternatives being considered

The promise of the Internet goes beyond these uses, but we're still figuring out which other uses are beneficial.

Mailing Out Key Technical Reports
or Environmental Documents

Many organizations produce large technical reports and environmental studies as part of decision-making processes. Simply putting technical reports or environmental documents at libraries or other repositories does not buy much in terms of credibility. Key documents need to be mailed directly to leaders of organized groups and interests, including business, environmental, or neighborhood groups. When you construct a mailing list, code the names of people being put into the list so that you can pull up a smaller list of people to whom copies of key reports will be sent. If people on your list have access to computers, you may find it much cheaper to send CD versions of documents rather than paper documents.

If you put these documents on your Web page, you may find it more effective to send a two- to three-page summary of the reports to the larger mailing list, advising people that they can access the full report on the Web page. Most people read the summary and never bother with the full report. If you are sending out a regular newsletter, you could describe the study results in your newsletter and refer people to the Web page or provide a clip-out request form for those who want copies of the study. This approach can sharply reduce the number of copies of thick reports that need to be sent out.

Mass Mailings

If you need to reach the general public, you may need to prepare a publication and mail it directly to people's homes. An alternative is a newspaper insert (discussed below).

There are companies in most communities that have mailing lists that will allow you to target your audience (usually by mail code) and will do the mailing. You deliver the publications, and they take care of the rest.

One caution with mass mailing: be sure the mailing doesn't look slick or expensive. The public is very sensitive to what they perceive as efforts to buy their support through flashy material. This is particularly true for government agencies. For this reason, if you are sending a large volume of mail, you may want to print it on newsprint so that it doesn't look expensive.

Media Interviews and Appearances on Talk Shows

Normally agencies want to respond to requests for a media interview or any opportunity to appear on a radio or television talk show. You may seek out such opportunities as a way to get information out to the public. If the public has a better understanding of what the agency is doing, it is more likely to support the agency (although this is not always the case). Interviews are an opportunity to say what you want to say. An interview that will be broadcast on radio or television also gives you a chance to talk directly to the public and set the record straight without filtering by the reporter.

Establish who in your organization handles initial inquiries about interviews. Many agencies require that the organization's public affairs officer be the initial point of contact. This person will then call on agency staff to give the interviews, as appropriate. In other cases, contacts may come directly to technical people involved in the public participation program. Be sure you have a protocol worked out for how you will handle requests for interviews that come directly to technical people. In some cases, public affairs officers are comfortable just being informed that the interview is occurring, because they know the particular technical person has the experience and skills to handle the interviews. In other cases, the public affairs officer will want technical people to refer all requests for interviews to him or her.

One thing a public affairs officer will do (and any technical person should do if handling a request for an interview) is get the details:

- The name of the reporter and the publication, station, or organization
- Ground rules
- The topic and angle
- The reporter's questions, or at least the subjects to be discussed
- From what viewpoint the questions are posed
- The objective
- When the interview will be printed or aired

Many technical people feel obliged to respond to any request for an interview without asking these questions. But the reality is that an interview is a mutual benefit situation, something like a business deal: you get your message out to the public, and the reporter gets a story that provides content for his or her organization and is perceived as fulfilling a public service. Since it is a mutual gain situation, you have every right to discuss what is going to take place and, if need be, negotiate what you are and are not willing to discuss. You also have the right to ask for reasonable time to prepare.

Find out as much as you can about the audience for this particular reporter or medium. Many broadcast media have a specific audience, and the more you can present the story in a way that is relevant to that audience, the more effective you will be.

After you have learned all you can about the audience, define at least three important messages you want to be sure will come across during the interview.

This could be as simple as (1) the topic of the public participation program, (2) that you are holding a meeting at a particular time and place, and (3) that the purpose of the meeting will be to discuss alternatives. Or the three messages might be considerably more complex. What is key is that you are defining what you want to say and which of your points are the most important.

You may also want to do some advance preparation for the questions you may be asked to address. Try to determine the five best questions you could be asked and the five worst questions you could be asked. You might prepare an opening and closing line, something short and to the point, even if you end up not using them.

If you are preparing for a particularly important or challenging interview, practice, practice, practice. Your public affairs officer might pretend he or she is the reporter, for example, and ask you a series of questions in a role-play interview. Practice making short, simple responses; most professional media try to hold their responses to twenty-second chunks of information.

Your public affairs officer may also train you in phrases you can use to be sure you communicate the most important messages and refrain from saying anything that is inappropriate—for example:

- Ways to avoid an inappropriate question: "The answer to that would be pure speculation"; "My personal opinion isn't important; what is important is . . ."
- Ways to bridge to another key message: "Just as important is . . . "; "Another important point . . . "; "I don't know about that, but what I do know . . ."
- Flagging points that are particularly important: "Don't lose sight of the fact that . . . "; "The most important thing is . . . "; "I think it boils down to . . ."

Media Kits

One way to help reporters is to prepare a media kit that provides a summary of the key information they might need throughout the decision-making process. Often a reporter, under pressure to meet a deadline, will find it difficult to contact you by telephone but will turn to the media kit as an authoritative source of information.

Typically a media kit consists of a folder with pockets that contain short summaries of project need, the decision-making process, summaries of key technical studies or environmental documents, and other relevant information. Keep in mind that reporters work under extreme time pressures, so information must be in summary form. If you publish a regular newsletter, include past copies in the media kit, because they often present the important background information at the level of information a reporter needs to prepare a story.

Once a media kit is prepared, identify the reporters or editors you believe will be interested in the story and arrange to drop in, deliver the media kit, and answer any questions on the spot. If the issue starts to attract attention, be sure that you provide the media kit to any reporter who inquires about the process.

News Conferences and Media Briefings

A news conference is an event to which you invite the media and at which you make an announcement or give a briefing. Usually there is an opportunity for questions from the media.

The topic of the news conference or the person conducting a news conference must be newsworthy, or no one will show up. News conferences are usually reserved for major announcements or for a time when a well-known spokesperson is available. Getting a major elected official or senior official to hold the news conference increases media interest.

The major advantage of a news conference, particularly when you are dealing with radio and television audiences, is that your spokesperson can speak directly to the public. Even if the reporting from the news conference is reduced to seconds on the evening news, there will usually be short sound bites from the news conference included in the news coverage.

News conferences are another way to stimulate the interest of the media in doing feature news stories.

A variation on the news conference is the field trip. For example, invite the media to take a field trip out to the site of a potentially controversial project. Load up a bus, and brief reporters en route to the project.

Newsletters

Organizations frequently publish and distribute periodic newsletters during public participation programs. Newsletters are an effective way of keeping the people who are most interested in the decision-making process informed and at a level of detail you could never achieve through the media. Newsletters are a means of sustaining interest throughout a decision-making process that may last for months. They document the fact that the public has been kept fully informed throughout the process and provide good background information in press kits.

Typically, newsletters are targeted at the people who are most interested in the issue. They might include neighbors, leaders of interest groups, elected officials, agency representatives, or anybody who has participated in public meetings or other public participation activities. On controversial issues, mailing lists can be as large as five thousand to ten thousand people.

The value of a newsletter depends in part on how well it's done. A newsletter that is visually attractive, with plenty of graphics, and written in simple, everyday language will usually be widely read.

Newsletters can be expensive to produce. It takes staff time to write the newsletters, the time and effort taken up by all the internal approvals can be exhausting, and there are printing and mailing costs.

An e-mail mailing list can sharply reduce printing and distribution costs. Alternatively, if your organization does regular mailings to customers, such as sending a monthly utility bill, design the newsletter to be part of this regular mailing. Usually this requires significant format changes and a shorter newsletter, but it does reach a larger audience.

Newsletters used as part of public participation programs must be written objectively. If they are a promotion piece for a predetermined position, they will lose credibility. To ensure objectivity and protect credibility, you might have the wording of the newsletter reviewed by a citizen advisory group or a peer review panel, since such a group is usually highly sensitive to political nuance. In highly polarized situations, a newsletter could be published by another governmental entity or a neutral organization.

Newspaper Inserts

One way to reach a whole community with the same information is to prepare the information in the form of a newspaper insert. As long as the insert is prepared to the newspaper's specifications, the cost can be moderate. This is one way to reach beyond the most actively involved citizens and be sure that the public at large has an opportunity to be informed. It can also generate a lot of interest in a hurry. Just like newsletters, the more attractive the insert is and the easier it is to read, the more impact it will have on the community.

Once again, be sure that the insert presents information in an objective and balanced manner. Use of public funds to circulate information that is seen as advocacy can stir a strong negative public reaction.

News Releases

News releases are typically one to three pages in length and make an announcement about an upcoming event or discuss a decision that has been made. Occasionally a news release shows up in a newspaper or on the air just the way you wrote it. But more often, it is used to convince an editor to do a story, and the reporter assigned to the story will contact you for follow-up information. Be sure to include the name and number of somebody in your organization whom the media can contact if they need more information.

If you are in a small community, your story is likely to receive attention in the local paper. If you're in a larger community, you are competing with lots of other news stories to get the attention of the media. As a result, news releases are often written with a hook, that is, a slant or human interest feature to the story, which immediately convinces the media that their readers or viewers should be interested. If you are in a competitive news market, follow up on the initial mailing with a telephone call to the editor to offer additional information and encourage attention to the story.

Write news releases with the most important information in the first sentence, the second most important information in the second sentence, and so on. If editors trim a story to fit into a smaller space, they usually trim from the bottom. So be sure you have the most essential information at the very beginning of the news release.

Paid Advertisements

Paid advertisements are one sure way to make an announcement or present information to the public in newspapers or on radio or television. The chief advantage is that you control what is said and how it is presented.

Paid advertisements are expensive, however. One major consideration in paying for advertising is how the public will react to the expenditure of funds by your organization for this purpose. The public is normally quite appreciative of paid advertisements announcing public meetings, particularly if they are visually attractive, or provide information people need to participate in a decision-making process. Occasionally, though, there is criticism of large ads, even if they are providing information. There is almost sure to be criticism of any advertisement paid for with public funds that is considered a form of advocacy.

Panels

Panels are one way of providing information during a briefing session or public information meeting. Instead of having just one speaker, select a panel of individuals representing differing points of view to discuss the issue. This can be followed by questions or comments from the audience or small group discussions.

The term *panel* is sometimes used even if each person on the "panel" makes a prepared speech and there is no interaction among the panelists. This is not actually a panel; it is a series of speakers who address a related topic and sit at the same table. This may be acceptable for communicating information, but it loses virtually all of the benefits of a panel.

Panels are interesting when there is interaction and discussion among the panelists. They can engage and stimulate the interest of the audience in the subject. Just like a movie or drama, panels are more interesting when there is conflict or views differ.

If the circumstances require that each panelist make a presentation, you can increase interaction by asking other members of the panel to comment on or discuss each presentation, to be followed by the next presentation, discussion, presentation, and so on. But the best way to stimulate interest in the topic is to present a topic and let panelists discuss it in some depth. Panels often need to be moderated, to put time limits on subject matter, lead the discussion to new topics, or keep panelists from interrupting each other.

Presentations to Community Groups

One effective way to communicate with influential people in the community is to arrange presentations to civic groups, business association meetings, environmental groups, neighborhood groups, or home owners' association meetings. If you'll be making a number of presentations, it's advisable to prepare a slide show or other visual aids. A visual presentation is not only more interesting to the audience; it communicates more information in a short period of time. You may be able to prepare a slide show in modules, so that you can customize it to match the interests of an audience.

You can build credibility for your technical studies by making presentations to professional societies of engineers, planners, or other professional groups. These presentations help to create a general perception in the technical community that you are doing a professionally competent study. You do need to tailor your presentation to the technical interests of your audience.

Public Service Announcements

In the United States, radio and television stations used to be required by the Federal Communications Commission to broadcast, without charge, a certain number of announcements on behalf of charities, government agencies, and community groups. This is no longer a formal requirement, but many stations still broadcast announcements as a public service. In particular, they are likely to run announcements of public meetings, events, or other opportunities for the public to participate.

The problem with public service announcements is that there is no guarantee that an announcement will be run, particularly if the issue is not particularly controversial. The announcement may also be aired at odd hours when relatively few people are listening.

Some organizations have increased their chances of being aired by submitting prerecorded cassettes with background music or using a celebrity announcer (a local political figure, a sports figure, or a local comedian, for example). An entertaining announcement is more likely to be broadcast and more likely to have an impact. But in the end, the radio or television will evaluate your announcement based on whether the public will see this as a service, not whether you think it is. So if you are publicizing an opportunity for the public to participate, you're likely to get some coverage. If you are pushing a point of view, which you shouldn't be doing in the context of a public participation program anyway, you are less likely to get coverage.

Symposia

One way to inform the community, or at least the part of the community that is highly interested in an issue, is to invite them to attend a symposium on the subject. A symposium is a meeting designed primarily to inform participants without asking attendees to take a position on the topics under discussion. Typically a symposium consists of a series of presentations, panel discussions, and question-and-answer periods, possibly including some time for attendees to discuss the topic in smaller groups. The presenters and panelists are established experts on the topic, representing a range of viewpoints, as well as a range of organizations. If there's no disagreement, the symposium is likely to be boring and uninteresting. The reason for using outside experts is to increase interest (and attendance) and make the symposium more credible; if all the presentations are from the viewpoint of your organization, they will not be credible. Symposia are an opportunity to stretch people's thinking by exposing the audience to ideas with which they may not be familiar. Although a symposium does not result in an expression of public sentiment, participants' viewpoints sometimes coalesce into a climate of opinion that can be influential.

CHAPTER SEVEN

TECHNIQUES FOR GETTING INFORMATION *FROM* THE PUBLIC

The essence of public participation, as distinct from simply public information, is two-way communication and interaction between the organization reaching a decision and people interested in or affected by the decision. This chapter discusses techniques that can be used to elicit participation from the public. Some of the techniques also provide for interaction, with communication in both directions. Some of these techniques are general-purpose tools, and others serve more specialized purposes.

Within this list of techniques, there is considerable difference in the levels of interaction, depending on which technique you use. A public hearing provides a somewhat ritualized and formal interaction, with people making speeches to (and sometimes at) each other. Workshops or advisory groups provide high levels of interaction, although the agency retains the ultimate decision-making authority. The highest level of interaction is joint decision making, such as a negotiation. The goal is to match the technique to the level of interaction you need at a particular stage in the public participation process. That's why the thought process set out in Chapter Four has you spend so much time writing out public participation objectives and defining the information exchange (the flow of information that must occur both to and from the public). That information provides the specifications for assessing what technique you should use. The challenge is to use the techniques that best meet those specifications.

Advisory Groups and Task Forces

Next to public meetings, the public participation technique most often used is a citizens' advisory group. An advisory group is a small group of people (usually fewer than twenty-five) representing various interests, points of view, or fields of expertise that is set up to advise an organization on its programs or proposed actions. Some organizations use advisory groups as a primary mechanism for involving the public. Others use advisory groups under specific circumstances, as an adjunct to other kinds of public participation activities.

More information about advisory groups is provided in Chapter Twelve.

Appreciative Inquiry Summit

Appreciative Inquiry Summit is one of several techniques described in this chapter (the others are Future Search, Open Space, and charrette) that are multiday events, usually involving large numbers of people, designed to bring people together to agree on changes needed in an organization or community. The technique was created as part of the organization development field and designed to bring about whole system change. Recently it has been used in communities as well.

Each summit, unique in design, typically lasts from two to five days. The number of participants ranges from one hundred to twenty-five hundred. A four-day design might have the following activities:

Day One: The first day is designed to discover the organization's (or community's) positive change core—those positive characteristics of the community or organization upon which change can be built. This could involve such activities as having all participants conduct one-on-one appreciative inquiry interviews (an interview utilizing questions designed to elicit information about positive attributes or strengths of individuals, organizations, or communities) of other participants; small group sharing of highlight stories and best practices discovered during the interviews; creating a visual map illustrating the strengths, competencies, positive hopes, and feelings of the organization; or identifying the factors that have sustained the organization over time and are desirable in the future.

Day Two: The second day is spent envisioning the organization's greatest potential for positive influence and impact in the world. This could involve exercises such as: "Imagine it is 2010 and your organization has just won an award for the outstanding socially responsible business of the year. What is the award for?" Small groups may discuss dreams for the organization they collected during interviews and make presentations of these dreams in skits or other creative presentations to the whole group.

Day Three: During Day Three, the participants work on designing an organization in which the positive change core identified on the first day is built into the strategies, processes, and systems of the organization.

Day Four: Small groups brainstorm possible actions and share them with the large group. Individuals declare publicly their intention for action. Using the open space technique (see below), small groups are formed of people interested in implementing specific programs. This is followed by a closing activity with the large group.

At the core of this approach is a constant focus on the existing strengths, capabilities, and positive feelings of the participants, in contrast to approaches that start out by defining organizational (or community) needs or deficiencies.

Beneficiary Assessment

Beneficiary assessment is a consultative methodology used by the World Bank and other development agencies to ensure that project beneficiaries, including the poor and those lacking political power, can provide insights on how a project will affect them. It was developed as a technique for use in the slums of Latin America. Beneficiary assessment is designed to solicit qualitative information, including subjective opinions, on a development activity. However, beneficiary assessments do seek a sufficiently large sample that quantitative results can be developed.

The techniques used in beneficiary assessment include a kind of conversational interview, focus group discussions, and participant observation. Focus groups, as used in beneficiary assessment, are facilitated discussions with a small group of people who share common concerns (but they are not the highly structured kind of focus group used in market research). Participant observation involves having researchers reside in a community of potential beneficiaries for periods from several weeks to several months. The observers attempt to develop sufficient rapport and involvement in the beneficiaries' everyday activities to develop an in-depth understanding of their motives and attitudes.

Charrette

Charrette is a French term. In the nineteenth century, proctors from the École des Beaux-Arts carried architectural students' drawings and projects to the school in a cart called a charrette. Occasionally students ran alongside the cart trying to make last-minute improvements as the charrette approached the school. The term has evolved over time to describe a type of workshop. The technique is increasingly used in the fields of architecture, planning, and design. It has also been used in education and social services.

A charrette, or design charrette, is an intense effort that lasts for several days to solve a problem or come up with a design in a limited time. It is focused on a single issue or issue, such as designing a building or planning a neighborhood.

There are several versions of the charrette. In one version, participants agree to work together for three or four days. After an initial kick-off session, participants are broken into small groups, and each group is given the same assignment, for example, designing a community center. Each small group is assigned one or more artists or architects who capture the group's ideas and portray them visually. The groups then discuss what they like and dislike about the proposals developed in the small groups. The small group assignments and large group discussions can be repeated as many times as needed until there is broad general agreement on an approach.

Another version of charrette has many of the same elements (a series of sessions spread over multiple days and a design team) but doesn't try to hold the same participants for the entire period. At the core of the process is a design team, typically a multidisciplinary team of professionals. Their job is to take what they are hearing from the public and translate it into a form that could be implemented. This might be designs, but it could also be an educational policy or new zoning regulations, whatever the topic of the charrette may be. Stakeholders are specifically invited to attend two public meetings, several days apart, but they are also invited to drop in at a charrette studio, where the design team is working to translate what they hear from the public into implementable designs, plans, or programs.

The first step is for the design team to set up the charrette studio, the physical space in which the design team will work and which will be a constant open house for anyone who wants to drop in and discuss the topic of the charrette. Because it is both workspace and discussion space, the design team does its work in a highly visual manner, posted on walls, so that the public can see what they are doing.

The first public meeting is a kickoff meeting (and a site tour if the issue under discussion has to do with a physical space) followed by a hands-on workshop. The next day, the design team begins to develop alternative designs, plans, or programs based on what they heard in the workshop. All participants are invited to drop in at the charrette studio to discuss the issue further or react to the materials the design team is developing. The design team may also go out into the community and conduct interviews with key stakeholders.

For several days, the design team keeps refining the plans until it has a proposal to present to the community. There is then a public meeting during which the proposal is presented to the public for comment or approval.

Over the next several weeks, the design team continues to refine the proposal and may continue to interview stakeholders. Approximately one month after the charrette, there is a final public meeting to review the documents prepared by the design team.

One of the keys to the success of a charrette is a well-planned public relations effort prior to the charrette to get the interest and involvement of the community in the charrette. The other key is the skill of the design team. The team must have the ability to take what they hear from the public, providing sufficient detail so that is implementable, yet keeping their own ideas and biases out of the process sufficiently so that the final product is recognizable to the public as a translation of what they told the design team.

City Walk

People's interactions with their environment often become so routine that they no longer see (or at least no longer have emotional reactions to) features in their environment that are either problems or opportunities. The term *City Walk* was coined by Lawrence Halprin, a distinguished landscape architect and urban planner, to describe a workshop designed to resensitize people to community problems and opportunities to which they may have become inured. Many others have since designed other variations of this kind of workshop, sometimes calling the event by a different name (for convenience, I'll continue to use Halprin's term).

In a City Walk, a group of community leaders agree to participate in an event during which they reexperience their community or a portion of their community, and then draw on their observations to recommend planning policies or standards. Initially a planner or group of planners identifies key issues, problems, or opportunities and places in the community that illustrate these. The planners prepare a series of instructions, that is, a script, that directs people to particular locations and gives them instructions to interact with people or facilities in those areas, for example, "order a cup of coffee and sit and take notice of other people who are sharing this space" or "take a ride on the subway to Park Avenue, recording your observations about the kinds of people riding the subway." Although the script directs people to focus on certain experiences, it is written so that it does not tell people what their emotional reaction to that space or amenity should be.

Participants record their observations and experiences in notebooks, then gather and discuss their experiences. This final workshop may include various structured activities in which people draw on their observations during the City Walk to develop planning recommendations.

Coffee Klatch

A coffee klatch (or *klatsch*) is a small, informal discussion with a group of people in a private home, usually with light refreshments. Originally the term simply meant people getting together for coffee and conversation. But for public participation purposes, a coffee klatch is more like the coffees scheduled by politicians during a campaign. There is usually a short presentation, followed by questions, answers, and discussion.

The fact that the coffee klatch is held in a private home changes the dynamic considerably from a public meeting, as participants are usually on their best behavior because they are guests in a home. Participants discuss issues informally. The more intimate setting allows people to get to know each other personally, not just in roles or as representatives of organizations.

Because the number of people who can meet in a private home is limited, you may need to hold a series of coffee klatches to reach more people.

Coffee Klatches in Action

A federal agency was conducting a study that potentially was highly controversial because it involved reassignment of existing water rights. If the agency used typical public comment meetings, the possibility of angry polarization was high. Instead, the agency held a series of coffee klatches to gather information before developing alternative proposals. The agency contracted with the League of Women Voters, a volunteer organization that encourages civic involvement, to line up people who would volunteer the use of their homes for a coffee klatch. The coffee klatches worked well to diffuse the polarization and produced many insights. But they also proved to be very staff intensive.

Computer-Aided Negotiation

Over the next few years, I expect to see far more use of computer modeling as a tool during workshops. Some of this is already occurring. In the water field, there are now several computer models that can replicate the flows of water in river basins using a laptop computer. For example, the U.S. Army Corps of Engineers Institute for Water Resources (www.iwr.usace.army.mil) has developed a number of models using a software package called STELLA. A private consultant, Dan Sheer, has developed a software program called OASIS that he and his firm, HydroLogics (www.HydroLogics.net), have used in computer-aided negotiation. If there is a controversy over allocation of water in a river basin, these computer models provide quick information that allows participants to search for alternatives that do the best job of meeting everybody's needs.

During the first step in the process, consultants work with decision makers representing the key stakeholders to identify the necessary attributes of the model of the hydrologic system. This includes identifying performance measures that will be used to evaluate which alternative strategies are better. This important step results in a model that decision makers can trust, because it was built to their specifications.

Once the model has been developed, representatives of stakeholder groups, such as a number of water districts or agencies managing instream flows for fisheries, can meet and prepare a set of demands for certain quantities of water at certain times of the year. The model provides immediate feedback on how well the river basin could meet those demands and which demands went unmet during which time of the year. The negotiation can continue as a sort of game with successive rounds of play, with the players adjusting the demands in an effort to find the set of demands that the river basin can meet and does the best job of meeting the needs of all the users. Typically decision makers learn a great deal about the capability of the river system to meet the competing demands. Participants also learn a great deal about each other's objectives. Finally, decision makers can refine alternatives to optimize benefits to all the parties.

This approach differs considerably from other efforts to use computers to evaluate alternatives, because it focuses on providing the information in a manner that empowers decision makers to understand their own resources better and gain a better understanding of how problems could be solved.

Consensus Building

Consensus building is a term that is used to describe efforts to get agreements to resolve public controversies. There is no one single technique that is used. Consensus building programs may use facilitation, mediation, arbitration, and somewhat more specialized techniques such as disputes review panels, mini-trials, and negotiated rule making in an effort to reach agreements.

Typically consensus building involves establishing a panel representing all the various interests and seeking to reach agreement within that panel. If that panel is able to reach agreements and make commitments on behalf of the constituencies represented on the panel, the issue may be resolved. There have been occasions when agreements were reached but the controversy continued because the panel was not considered sufficiently legitimate as to make decisions on behalf of the larger public.

In most public participation processes, the agency makes the final decisions after consultation with the public. In consensus building, the agency is either one of the parties at the table or is neutral on the outcome of the decision as long as there is resolution. In this sense, consensus building is a somewhat different process from public participation. However, the fields overlap considerably, and many practitioners move back and forth between the fields. In some cases, public participation results in high levels of agreement, which the agency then ratifies. In other cases, the consensus-building panel is surrounded by a larger public participation process.

While *consensus building* is the term currently in vogue, it is an outgrowth of two related fields known as environmental mediation and alternative dispute resolution. Environmental mediation was a movement in the 1970s and 1980s to apply techniques from labor-management dispute resolution, such as mediation, arbitration, and fact finding, to environmental disputes. Alternative dispute resolution (ADR) uses techniques that result in mutual agreements between two or more parties, as an alternative to expensive and unpredictable litigation. ADR uses many of the same techniques as consensus building. In fact, consensus building can be viewed as the application of ADR techniques to public policy issues.

Consensus Conference

The consensus conference is a technique designed to incorporate citizen opinion and values into decisions about complex technological or scientific issues. The technique seeks to inform a panel of citizens about a technology and its implications, who then formulate a consensus position on the implications of uses of the technology.

Some people claim that the technique originated in the United States as a technique known as a citizen jury, but in Europe, the Danish Board of Technology is widely recognized as the originator. Consensus conference is one of a suite of techniques used as part of a field called participatory technology assessment.

The conference is a dialogue between experts and a panel of laypeople. There is an education phase, followed by three days of panel deliberations, which are open to the public.

The panel consists of laypeople of divergent background. They are found by sending out an invitation to about a thousand randomly selected people over the age of eighteen. From those who express interest in participating, twelve to sixteen citizens are selected, with an effort to get a mix of people based on age, gender, education, profession, and geography. The time commitment on the part of the citizens is substantial, so they must be motivated by a strong interest. However, panel members are not selected to represent particular groups of points of view. In fact, it is essential that they be open-minded.

Topics suitable for a consensus conference must have current social relevance, expert contributions must be available, and the topic must be both important and have clear enough boundaries so that it can be defined and addressed. Typically a topic is selected before societal opinions have hardened in an effort to inform deliberations in the broader society. Examples of topics on which consensus conferences have been conducted include gene therapy, electronic surveillance, genetically modified food, and human genome mapping.

Several European legislatures have established technology assessment organizations that are advisory to the parliament. When a consensus conference is run by one of these organizations, the results of the consensus conference are handed to the parliament. A number of recommendations from consensus conferences have made their way into legislation. Citizens are more willing to donate their time when they know that the results could be influential.

The consensus conference process is normally managed by a steering committee of people familiar with the technique or who provide recognized expertise in the subject matter of the conference.

The first step in the process is to educate the panel. Panel members participate in two weekends during which they receive information about the topic and prepare a list of the questions they want to ask technical experts. The panel members also get to know each other. The background materials presented to the panel must be both complete and objective. Typically these materials are screened by the steering committee to ensure that it is complete, factual, and unbiased.

During the first day of the consensus conference, the experts make short presentations and address the questions identified by the panel. They might, for example, hear from twelve to fifteen experts on the financial, biological, legal, social, and ethical aspects of the issue.

On the morning of the second day, panel members ask questions of the experts in an effort to get them to elaborate on or clarify their presentation. The audience also asks questions of the experts. For the rest of the second day, the panel works on a draft of their consensus report. Facilitation is provided if needed, and editors and secretaries are also available. The panel prepares a report summarizing their points of agreement or disagreement. Typically, the first draft is ready for discussion by the panel in the evening of the second day. The panel may break into smaller groups for discussion of critical issues. The panel strives for unanimity. (Some consensus conferences take four days, providing two days to complete the task of getting agreement on the contents of the report and putting the conclusions into a presentable report.)

On the third and last day, the panel presents the final document to the experts and audience, including the media. The experts are invited to clear up misunderstandings or outright factual misstatement but are not to comment otherwise on the panel's conclusions. The final report of the panel, along with all the written materials from the experts, is compiled into a report that is sent to the parliament (or some other influential body) and made available to the public. Typically there is extensive media coverage of the panel's conclusions. In many cases, there is a major news conference designed to maximize media coverage of the panel's conclusions.

The consensus conference is not designed to result in a specific decision, although they have contributed to subsequent legislative action. Instead, the purpose is to inform the public discussion and knowledge of the issue in a way that combines expert knowledge and citizen values.

Facilitation

Facilitation is a set of skills and a style of meeting leadership that is particularly suited to leading public meetings. A detailed description of facilitation is provided in Chapter Ten.

Field Trip

Public participation meetings often occur in large cities, well away from the area where the impact of a project or decision will be experienced. In some cases, active participants may never have experienced the area where the impacts have occurred. Many proposed actions look very different when you are actually out on the ground looking at the resource under discussion. It's one thing to discuss impacts when they are an abstraction or an image in people's heads, and quite another to engage with the actual reality on the ground.

Imaginary Field Trips

People often have trouble visualizing what a project might look like when completed. One electric utility flew over the alternative routes of electric transmission lines, making a video of the routes from the air. The company then showed the video at a public workshop discussing the proposed routes. This way people could see where the routes might go, at least from a bird's-eye view. More recently, other utilities, using modern computer techniques, have inserted true-to-scale pictures of proposed transmission towers into videos of proposed transmission routes, so that people can see the visual impact of the towers.

Modern computer technologies also allow you to see a model of a building inserted into an actual physical location, allowing you to rotate the image so you can see it from all sides, and even to look out from the proposed building at the surrounding buildings.

Typically field trips are organized so that people meet at a single location and then ride together on a rented bus to the location. Because everybody is in the same vehicle, it's possible to conduct informational briefings en route. It is essential, however, that these briefings be factual in nature, not biased information presented to a captive audience. Be sure to allow time for informal conversation on the bus, as the informal interaction that takes place has a team-building effect as people come to know each other as human beings not just roles.

Once you arrive at the site, allow time for people to express their reactions. If the site has no suitable place for discussion, assemble afterward in another location where people can discuss their experience and ask further questions.

In some cases, there is no place you can take people because you are asking them to visualize how a location with which they are familiar will look after a project has been built. One solution is to find a similar facility in another location and provide transportation to see that facility. For example, one city wanted to site a new gas-fired power plant within its city limits. Modern gas-fired power plants are much smaller than the kinds of power plants with which most people are familiar and can be fit comfortably (and aesthetically) in an office park or industrial area. When participants were unable to visualize anything but a giant smoke-belching monster of a power plant, the city conducted a field trip to a nearby city where one of the new facilities was located. Pictures of this new facility were also prominently displayed in all informational materials. In another case, city officials from a city on the West Coast of the United States were flown more than twenty-five hundred miles to visit an existing oil port on the East Coast to assess whether they would find a proposed oil port near their own city to be acceptable.

The key point is that people build up pictures in their minds about what the impact of a project will be and participate in public participation programs based on those images. Field trips provide an opportunity for people to match their images to the reality of the actual resources.

Focus Groups

The focus group technique was developed by the advertising and market research industry as an alternative to expensive polling or surveys. Think of a focus group as conducting an interview but with a group rather than a single individual. Focus groups are small discussion groups whose participants are selected either randomly or to approximate the demographics of the community or target market. The group is conducted by a trained moderator who draws out people's emotional reactions to a product, publication, idea, or whatever else is under discussion. Normally, several focus groups are held until the researchers are confident they have valid information.

A focus group can help identify emotional reactions, issues, data needs, and the language laypeople use to talk about an issue. They are not helpful in predicting the number of people in the larger community who will take a particular position because they do not have statistical validity. But focus groups still have their uses. For example, some organizations use focus groups to review draft publications to ensure they are understandable and perceived as objective. Some utility companies have used focus groups to help design a user-friendly bill.

In the context of a public participation process, a danger of focus groups is that the public may view them as an effort to learn information that can be used to manipulate the public rather than learn from the public. Even if researchers gather useful information, the public does not see focus groups as a substitute for other forms of direct participation.

Increasingly the term *focus groups* refers to small, informal meetings that the organization uses as a sounding board, with no effort to follow the strict protocol of a formal focus group. Sometimes these meetings are targeted at specific stakeholders. For example, one meeting might be held with environmental groups, another with industry, and another with regulatory agencies. When the term *focus group* is used, be sure to ask a few more questions to determine whether it is being used to describe the market research format or simply informal meetings with stakeholders.

Here's some information on each step in conducting a focus group.

Identify Target Population

Is your goal to learn how specific stakeholder groups feel, or is it to understand the reactions of a broad class of people, such as a cross-section of people who use a service or rate payers? The first task is to identify who to include in the focus group to get the information needed.

Recruit Participants

The next step is to recruit participants from the target audience. If the people needed are easily identified stakeholder groups, then begin calling individuals from these groups. If you are trying to get a representation of the views of a large class of people, obtain lists of people with names and telephone numbers of people from that class.

With active stakeholders or people with a strong interest in a particular service, you may be able to draw on their public spirit to get them to attend. If you are trying to involve the general public, you may need to offer some compensation, such as twenty-five dollars to participate in a ninety-minute session.

The ideal focus group is about eight to ten people. To get this number, you may need to sign up at least twelve people who agree to participate, because typically one or two who have agreed to participate will not show up. (If they do, proceed with the larger group.)

Follow up the telephone calls with a letter confirming all the details. People should receive this letter seven to ten days before the actual session. Then follow up with telephone reminders three days before the session.

Room Setup

Focus groups are typically conducted with people sitting around a table, so they can see each other.

The groups are usually recorded with either audio or video recording equipment. The room setup therefore needs to take into account how to locate equipment such as video cameras or recording devices and microphones.

Question Preparation

Prepare the questions you want answered in advance, and try them out on a few people to be sure they elicit the kind of answers sought. Typically you will need a minimum of five or six questions for a ninety-minute session (some people recommend preparing a few more). The same rules apply to your questions as apply to any other interviewing: use open-ended questions, and don't ask leading questions.

The Facilitator or Moderator

Focus groups are usually moderated by a trained focus group facilitator or moderator. This is particularly important if you are going to try to use the information you receive to perform a sophisticated statistical analysis. If you decide not to use a professional focus group leader, be sure to pick a meeting leader who has good interviewing skills and is capable of interacting with participants without showing any bias.

Numerous Web pages offer the services of professional focus group moderators. For example, www.FocusGroups.com provides both a U.S. and international directory of moderators and focus group facilities.

The Session

The moderator poses a question, asking participants to jot down notes and then to share their ideas. The goal is to get comments from each participant on each question. The moderator has to control the discussion so a few individuals don't dominate the discussion. Sometimes this is done simply by taking turns going around the room. The moderator may ask a few follow-up questions to clarify information or explore a topic in more depth. But typically the moderator has to be careful to save time to be sure he or she gets to ask all the scheduled questions.

When focus groups are done for market research, the groups are often conducted in rooms with one-way mirrors so that researchers can observe the discussion. In other facilities, researchers watch the discussion on a television feed from the video camera. Having researchers in the room with the participants could skew the results and make participants uncomfortable, leading to less participation.

In public participation programs, some people may feel uncomfortable being observed. So researchers are more likely to view or listen to the videotape or audiotape after the discussion rather than observe through one-way mirrors.

Participants are usually promised that they will receive a copy of the report discussing the results of the focus group. This provides reassurance that the focus group is not being used for manipulative purposes and also provides an opportunity for people to comment on the summary.

After the Focus Group

Immediately after the focus group, check to be sure that the recording equipment worked. If it did not, it is imperative to get your impressions down on paper as soon as possible. Even if the equipment worked, write down observations you made during the session.

Written Report

The written report is typically organized around the questions asked during the focus group. The report could include a brief background and objectives section, the methodology, a summary of responses to the questions, and highlights of the findings.

Future Search

Future Search is a two-and-a-half-day event designed to result in a common vision of the future. It is a sibling to Appreciative Inquiry Summit and a cousin to charrette and visioning. The creators of the Future Search technique consider sixty-four participants to be an ideal number, because they can be divided into eight groups around eight tables. Ideally the participants are representative of the community and have the power and influence to make something happen in the community.

The event is organized into five tasks, each lasting three or four hours. The first task is for people to review the past, usually the past thirty years. They share their personal histories and their perceptions of what happened in the community or organization under discussion during those years. Participants then create three time lines on the wall: the key events in their lives, in the world, and in the community (or organization) in the past thirty years. This is followed by a general discussion addressing questions such as "What did you get out of that? What did you learn? What did you hear?"

The second task is to create a group mind map of all the trends in the world, in society, that are affecting them right now. A mind map is created on a wall-sized sheet of paper, with group members writing, drawing, or posting words or symbols to show trends or events, and the interconnections between them. As participants put items on the visual mind map, they are asked to share their experiences surrounding that event. Each stakeholder group is given seven or eight colored dots and asked to put them on the trends they believe are most important.

Then the participants are organized into homogeneous groups (for example, the environmentalists, industry representatives, and students). The idea is to identify seven or eight highly differentiated points of view about the issues. These groups are asked to reinterpret the mind maps from their own point of view, identify the key issues, and report on what they have done.

Then groups are asked to discuss their feelings about the issues they've identified. For example, they might be asked: "Looking at what you personally or other members of your stakeholder group are doing right now about these issues, what makes you really proud? What are you doing or not doing right now about which you are really sorry?" The point of the exercise is not to point blame, but to get everybody in touch with their own feelings about how they are addressing the issues.

Then the participants are reorganized into mixed groups and asked to put themselves ten to twenty years in the future. The question may be framed: "The date is . . . . You have made this community into the kind of community you really want. What are the characteristics of this community?" After each of the small groups reports to the larger group, each is asked to identify common futures, potential projects, and unresolved differences.

In the final activity, each small group is asked to meet briefly and consider what they would like to do in the short and long terms. This is followed by a second session where people reorganize themselves into committees or task forces to take on some activity. At the end, each committee shares its commitment for action.

One of the challenges of Future Search (as well as Appreciative Inquiry Summit and some forms of charrette) is getting participants to commit to participate in a multiday program.

Groupware

Groupware is a term that is used for a large number of electronic technologies designed to support collaboration (in person or virtually), including meetings. Typically, groupware consists of both hardware (computers, personal digital assistants like a Palm Pilot or Pocket PC, keypads, or computer-linked white boards) and software that allow this technology to be used for highly sophisticated collaborative activities. Several kinds of groupware have strong potential for use in public participation.

One product with immediate applicability is computer-linked white boards. Anything recorded on these boards can be immediately downloaded into a computer and then shared (using wireless technology) with every other computer or digital assistant in the room. Similarly, people with keypads, personal digital assistants, or laptops can transmit information to the white board. SMART Technologies, a leader in this technology, has developed a number of sophisticated software programs that allow the meeting leader to move items around on the white board or change the order of items on a list with a tap of a finger. Diagrams can also be built up in layers, so that participants can tap on an item in a flowchart, for example, and this will allow them to access other layers of information embedded beneath the top layer.

So far, the technology that has been used most frequently for public participation purposes is keypad electronic meeting systems. Keypad electronic meeting systems are designed to let people vote on a 0–10 scale by moving a control knob up or down or typing in a number, with the combined group answers almost immediately visible on a large display at the front of the room. A meeting facilitator can pose questions to the audience and immediately get votes that show not only people's position but also how strongly they feel about their position. Participants' responses are anonymous, so people feel safe recording their responses. Questions can also be posed in such a way that people identify both a position and an affiliation, and answers can be recorded in such a way that they show how people with a particular affiliation feel compared to people from a different affiliation but without individuals being identified. People who have used these systems find they permit audiences (even large audiences up to several thousand people) to prioritize lists, state preferences, or weight values quickly. Two of the best-known systems using keypad technology are Council and OptionFinder.

One of the challenges that face makers of keypad technology is that personal digital assistants and laptops can now be connected by wireless technology. Although they are more expensive and more complicated to operate, they can also do more. For example, people in a meeting can generate brainstorming items on their laptop computers and have them show up on a giant screen at the front of the room. They can also submit comments, not just numbers. The simplicity and lower cost of the keypad is an advantage, but the versatility of personal digital assistants or laptops may soon dominate.

Hotlines

Have you ever tried to call a large organization in an effort to find that one person in that organization who knows about an issue? You are often transferred back and forth between five or six people before you find the right person. Many callers give up long before that.

If your organization is large and you are working on an important issue, consider setting up a hotline so people don't have this problem. A hotline is a widely advertised telephone number that rings through to a person who can answer questions. Usually it's set up so that there are several lines that answer to that number, so callers don't get a busy signal. The number is announced in newsletters, news releases, meeting announcements, or any other place where people are encouraged to ask questions or comment on an issue.

Hotlines can be a form of two-way communication. Some people call a hotline to ask a question and others to comment. A hotline can also be used for coordination purposes. Advisory group members, uncertain about the date of the next meeting, can call the hotline. Some hotlines allow people to select from a menu of topics in which they may be interested, allowing them to access prerecorded tapes on these topics by pushing numbers on their touch-tone phones.

The key to an effective hotline is a well-trained person at the receiving end of the line. Callers must get the feeling that the person taking their calls is interested in what they have to say and is both knowledgeable and responsive. If the person answering a call doesn't have all the information, he or she must take responsibility to search it out, and get back to the caller.

As Internet usage becomes universal, Web-based hotlines may increasingly replace telephone hotlines. Much more information can be posted on a Web page. For example, people can sign on and leave or pick up messages, get information from or make a copy of a report, and review and comment on the language of a task force recommendation.

Internet

The Internet is clearly a powerful tool for informing the public. The potential for using the Internet as an interactive tool is very high. Future participation programs may use chatrooms, Web conferencing, or other virtual communication as a primary mechanism for participation.

But so far, the Internet is not yet a truly interactive forum. Some of the most technologically advanced companies in the world are working on the technology to use these same forms of participation in virtual teams around the world. Even when provided with substantial technical assistance, however, the technology is somewhat cumbersome and at times unreliable.

That doesn't mean that Internet doesn't have its uses, even at the current level of technology. Increasingly agencies are encouraging people to submit comments by e-mail, along with written mail or telephone. The U.S. Environmental Protection Agency is putting in place a procedure that will allow people from throughout the United States to access information about proposed rules and policies and then submit their comments by e-mail.

Is There a Digital Divide?

There continues to be concern about a digital divide, with low-income and minority populations having less access to the Internet, even in industrialized countries. That reality persists, but inventive people are finding a way around it. I recently was involved in a public participation process where homeless people participated using computers in their local libraries. In the United States, at least, free or low-cost access to computers is available in many local public libraries.

The U.S. Department of Energy has a program to provide surplus computers to community centers in minority communities, along with computer training. The province of São Paulo in Brazil is setting up numerous cybercafés in the slums to provide access to the Internet and as a mechanism for public participation.

Increasingly the barrier to use of the Internet may not be a problem of access, but a lack of comfort with and confidence in the technology.

One of the primary constraints on Internet use has been that not everyone has access. Recent studies show that in 2004, nearly 70 percent of the North American population had access to the Internet at work or home. There are similar or higher access rates in Europe and some Asian countries. Access rates are much lower in developing countries.

Even when people have access to the technology, there is still the problem of whether they know how to use it. One of the barriers in corporate virtual teams is the additional training that people need to be able to use the technology. This is a problem even when the technology is part of people's jobs. If the same learning were required before people could participate in public decision-making processes, it could be a considerable barrier to participation.

Nevertheless, the technology is improving rapidly and becoming more user friendly. Once people get used to e-meetings and Web conferencing in other settings, the potential for their use in public participation is considerable.

Interviews

Interviews can be an effective part of public participation programs. A series of thirty- to sixty-minute interviews with representatives of the key interests can provide a quick understanding of the issue, the dynamics between the interests, and the intensity of people's interest in the issue. Several days of interviews can often produce a large amount of information.

More information about conducting interviews is provided in Chapter Thirteen.

Large Group/Small Group Meetings

In a large group/small group meeting, the entire audience meets, and then the audience is divided into small groups of five to ten people to complete an assignment, such as identifying alternatives or ranking alternatives. Then everybody reassembles and hears reports from the small groups. This can be the end of the meeting, or there can be additional discussion or conclusions reached with the whole audience. The large group/small group meeting format is a method for increasing the level of interaction while still conducting a meeting for a large number of people.

A number of structured small group activities can be used to structure the small discussion groups. Chapter Nine discusses how to design interactive public meetings.

Meetings, Hearings, and Workshops

Meetings of some kind, whether town meetings, public hearings, workshops, or any of many other kinds of gatherings, are by far the most widely used public participation techniques. There are a number of different kinds of meetings formats, and the various types of meetings are listed throughout this chapter.

Chapters Eight through Eleven provide more information on designing and conducting public meetings.

Multiattribute Utility Analysis

Researchers in the decision analysis field have developed new tools for helping decision makers evaluate alternatives. One of these tools is multiattribute utility analysis (MAUA). In recent years, a number of organizations have involved the public, or at least citizen advisory groups, using one of several variants of MAUA.

An underlying premise of MAUA is that as long as there is only one value under consideration, whether that value is the protection of endangered species, cost-benefit ratio, or social well-being, then experts are good at evaluating how well alternatives perform on that single dimension. If you ask experts to tell you which alternatives are cheapest over the long run, they can do that with some precision. If you ask them which alternatives have the fewest impacts on endangered species, they will probably be able to do that as well (although this is somewhat more difficult because an alternative that protects one endangered species may threaten another). But the idea is that as long as experts are confining themselves to only one value at a time, they are good at evaluating alternatives.

The problem comes when you have to compare those values to each other. When you are evaluating alternatives, which is more important: the environment, economic development, social well-being, or something else? As soon as you try to assign weight or importance to these various values, you are in the realm of political philosophy and beliefs about what is "good." These decisions are inherently political, even if they are not partisan, in that they have to do with beliefs, not science. These values choices are precisely the kinds of issues that are appropriate for public participation. They are also highly individual.

In MAUA, experts first identify a set of values dimensions, and they rate how well the alternatives perform for each of these dimensions. Then the public is asked to assign a weight or importance to each value dimension, for example:

Protecting the habitat for endangered species	0.40
Total cost (including operations and maintenance)	0.40
Jobs created in local community	0.20

There are several techniques for eliciting scores from the public. The simplest is to tell participants they have 100 points they can allocate between the values dimension as they wish. Another approach is to have people place the scores on a scale, such as that shown in Figure 7.1.

The most rigorous methodology, and the one favored by researchers concerned with statistical validity, is a series of forced-choice questions, such as, "Which is more important, A or B?" "How many times more important is A than B?" A series of these questions allows researchers to develop a precise weighting of the various values dimensions. As can be imagined, different individuals and groups produce very different weightings.

In the next step, the researchers compare the weightings they have received with the rankings given to the alternatives by the experts. For each individual or group,

FIGURE 7.1. A SIMPLE SCALE TO SHOW PRIORITY.

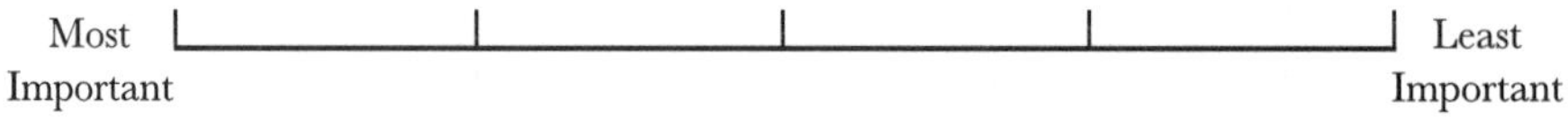

Most Important ⌞_____|_____|_____|_____⌟ Least Important

they can then provide feedback that says, in effect: "Given the weights you assigned, here's how well each alternative performed in achieving the values you thought were most important."

Participants can be surprised by the outcomes. People may be advocates for alternatives that do not do the best job of satisfying the values they say are important. This can lead to a discussion about whether the weights they assigned need to be adjusted or whether they need to reevaluate the alternatives in the light of the new information.

In its academic forms, MAUA is used to produce aggregate scores, averaging all the scores. The result is a single score that is used to say, in effect, "Given the aggregate weightings, this alternative performs best."

In my experience, this is the least beneficial use of MAUA, for several reasons. First, participants resent having their individual weightings lumped together statistically. As one participant put it, "That's like saying a man with one foot in a block of ice and the other in a bucket of boiling water is, on the average, comfortable." Second, the statistical manipulations that are done are so complex that the public becomes suspicious that the information they gave the researchers is being manipulated to produce an outcome the researchers want. And, third, some decision makers are all too prone to grab on to a quantitative answer and accept it without any understanding of what it does, and does not, mean.

Nevertheless, MAUA can produce important insights. Not infrequently, people find that the alternative they favored is not the alternative that performs the best to meet the values they said were important. Or they may find that another alternative not only meets their needs the best but also does the best job of meeting the needs of an individual or group they thought of as opponents. Finally, it can be used to test how sensitive the rankings are to changes in the weighting. If you ask, "How much would the weighting of attribute A have to be increased [or decreased] to change which alternative performs best?" you'll sometimes find out that a few small changes produce different results; at other times, you'll find that no matter how much you increase or decrease the weighting for a particular attribute, it doesn't change which alternative is superior. This more qualitative information can lead to important discussions, even to realignment of political forces.

Open House

An open house is an event to which the public is invited. Interested people can drop in at any time during an announced time period. The open house is held in a large room with space for a variety of booths, or stations, organized around specific topics. One booth might provide maps, another might be organized to discuss project need, and others might be organized around various environmental or health topics. Each booth is staffed by a technical expert on that topic. People can walk from booth to booth, engaging in conversation with the expert as they wish. Participants can examine the displays, chat with staff, form discussion groups, or just interact informally. People come and go at will.

An open house is particularly useful when the purpose is to talk with the public one-on-one or when the public primarily wants to get information about a project rather than comment on it. It may also be held in conjunction with a public meeting. For example, an open house held during the afternoon might be followed by a public meeting or workshop in the evening. Some people will come to the open house to learn what they need to participate effectively in the evening meeting; others will come to get the information they want and then have no need to attend the public meeting.

As people arrive at the open house, they are greeted by a staff person who explains where they need to go in the room to get the information they want. In some open houses, the host shows the participants around the room; in others, the participants simply rove at will to get the information they want.

Depending on the size of the audience, there may be extensive one-on-one discussions between the experts and the public, or people may gather in small groups for informal discussions. You may want to have a flip chart at each station, so staff can write down the questions or comments from the public. Or you may want to provide a hand-in response form that people complete after they've attended the open house.

A nice touch is to have coffee and cookies available, as this increases the informality of the session. You can even have recreational and social activities as part of the program, so that the open house is more like a fair. Some agencies have provided child care while parents are participating in the open house or have provided activities designed primarily for children.

If there are active groups who want to get their position out to the public and suspect the agency of stacking the decks, they can be invited to set up their own stations.

After the open house, gather the staff for a debriefing session to discuss their reactions and record the ideas they received during the open house.

There is a debate within the public involvement field about using open houses as an alternative to public comment meetings. Some specialists believe that open houses are far more productive. A large number of interested people can obtain information and register their views informally in a relaxed atmosphere. Other practitioners argue that a public comment meeting is still needed because at a public comment meeting, everybody can hear and see what everybody else says. They worry that agencies will use open houses as a way of keeping the public from hearing the opinions of those who oppose a proposed action. This may backfire, causing resentment that may lead to highly adversarial behavior. Many of these concerns can be addressed by combining open houses and public meetings, reserving open houses for those times when the primary purpose of the meeting is to inform the public, or allowing stakeholder groups to set up stations at the open house.

Open Space

Open Space is a type of meeting developed by Harrison Owen, president of H. H. Harrison and Company and a leader in the organization transformation movement. It has some resemblance to a charrette, in that participants may work together for several hours to several days on a specific theme. But the manner in which the agenda is set and controlled is entirely different. Open Space has these basic ground rules:

1. Conduct Open Space in a large room with either sufficient space for numerous breakout meetings in the same room or numerous breakout rooms nearby. You must be able to post flip chart sheets on the wall using masking tape.
2. The meeting facilitator opens by stating the theme of the meeting. Typically this is done in a way that will be evocative or even provocative as a way of stimulating some passion about the subject.
3. The facilitator asks members of the audience to identify issues or opportunities related to the theme about which they care deeply. The idea is that people identify ideas for which they will take personal responsibility, not ideas that "someone else ought to do something about."
4. Each person who has an idea writes a short title for the idea on a flip chart sheet, using a marker, and signs his or her name. Then each person who has an idea comes to the front of the room and says, "My issue is . . . , my name is . . . " Then the individual hangs the flip chart sheet on the wall.
5. Each person who has identified an idea then takes responsibility by specifying a time and place for a small group discussion on the topic. Typically there are wall charts available to simplify assignments to meeting rooms.
6. Participants go to sessions on whichever topics are of interest. They are encouraged to move around from group to group as they wish.
7. Each group prepares a summary of its discussion, and a bank of desktop computers and printers is available for people to prepare the summary from their group meetings. The summaries are submitted electronically to a central database, and any participant can read the summary.

8. The entire audience reassembles periodically (such as once each morning and at the end of the day) for announcements and news.
9. There is some sort of grand finale or closing session.

What work is accomplished and how it is implemented during the session ride on the energy and enthusiasm of the participants. Advocates of the Open Space approach report exceptional outcomes resulting from group initiative and commitment. My own experience as a participant in several Open Space workshops has been that there has been great energy and commitment for developing ideas. I have not always been clear on whether that resulted in implementation of these ideas.

Participatory Rural Appraisal

Participatory Rural Appraisal is a group of techniques used to enable local people to participate not only as sources of information, but in analyzing the information leading to a development project. Many of the techniques are designed so they can be used with nonliterate participants. Participatory Rural Appraisal offers a basket of techniques that generally group into four categories: interviews and discussions, mapping, ranking, and trend analysis. For example, residents might develop historical maps showing changes that have occurred in the community. Or maps might be drawn showing different households and their characteristics, such as relative wealth, number of school-age children, and involvement in community activities. Sometimes individuals are asked to draw maps to show their perceptions of community boundaries, the places that are most important to them, or their vision of how the community could be improved. Similar mapping techniques have been used for mapping institutions. On a map, participants show who cooperates, who shares information, and other information.

Ranking techniques also use visual approaches. For example, people are shown cards with drawings showing problems and are asked, "Which is the bigger problem?" After a series of such choices, results can be displayed in a matrix. Other techniques include developing seasonal calendars or daily activity charts drawn by residents.

Participatory Technology Assessment

Participatory technology assessment is not a single technique, but a movement in Europe to involve the public in science and technology decisions. In particular, it focuses on involving the public in identifying and forecasting of likely implications of future technologies. It uses a number of techniques, including consensus conferences, Future Search, and public hearings and workshops.

Participatory Television and Cable Television

Television can be used as a participation tool. For example, one regional planning agency used the fundraising setup at a local educational television for a kind of telethon. Alternative plans were presented to the community, and residents could call in with comments or questions, which the meeting moderators then presented to the television audience.

Cable television offers the potential for other forms of participatory television. Some communities, as part of contracting with companies to provide cable television in their community, have reserved community access channels that are owned and operated by the local government. They may be used to broadcast important meetings, such as city council meetings. These programs, however, rarely reach a significant percentage of the viewing audience.

An increasing number of television shows use a voter feedback system. For example, recent television shows used phone-in technology to select the winner of a national talent contest. Millions of people voted by calling in on different telephone lines to show who they thought should win the contest. This technology has potential for public participation, but it should be noted that in the case of the talent show, the voting audience was given the authority to determine the winner. In most public participation processes, voting is undesirable because it implies that a vote will determine the outcome when the organization sponsoring the process retains decision-making authority.

The potential exists for the creative use of television in public participation processes, but this potential has not yet been fully realized. It is not clear whether the constraints are technological or sociocultural.

Plebiscite

The ultimate test of whether a community supports a decision is a direct vote on the issue. In some communities, it is legally possible for the city council or other appropriate elected body to put an issue on the ballot for the next election. In other communities, changes might have to be made in the law before such a vote could be legally binding, although advisory plebiscites are usually possible. A plebiscite could be useful when a community is the ultimate decision maker. It is not usually appropriate if the agency will retain final decision making authority.

A Unique Use of a Plebiscite

A Canadian province wanted to site a hazardous waste repository. The crown corporation it set up to do the siting first did geotechnical studies and identified communities where the geology seemed to be suitable. Then it went to these communities and said: "We'd like you to consider being the host of a repository. We'll work with you to decide what studies need to be done to be sure it is safe. We'll also negotiate mitigation and compensation. But we want you to know going into it that we will not site the facility unless there's an actual community vote to accept the facility." Several communities voted to accept the facility. The day the provincial government announced which site was selected, another community took out a full-page ad criticizing the government for not selecting it!

The key to the success of this approach is that the election made the acceptance of the site voluntary. Risk communication research shows that when a risk is voluntary rather than imposed, perception of risk is dramatically reduced.

If the decision being made affects several communities, a region, or a whole country, then having a plebiscite in only one community is not appropriate. But if the political boundaries for the plebiscite correspond with the people most likely to be affected, a plebiscite could be useful and legitimate. Some people argue strongly on behalf of this form of direct democracy. Others argue just as vehemently that such an approach undermines the fundamentals of a representative form of government.

If a plebiscite is used, it should be preceded by active public participation, so that the proposal put before the voters takes into account the concerns of the interests within the community and has the credibility of open, visible participation during the proposal's development.

Polls and Surveys

Polls and surveys permit a quantitative assessment of viewpoints in the community. Polls, particularly telephone polling, have become considerably less expensive, and some organizations are using them as an adjunct to their public participation programs.

Polls and surveys are effective for assessing public opinion. Their advantage is that they provide a way to measure the proportion of opinion in the community at large, not just among those who participate in the public participation program. A poll or survey can help determine, for example, whether the opinions being expressed by advocates represent a large segment of public opinion or only a vocal minority.

Polls are conducted by trained interviewers who ask each person exactly the same questions and in a prescribed order. These questions are pretested to be sure they are clear and unbiased, and elicit the information desired. The interviewees will be part of a sample population chosen using rules accepted by professionals in the field to guarantee the randomness or lack of bias in the sample chosen. Statistical research has been conducted to establish standards for how many people must be interviewed from a total population to ensure reliability of the findings to certain levels of confidence (for example, that the figures are accurate to plus or minus 5 percent). The level of confidence can be increased by increasing the number of interviews conducted.

Surveys are conducted by trained interviewers but are often more open-ended than polls. As a result, they may elicit more information, including information other than that anticipated by the questioner. However, polls, precisely because they are not open-ended, have greater statistical reliability.

Before any claims of statistical validity or reliability can be made for the results of a poll or survey, the design of the sample (the people invited to complete the interviews or questionnaire) must meet rigorous standards to ensure that the sample is truly random. In addition, the questions need to be pretested to ensure that they are not biased and obtain the information they were designed to elicit.

This means that the design of any interview or survey protocol should be done by someone with professional expertise in poll or survey design. Amateurish polls or surveys may produce charges of bias or invasion of privacy and result in information that is not credible enough to be used.

The very virtue of polls and surveys—their ability to produce quantitative answers—is also their weakness if they are poorly done. Because results of polls and surveys are quantifiable, they have an aura of objectivity that no other technique can give. This can be very reassuring to a decision maker who must make a difficult decision in the face of strong opposition. But a poorly designed poll will be quoted as "fact" just as much as a well-designed poll. For this reason, polls and surveys should be conducted by people with extensive training. This usually means that external consultants must be used, increasing the cost.

There are important limitations to the validity of polls and surveys. Polls and surveys give a snapshot of public opinion at a particular time. Public opinion can change rapidly, particularly if the public starts out largely uninformed about the issue. A completely accurate picture of public sentiment at one time may not be at all accurate two months later. Polls and surveys give equal weight to all respondents, even though this does not reflect political reality. A person who cares deeply about an issue is given the same weight as an uninterested individual, whatever his or her political clout. Knowledge about the mix of views in the general public does not necessarily tell the political balance of power in the community.

Public Hearings

Public hearings are formal meetings at which people present official statements of position and assertions of fact, and comments are recorded, often by a court reporter. The term *public hearing*, as used in the United States, refers to a single meeting, usually no longer than a single day or evening (although similar meetings may be repeated in multiple cities if an issue is regional or national). The term *public hearing* is used in Canada for a major inquiry that may last weeks or months. The only equivalent in the United States is a congressional inquiry.

Normally, except where legally required, avoid public hearings. Their primary value is to serve the lawyers (the hearing results in a public record on which decisions can be based). The one positive value of public hearings is that everybody gets to hear whatever anybody else says. But public hearings also tend to exaggerate differences: leaders of organized groups have to be seen defending their group's interests and have to take more extreme positions than they would in private. Public hearings are also easily dominated by organized groups. People who simply want information have to sit through hours of speeches in order to get that information—and may never get it.

If a public hearing is the conclusion or wrap-up of an extended public participation process, then many of the negatives of public hearings are not as prominent. But if the public participation process relies primarily on public hearings, the negatives are likely to become pronounced.

If you must hold a public hearing, be sure to establish reasonable time limits for speakers and procedures for registering to speak, such as a sign-in card. The time limits need to reflect the number of speakers. If there are only three people who want to speak, then it is unreasonable to limit presentations to a brief period such as three to five minutes. But if there are fifty speakers, then time limits need to be established to guarantee that everyone will have a chance to speak. Explain any ground rules in terms of providing an equal opportunity for everyone to speak rather than as requirements of the agency. Enforce any ground rules consistently and even-handedly, if possible with a light touch.

Chapters Eight through Eleven provide additional information on designing and conducting public meetings.

Public Meetings

The term *public meeting* is used as an umbrella for all types of meetings, whether hearings, open houses, or workshops. It is also used to describe a specific kind of meeting: a large public comment meeting in which the procedures are less formal than in a public hearing but the audience stays together during the entire meeting and participants make comments to the entire audience.

The primary difference between a public hearing and a large public comment meeting is that a large public comment meeting does not necessarily require a verbatim record and the meeting procedures can be somewhat less formal. Somewhat greater interaction may occur among participants. But all large meetings (except those using the interactive methods discussed in Chapter Nine) have most of the same advantages and disadvantages as hearings. Everybody gets to hear what is said. But people tend to make speeches rather than discuss an issue, and large meetings often contribute to polarization.

Chapters Eight through Eleven provide additional information on designing and conducting public meetings.

Retreat

The idea behind a retreat is to get away from the workplace for a concentrated period of time in a setting that encourages social interaction as well as organized discussion. There is a much higher chance of building consensus when people can talk the issue through in a concentrated manner yet in an informal setting. A retreat might be very useful, for example, when an advisory committee is getting close to a key decision point.

If you schedule a retreat, you might want to retain a professional facilitator to assist with designing and conducting it. Also, be aware that if the retreat is held in a physically attractive setting, such as the beach or mountains, there is the potential for criticism about expenditure of taxpayer or rate payer funds for such a purpose, even though the attractive setting may increase the retreat's effectiveness.

Samoan Circle

The Samoan Circle is one form of large group/small group meeting. It is designed to permit the kind of interaction that occurs only in small groups but witnessed by a larger group.

The meeting room is set up with an inner circle of five or six chairs. The rest of the chairs are set up in concentric outer circles, with aisles that permit access to the inner circle. Initially everybody is seated in the outer circles. The topic is announced, and people are invited to make comments, but there is a firm ground rule that anybody who wants to speak must move to the inner circle. Once people have spoken, they return to their original seat. If all the seats in the inner circle are full, people who want to speak stand behind the chairs in the inner circle and wait for a chair to be vacated.

As long as the topic is one of strong interest to the audience, the discussion can extend for several hours with virtually no monitoring by a meeting leader (or a meeting leader can occupy one of the seats in the inner circle on a continuing basis).

This meeting format can be used with audiences up to several hundred people. Above twenty-five to thirty people, though, the discussion in the inner circle must be amplified with microphones so everyone can hear the discussion taking place.

See Chapter Nine for a more detailed description of Samoan Circle.

SARAR

SARAR is a collection of techniques that have been used within the development activities of the various United Nations agencies (such as the U.N. Development Program and UNICEF), as well as many nongovernmental organizations worldwide. The World Bank has also used SARAR extensively on development projects. The name *SARAR* derives from the five attributes the technique hopes to foster: *s*elf-esteem, *a*ssociative strength, *r*esourcefulness, *a*ction planning, and *r*esponsibility.

One of the strengths of SARAR is that the techniques are very visual and can be adapted to people who are unable to read or write. Although there are a number of techniques, a few will illustrate the approach:

• *Pocket chart.* A pocket chart is a wall hanging with pockets in which people can put tokens or votes. The pocket chart is used as a way to make choices or provide information. For example, across the horizontal axis, the pockets could indicate different water uses, such as cooking, washing, and drinking. On the vertical axis, people indicate which water source they use for that purpose, such as well water, river, or standpipe. By using tokens (sometimes small stones), people show which water source they use and for which purpose. Researchers then count the tokens and quickly determine which water sources are used for which purpose by the entire village. One of the advantages of a pocket chart is that it can be used over and over to address different questions.

- *Three pile sorting.* Participants are given a set of pictures showing a set of different activities, such as farming, sanitation, and irrigation, and are asked to sort them into piles showing "good" activities, "bad" activities, or "in-between." Then they discuss why they sorted the activities the way they did. These sorts can be used in many ways. For example, participants might be asked to describe why bad actions occur in their village or what needs to be done to increase the good activities.
- *Story with a gap.* Respondents are given two pictures, one showing an undesirable situation and one a desirable situation (such as children using latrines), and are asked to create a story describing what it would take to get from one condition to the other. Or people could describe a before and after situation.

The number of SARAR techniques continues to grow. The unifying theme is simple visual techniques that help people describe the experience of life in their village or community.

Task Force

Task forces are a specific kind of advisory group. Although most advisory groups are set up to last several years or indefinitely and consider a number of different topics, task forces usually complete a single major task and then disband.

Chapter Twelve provides a detailed discussion of advisory groups.

Town Meeting

In New England, the town meeting has an honored tradition. All citizens in the town can attend and speak on an issue. A vote is taken on all articles listed in the town meeting warrant and is binding on the community.

The term *town meeting* is sometimes used in the same way as *public comment meeting,* meaning a meeting at which everybody can express their opinions, except no votes are taken or decisions made during the meeting.

Chapters Eight through Eleven provide a detailed discussion of designing and conducting various types of public meetings.

Visioning

During the 1980s and 1990s, a number of cities and states in the United States engaged in visioning programs with names that looked to the new century, such as Chattanooga 2000 and Oregon 2000. Communities continue to use visioning, but, of course, the years now are more likely to be 2020 or beyond.

The goal of visioning is to get a community to define the future it wants. The visioning process is designed to get a broad cross-section of the people in the community to agree on where they want to go in the future instead of focusing on current needs and deficiencies.

Typically this involves an extensive series of meetings at which people are asked to define the characteristics of the future they desire for their community. The workshop must be designed so that those attending set aside their knowledge of the existing problems and constraints and talk about what the community or state could be like. For this reason, the time frame under discussion is usually at least ten years out in time, long enough that people can accept the possibility that significant change could occur.

After the initial workshops and meetings, the ideas that have been collected are formulated into goals. This may be done by a steering group or task force. But to maintain credibility, these goals may be presented at of public meetings, where they can be ratified.

The next step is to engage the public in defining action steps to meet these goals. This may be done through a series of public meetings, workshops, or task forces. In some visioning processes, there is a ratification step, when citizens are asked to vote.

The challenge comes in implementing the action steps. The hope is that enough enthusiasm, commitment, and energy have been generated by the visioning process that it will result in implementation. The track record is mixed. In some communities, visioning has been dramatically successful. In others, the process was exciting but led to few tangible outcomes.

Visioning is not a single technique. A visioning process might use virtually every technique described in this chapter. It can also employ virtually all of the public information techniques, as its success rests on generating high visibility and broad participation from the entire community.

Workshops

Workshops are highly interactive meetings, usually designed for a group of twenty-five people or fewer. Typically they involve completing a specific task or assignment, such as developing or ranking alternatives. They are particularly useful when dealing with complex topics because they provide time for detailed consideration and a high level of interaction.

Chapter Nine provides many techniques that can be used in workshops.

Putting It All Together

The effectiveness of public participation results not from using a single public participation technique but from combining involvement and participation techniques into a total program. (For examples of complete public participation programs, look at Chapter Eighteen.)

No one public participation technique fits all circumstances. That's why previous chapters outlined a detailed method by which you can analyze exactly what you're trying to accomplish with the public, which parts of the public are important to reach at particular stages in the decision-making process, and other considerations. This kind of analysis provides the framework within which you can select techniques appropriate to your situation.

References

Appreciative Inquiry Summit

Ludema, J. D., Whitney, D., Mohr, B. J., and Griffen, T. J. *The Appreciative Inquiry Summit: A Practitioner's Guide for Leading Large-Group Change.* San Francisco: Berrett-Kohler, 2003.

Beneficiary Assessment

Rietbergen-McCracken, J., and Narayan, D. "Beneficiary Assessment, Module V." In J. Rietbergen-McCracken and D. Narayan, *Participatory Tools and Techniques: A Resource Kit for Participation and Social Assessment.* Washington, D.C.: The World Bank, 1997.

Charrette

Segedy, J. A., and Johnson, B. E. *Neighborhood Charrette Handbook*, Sept. 2004. [www.louisville.edu.org/sun/planning/char.html].
Lindsey, G., Todd, J. A., and Hayter, S. J. *A Handbook for Planning and Conducting Charrettes for High Performance Projects.* Golden, Colo.: National Renewable Energy Laboratory, NREL/BK-710-33425, Aug. 2003. [www.eere.energy.gov/buildings/highperformance/charrette_handbook.html].

City Walk

Halprin, L., and Burns, J. *Taking Part: A Workshop Approach to Collective Creativity,* Cambridge, Mass.: MIT Press, 1975.

Computer-Aided Negotiation

HydroLogics. "Computer-Aided Dispute Resolution," Sept. 2004. [http://hydrologics.net/publications/cadr.pdf]

Consensus Building

Susskind, L., McKearnan, S., and Thomas-Larmer, J. (eds.). *The Consensus Building Handbook.* Thousand Oaks, Calif.: Sage, 1999.

Creighton, J., Priscoli, J. D., Dunning, C. M., and Ayres, D. A. *Public Involvement and Dispute Resolution: A Reader Covering the Second Decade of Experience at the Institute for Water Resources.* Alexandria, Va.: U.S. Army Corps of Engineers Institute for Water Resources, 1998. [http://www.iwr.usace.army.mil/iwr/pdf/pisecond.pdf].

Consensus Conference

Joss, S., and Belluci, S. (eds.). *Participatory Technology Assessment in Europe: Introducing the EUROPA Research Project.* London: Centre for the Study of Democracy, University of Westminster, 2002.

Joss, S., and Durant, J. *Public Participation in Science: The Role of Consensus Conferences in Europe.* London: Science Museum, 1995.

Focus Groups

Bader, G. E., and Rossi, C. A. *Focus Groups: A Step-by-Step Guide.* (3rd ed.) San Diego, Calif.: Bader Group, 2002.

McNamara, C. *Basics of Conducting Focus Groups, 2002.* [http://www.mapnp.org/library/evaluatn/focusgrp.htm].

U.S. Army Family Advocacy. *Using Focus Groups to Create Excellence.* 1996. [http://child.cornell.edu/army/focus].

Future Search

Weisbord, M. R., and Janoff, S. *Future Search: An Action Guide to Finding Common Ground in Organizations and Communities.* San Francisco: Berrett-Kohler, 2000.

Groupware

Groupware technology is changing so rapidly that anything that can be written about it is quickly out of date. Below is a text in the field, but you may do better on the Internet:

Coleman, D. (ed). *Groupware: Collaborative Strategies for Corporate LANS and Internets.* Upper Saddle River, N.J.: Prentice Hall, 1997.

Multiattribute Utility Analysis

Von Winterfeldt, D. "Decisions with Multiple Stakeholders and Conflicting Objectives." In E. Weber, J. Baron, and G. Loomis (eds.). *Conflict and Trade-Off in Decision-Making.* Cambridge: Cambridge University Press, 2002.

Open Space

Owen, H. *Open Space Technology: A User's Guide.* Potomac, Md.: Abbott Publishing, 1992.

Participatory Rural Appraisal

Rietbergen-McCracken, J., and Narayan, D. "Participatory Rural Appraisal, Module III." In J. Rietbergen-McCracken and D. Narayan, *Participatory Tools and Techniques: A Resource Kit for Participation and Social Assessment.* Washington, D.C.: The World Bank, 1997. [www.worldbank.org/wbi/sourcebook/sba104.htm].

Participatory Technology Assessment

Joss, S., and Belluci, S. (eds.). *Participatory Technology Assessment in Europe: Introducing the EUROPA Research Project.* London: Centre for the Study of Democracy, University of Westminster, 2002.

Polls and Surveys

Rea, L. M., and Parker, R. A. *Designing and Conducting Survey Research: A Comprehensive Guide.* San Francisco: Jossey-Bass, 1997.

Weisbord, H., Krosnick, J. A., and Bowen, B. D. *An Introduction to Survey Research: Polling and Data Analysis.* Thousand Oaks, Calif.: Sage, 1996.

SARAR

Rietbergen-McCracken, J., and Narayan, D. "SARAR, Module IV." In J. Rietbergen-McCracken and D. Narayan, *Participatory Tools and Techniques: A Resource Kit for Participation and Social Assessment.* Washington, D.C.: The World Bank, 1997. [www.worldbank.org/wbi/sourcebook/sba105.htm].

Visioning

Ames, S. C. *Guide to Community Visioning.* Chicago: APA Planners Press, 1998.

Okubo, D. *The Community Visioning and Strategic Planning Handbook.* Denver: National Civic League, 1997.

PART FOUR

PUBLIC MEETING TOOLS

Inside every experienced public participation practitioners' techniques tool kit is a large section set aside for techniques related to public meetings. Public meetings are the most frequently used technique during public participation programs. Knowing how to plan effective meetings that are appropriate to a specific situation or issue is an essential skill for all public participation practitioners. For this reason, I have devoted this part of the book to designing and conducting meetings and workshops.

There are many different types of public meetings. Each has value in some circumstances, and each has limitations that make it inappropriate in other circumstances. Some offer high levels of interaction. Others are very formal. Table P4.1 presents an overview of the major types of meetings, as well as my evaluation of their general usefulness and limitations.

How do you determine which type of meeting is appropriate in your public participation program? Once again there is no cookie-cutter answer. So in Chapter Eight I present a thought process, somewhat similar to the thought process for designing a public participation program discussed in Chapters Three through Five, that you can use to think about the key issues you should address when considering what meeting format to use.

I strongly recommend using interactive meeting formats rather than formal meetings such as public hearings. Typically the formal approaches provide only an opportunity for people to be heard officially, taking fixed, predetermined positions.

TABLE P4.1. TYPES OF MEETINGS.

Technique	Usefulness	Limitations
Public hearing	Anyone can make a comment and have it recorded (verbatim) Highly transparent; everybody can hear what everybody else said	Often results in speeches rather than discussion Can be controlled or manipulated by an organized group Little or no interaction
Public comment meeting/town meeting	Anyone can make a comment and have it recorded (but not usually verbatim) Highly transparent; everybody can hear what everybody else said Somewhat less formal than a public hearing	Often results in speeches rather than discussion Can be controlled or manipulated by an organized group Little or no interaction
Briefing, question and answer	Useful for providing information to the public Question-and-answer period permits clarification	No value for obtaining public comment, although the session can be followed by a comment period
Panels	A more interactive way of conducting a briefing Permits discussion of informed viewpoints	No value for obtaining public comment, although the panel can be followed by a comment period.
Large group/ small group	Combines the benefits of large meetings (everybody receives the same information) with the interaction provided by small group discussions Can be used to produce a product or complete a task, but the agency will need to resolve differences in products produced by the small groups Interaction leads to higher audience participation and enthusiasm than other large meeting formats	Logistics can become cumbersome; careful planning required An angry audience may refuse to break into small groups Organized groups may dominate a few small groups (but not the entire meeting)
Workshop	Targeted at producing an actual product or completing a task (for example, identifying a set of alternatives or ranking alternatives) Highly interactive Can produce agreements	Typically for twenty-five participants or fewer; may need to be repeated multiple times if more people want to participate

TABLE P4.1. TYPES OF MEETINGS, Cont'd.

Technique	Usefulness	Limitations
Open house	Allows participants to come to the meeting whenever they want (during the announced hours), get information, then leave Allows prolonged interaction between individuals and experts on topics of interest People can leave comments on flip charts at each station or on hand-in response form	No visibility for what other people are saying Activist groups often do not like open houses because they do not give them an audience to address
Coffee klatch	Provides an opportunity for in-depth discussion in an informal setting Meeting in a private home leads to a friendlier, less adversarial setting	Can be staff intensive; may need to hold a number of coffee klatches to reach the intended audience
Symposium	Opportunity to provide information, including conflicting viewpoints, in a setting where people can think about the information without being put on the spot to respond	Not a forum for gathering public comment
Samoan Circle	Gives the experience of a small group conversation or dialogue, but can be observed (and participated in) by a much larger audience Largely self-monitoring (no meeting leader required once meeting started) Leads to interaction but not necessarily to agreements	People may be skeptical at first, since the format is unfamiliar
Open Space	People get to discuss the topics of greatest concern or interest to them Process is open and visible; people can move around to other groups whenever they want	Agency cannot prescribe the topics to discuss, so it is possible participants will not address topics of concern to the agency Requires meeting space with many venues for discussion and substantial premeeting logistics Format typically requires two to three days

Interactive meetings provide a chance for real learning to take place. People with different viewpoints can work together to complete tasks that give them a sense of common purpose.

But how do you have an interactive meeting when you have three hundred people in your audience? Don't give up hope. Chapter Nine provides suggestions for how to turn large meetings into interactive meetings.

The manner in which you conduct a public meeting can bring people together or turn the audience into screaming adversaries of the agency. Chapter Ten provides guidance on how to lead, that is, facilitate, public meetings.

Finally, meeting logistics can make or break a meeting; as a professional colleague says frequently: "God is in the details." Chapter Eleven identifies some of the key logistics issues you need to consider when designing a public meeting or workshop.

CHAPTER EIGHT

DESIGNING PUBLIC MEETINGS

During the course of a public participation program, you may design a number of very different kinds of meetings. You might have a planning meeting with internal staff. You might have a meeting with a task force. You might meet with a landowners' association or neighborhood group, or you might conduct a highly interactive workshop. You might lead a large community meeting in which several hundred people participate. There could be a formal public hearing. Each of these meeting formats has strengths and challenges. This chapter provides guidance on how to identify what type of meeting is appropriate for the task you want to perform.

Steps in Designing a Public Meeting

The first rule for designing effective meetings is that format follows function. Put another way, the format of the meeting is determined by what you want to accomplish during the meeting. This seems obvious, but an astonishing number of people start out with a meeting format in mind, usually based on how meetings have been conducted in the past at their organization, and end up with a format that is grossly inappropriate to what they need to accomplish.

This chapter provides a thought process to use in designing a public meeting. This process is designed to help you identify the purposes of the meeting and select a meeting format appropriate to those purposes. Figure 8.1 shows the same thought process laid out in graphical form. One way to involve the planning team in using the thought process is to take this figure and blow it up in size (using a photocopier or blueprint machine) until it can serve as a large chart hung on the wall. Having the chart on the wall helps the team stay focused and clarifies the relationship of the steps to each other.

Here are the steps in the thought process:

1. Review the public participation objectives and information exchange (discussed in Chapter Four) in your public participation plan for the stage of the decision-making process during which the meeting will be held.
2. Get agreement on what you hope to accomplish with the public during this meeting.
3. Discuss how you will use the information you receive from the public.
4. Identify the audience (stakeholders) you expect to participate.
5. List the topics that need to be covered.
6. Identify the level of interaction you need or want for each topic.
7. Select meeting activities for each topic to achieve the level of interaction you need to accomplish the objectives.
8. Allocate time to the various topics.
9. Prepare an agenda.
10. Determine seating arrangements and logistical needs.

More information on each step in the thought process is provided.

Step 1: Review the Public Participation Objectives and Information Exchange for the Stage You Are At in the Decision-Making Process

If you followed the thought process presented in Chapters Three through Five to develop a public participation plan, you identified the stages in the decision-making process for this issue, public participation objectives for that stage, and the information exchange that must take place between you and the public. Begin the meeting planning by reviewing these objectives and the information exchange, because they will help clarify the purpose of your meeting.

Step 2: Get Agreement on What You Hope to Accomplish with the Public During This Meeting

Meetings may be held for a number of purposes—for example, to provide information to the public; solicit views, preferences, or ideas from the public; encourage interaction between groups; or obtain agreements.

FIGURE 8.1. MEETING PLANNING WALL CHART.

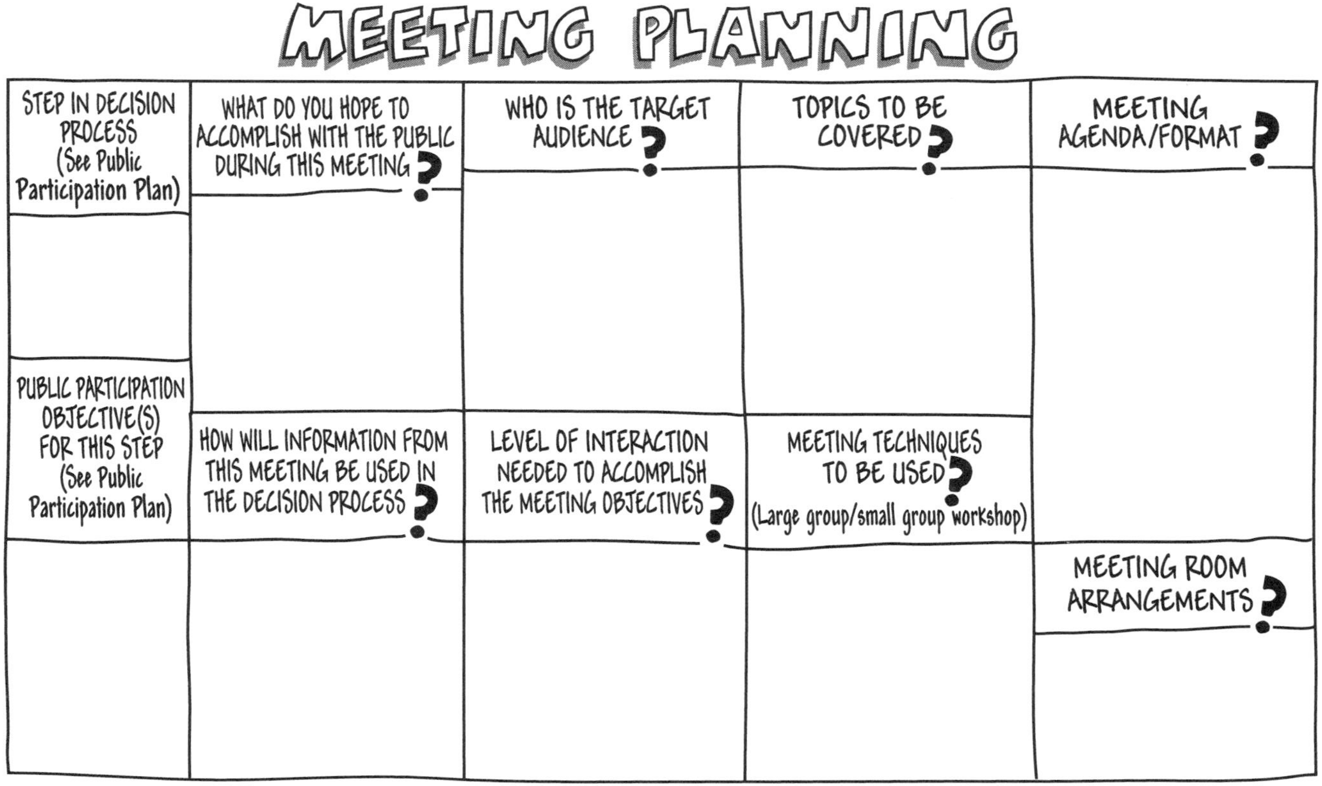

MEETING PLANNING

STEP IN DECISION PROCESS (See Public Participation Plan)	WHAT DO YOU HOPE TO ACCOMPLISH WITH THE PUBLIC DURING THIS MEETING?	WHO IS THE TARGET AUDIENCE?	TOPICS TO BE COVERED?	MEETING AGENDA/FORMAT?
PUBLIC PARTICIPATION OBJECTIVE(S) FOR THIS STEP (See Public Participation Plan)	HOW WILL INFORMATION FROM THIS MEETING BE USED IN THE DECISION PROCESS?	LEVEL OF INTERACTION NEEDED TO ACCOMPLISH THE MEETING OBJECTIVES?	MEETING TECHNIQUES TO BE USED? (Large group/small group workshop)	MEETING ROOM ARRANGEMENTS?

You need to define exactly what is it that you have to accomplish with the public during this meeting before you can begin to talk about what sort of format is appropriate.

Step 3: Discuss How You Will Use the Information You Receive from the Public

One way to clarify the purpose of the meeting is to ask yourself, "How will we use the information we receive during this meeting?" For example, the information you receive might be used to help you define the range of alternatives that will be considered, or it might help you select a preferred alternative, or it might help you define mitigation measures that need to be taken to protect the environment. Once you know what you need to learn from the meeting, that tells you the purpose of your meeting.

Step 4: Identify the Audiences (Stakeholders) You Expect to Participate

Meetings have different audiences. If the purpose of the meeting is to get agreement on the methodology for assessing habitats or determine the net present cost of the alternatives, the audience will be an expert audience drawn from technical people from other agencies or organized groups that can afford professional staff or are technically knowledgeable. At the other extreme are meetings where the purpose is not served unless you hear from as broad a representation of the public as you can reach. The way to frame the question is, "Who [what audience] needs to participate in order to achieve the purpose of this meeting?"

Step 5: List the Topics That Need to Be Covered

Once you are clear on the purpose of the meeting and the audience you are trying to reach, list the topics that must be addressed. This is the beginning of the meeting agenda.

Step 6: Identify the Level of Interaction You Need or Want for Each Topic

Identify the kind of interaction you need on each topic to achieve the objectives for the meeting (Exhibit 8.1). One item on the agenda may be informational. On another item, you may seek agreement. On still another, you may want the participants to interact, although agreement is not necessary.

EXHIBIT 8.1. LEVEL OF INTERACTION, BY TOPIC.

Topics	Interaction Needed
Study progress	Inform the public. Respond to clarifying questions.
Evaluation criteria	Seek high level of agreement on the criteria.
Acceptability of alternatives	Promote discussion between stakeholders, and solicit rankings of the acceptability of the alternatives.
What happens next	Inform the public.

Step 7: Select Meeting Activities for Each Topic to Achieve the Level of Interaction You Need to Accomplish the Objectives

Now you can begin to talk about what kinds of activities will provide the level of interaction you need. This will help you determine what type of meeting format you want, for example, town meeting, workshop, open house, or focus group. Since different topics require different levels of interaction, a single meeting may include different types of activities providing different levels of interaction. A brief presentation could be a good way to inform the public. Then, in order to get interaction, you might break into small discussion groups. If you have a large audience but you are seeking agreement, you may need to break the audience into small groups for discussion, followed by reports back to the full group, and then discussion by the entire audience. If you need the audience to rank alternatives, this could be done in small discussion groups, or it could be handled by asking people to complete a ranking form that they then hand in.

Step 8: Allocate Time to the Various Topics

Once you know the topics and the kinds of activities you need, you can begin to allocate time. Keep in mind that more participative activities always take more time, so if you need higher levels of interaction, allow more time for the activity.

Step 9: Prepare an Agenda

You now have all the information you need to prepare an agenda showing the topic, the type of activity, and the time allotted for each activity. If you are using a participatory activity, talk with those who have experience using these types of activities to be sure you've allowed enough time. The most frequent problem with participatory activities is to try to do too much and find yourself pressuring people to complete the activity just to stay on schedule, even though this may prevent them from completing the activity to the satisfaction of the participants or even your own satisfaction. This can build ill will and give participants the feeling that you are more concerned about staying on schedule than you are hearing what they have to say.

Step 10: Determine Seating Arrangements and Logistical Needs

Each type of meeting has different seating arrangements and meeting logistics. More information on these topics is provided in Chapter Eleven.

Other Factors Affecting Selection of Meeting Type

Although the purpose of the meeting always drives the format of the meeting, other factors can have an influence on meeting design.

Audience Size

Sometimes because of public interest, you know you are going to have a large audience, even though you might also want a higher level of interaction than is normally possible in a large meeting. It is possible, of course, to break the audience into small discussion groups. But if an audience is very large, it may become cumbersome to use small group processes. If the audience is broken up into small groups, for example, the logistics (for example, providing flip charts and meeting rooms) for all the small groups becomes complex.

Familiarity with Meeting Formats

If people have participated previously in meetings where small group processes were used successfully, they will be more comfortable in using this kind of format again. Otherwise there may be discomfort with less conventional meeting formats.

Credibility

Whenever a meeting format is used that is new or different, the public's willingness to accept that format may depend on the motives they attribute to the agency for selecting that format. If they are suspicious that a new format is being proposed to control them or divide and conquer, they will resist that format.

CHAPTER NINE

DEVELOPING INTERACTIVE MEETINGS

Many agencies hold public comment meetings in which speaker after speaker stands up and makes a comment to the entire audience. For some agencies, this is the only kind of public participation they have ever considered. But before you adopt a large public comment meeting format, carefully evaluate whether a more interactive meeting format, with genuine discussion among participants, would serve your purposes better. In my consulting practice, I advise clients to consider alternatives to the public comment meeting format. My experience is that this type of meeting lends itself to speechmaking rather than real dialogue, often results in increased polarization (because leaders of organized groups must be seen as strong defenders of their groups' positions, leading them to take more extreme positions in the meeting than they would in private), and is easily dominated by organized groups that have learned how to game public meetings so that their position appears far more dominant than their actual numbers deserve. With just a few exceptions, if I have a choice I avoid the large meeting format.

One obvious exception is when there are legal requirements to hold a public comment meeting. Some agencies are required by law or agency procedural requirements to conduct public comment meetings, with court reporters present to develop a formal record. Typically this requirement applies to a public meeting that must take place just prior to final decision making. If you've done a good job of public participation, this meeting will be simply a wrap-up of a process that has been ongoing for weeks or months. During earlier stages of the process, you may have held open houses, workshops, or other types of highly interactive meetings. When this is the case, your final public comment meeting is simply a summing-up meeting, and there are likely to be fewer problems. But if the only opportunity for the public to participate in a controversial decision takes place in a large public meeting—this is the one and only meeting in your public participation process—then the chances that the meeting will become dysfunctional are increased.

Keep in mind that legal requirements for public hearings (as distinct from customary practice) are often less restrictive than they seem. In the United States, for example, there are typically three fundamental legal requirements for public hearings: (1) there must be adequate advance publicity, (2) there must be a designated hearing officer (meeting leader), and (3) the agency must keep a complete record of comments. If you are doing a good job of public participation, you will probably exceed the legal requirements for prior publicity of the meeting. You'll have a meeting leader who can be designated the hearing officer without any real constraint on how the meeting is conducted, except that the meeting leader must be fair or impartial. So that leaves the complete record as the only real constraint.

Most lawyers interpret "complete record" to mean a verbatim transcript. But that does not automatically mean a court reporter must be present. There is no reason you couldn't break into small groups and have the small group discussions recorded on audiotape or videotape and transcribed after the meeting. The logistics might be a bit challenging, but it would fulfill the legal requirements.

To illustrate, assume you are holding a public hearing for a river basin study. River basin studies typically have a curvilinear public, that is, the public consists of a number of communities up and down the curves of the river. You could place advertisements in newspapers in communities along the river, announcing the day and time you would be in that community. You could rent a large van in which you carried a rug, folding chairs, an awning, and a tape recorder. You would drive to the designated meeting place, often a town square, put out the rug, set up the awning, set out the chairs, and insert a fresh tape in the tape recorder. At the designated time, you would conduct a meeting with those who showed up, recording their comments. Each night you would mail the tape to your office for transcription. This would meet all the hearing requirements: there would be adequate advance notice of the meeting, you would have been the designated hearing officer, and there would be a verbatim transcription of the public comments.

This particular format might not serve your purposes, but the example does illustrate an essential point: legal requirements may not be as constraining as they at first appear to be. Use your creativity to develop a format that serves the purposes of your public participation program rather than conforms primarily to custom.

The other circumstance that can drive you to using a large meeting format is the size of the audience. If the number of participants could be several hundred, you won't be able to hold a single workshop, for example, because workshop size is best limited to about twenty-five participants (although you could do a number of workshops). If you plan to do coffee klatches, you'd be doing a lot of them. If audience size is large, you probably have to go to the second strategy discussed in this chapter, making the format of your large meeting more interactive.

Making Large Meetings More Interactive

Just because you have a large audience does not mean that you must use the public comment meeting format. Many large meetings can have virtually as much interaction as in a small workshop by using variations of the large group/small group meeting format. Here are some suggestions for how to accomplish this.

Samoan Circles

As described in Chapter Seven, the Samoan Circle is a technique that permits everybody to talk and everybody to hear what is said, but in a setting that is more like a small group discussion than a series of formal speeches or comments (Aggens, 1998).

Chairs are set up in concentric circles surrounding an inner circle (which can be set up around a table), with aisles permitting access to the inner circle. The topic is announced, and anybody can make comments on the topic, except there is a ground rule that no one can speak unless they are seated in the inner circle. This means that anyone who wants to speak must stand up, walk to the inner circle, take one of the seats, and join the discussion going on at that time. No one is forced to leave the inner circle, but whenever someone wants to speak and all the seats are taken in the inner circle, people wanting to speak stand behind chairs in the inner circle. Peer pressure usually clears chairs for those who are waiting to speak.

Because people in the inner circle are seated in what amounts to a small group discussion configuration, conversations have the quality of an informal discussion or dialogue rather then speechmaking. Microphones do need to be provided for the inner circle so that everyone in the audience can hear what is being said.

I've used the Samoan Circle format very successfully during scientific and technical workshops, where the objective was to have an in-depth discussion of an issue, but with everybody hearing the discussion and feeling as if they could participate if they wanted. The only time I've experienced a failure with the Samoan Circle was in a training class where participants were not really interested in the topic of discussion. They didn't care enough about the topic to get up out of their seats and move to the inner circle to participate.

Large Group/Small Group Meetings

The Samoan Circle format gets away from having just one person making a speech or comment, but even more interaction can occur when a large audience is broken into small discussion groups, so that everyone has the experience of participating in the discussion. This is the large group/small group format.

In a large group/small group meeting, everybody assembles as a large group for an initial briefing. Then the audience is broken into small groups, and the small groups are all asked to complete an assignment. After completing the assignment, the participants reassemble as a large group and hear summary reports from the discussion groups. This is sometimes followed by opportunities for comments in the large group.

In most cases, participants prefer the large group/small group format over the public comment format because everybody gets the maximum amount of "airtime" possible given the size of the audience. There are a few exceptions, however. Members of organized groups opposed to a proposed action by an agency often prefer the public comment meeting format because they get a chance to try to persuade the entire audience to their point of view. Elected officials who come to the meeting to impress their constituency may have the same reaction: they want everybody to hear them. But for the average meeting participant, the large group/small group format provides a more satisfying experience.

The one exception is when a large percentage of the audience opposes a proposed action that is being discussed. Then the audience may resist breaking into groups, believing that the agency is attempting to divide and conquer. When a large audience refuses to break into small groups, there is nothing a meeting leader can do to make them do so. If there is a chance this could occur and the audience might refuse to break into discussion groups, discuss the meeting format with the organized groups several days in advance of the meeting to be sure that the format you propose is acceptable.

Here is some information about the mechanics of running a large group/small group meeting.

How to Break into Small Groups. One of the ways to break people into small groups is based on where they are seated in a room, for example, "All of you over here be a group, all of you over here be a group," and so on. But since people with similar viewpoints tend to sit together, this may produce some groups with relatively homogeneous viewpoints. Usually the goal is to have diverse viewpoints in each small group.

One way to get this diversity is by preparing for the meeting by putting different colored dots on stick-on name tags. If you have five to ten colors, prepare the name tags so that they are stacked in colored sets (one green, one blue, one red, and so on). As participants arrive at the meeting and sign in, they receive a name tag with a colored dot. The meeting leader can then make assignments to tables based on colors: "If you have a red dot on your name tag, go to Table 1, if you have a green dot . . ."

Name tags can also be numbered to accomplish the same thing. When there will be more discussion groups than there are colors, numbering may be a simpler approach. People can be assigned to a discussion group by table number.

Alternatively, each table can be assigned a topic, and participants can self-select which topic is of interest to them. You can put signs on the tables with the topic or post the topic on flip chart sheets on the walls immediately behind the tables. This approach means that everybody at a table will be interested in the same topic, but some tables may have more people than are manageable while others may have too few participants to support a lively discussion.

Use of a Small Group Facilitator. Small group discussions can benefit from skilled meeting leadership or facilitation. Depending on the circumstances, agencies sometimes provide a facilitator to assist each small group. There are two major constraints. The first is that there can be far too many small groups for the agency to provide qualified facilitators. The other issue is whether the participants will accept facilitation as something helpful or see it as an effort to control their participation. My experience is that if the agency's credibility is good, a facilitator provided by the agency will be accepted and will be seen as adding value. This is not true, though, when the primary objective of participants is to block an action by the agency. Under these conditions, participants are likely to see agency staff as "the enemy" and will resists efforts to "control" them.

I've led a number of successful meetings where participants selected by the small groups themselves served as meeting leaders for the groups. I spend considerable time when giving instructions for the exercise describing what the facilitator role is. (See Chapter Ten for a detailed discussion of the facilitator role.) For example, I stress the neutrality of the facilitator. I emphasize that the facilitator is the servant of the group, which means that the small group has the power to give guidance to the facilitator. I also point out that being the facilitator puts constraints on this person's ability to be an advocate for a position. I suggest that those who feel strongly about the topic under discussion and want to advocate for that position may not want to be facilitator because this role will limit their ability to advocate.

On occasion I've used facilitators from third-party groups. For example, I've asked the local chapter of the League of Women Voters or some other more or less neutral group to provide facilitators. If you do this, you will need to hold a short training session for the facilitators so they understand their role in the meeting and understand the exercise instructions completely.

Recording Comments Made During Small Group Discussions. Normally no effort is made to capture every comment made in a small group. Instead, each group is provided with a flip chart on which to keep a summary of its discussion and conclusions. Groups do need, however, to have someone clearly designated as the recorder or scribe for the group. There are basically three ways to do this: (1) the agency can provide someone who acts as the recorder, keeping a summary on the flip chart; (2) the facilitator, whether provided by the agency or selected from the participants, can act as the recorder; or (3) the group can pick a participant who serves as a recorder. The advantage of providing a staff person is that this person is focused solely on maintaining the summary, so the summary is usually more complete. But this approach does require extensive staff support for the meeting, and you will also need to conduct advance training so that all reporters understand their role.

The meeting leader needs to make sure that exercise instructions include a description of the recorder role. The recorder's job is to provide a summary of the meeting to the satisfaction of the group. If the group wants the facilitator to change the summary or record additional material, the recorder takes direction from the group. The recorder should not use that role to inject bias or editorializing into the summary. The recorder is a servant of the group.

Getting Reports from Small Groups. Once the exercise is completed or when the announced time is up, the participants return to the large group to hear and discuss what happened in the small groups.

Typically the exercise instructions ask each small group to select someone from their group to make a report on behalf of their group. This person is sometimes called the spokesperson. If participants selected their own facilitator from among themselves, the facilitator often gets named spokesperson as well. But this is not automatic. The meeting leader, in giving the exercise instructions and again when beginning the report-back session, will emphasize that the spokesperson's job is to provide a summary of what the entire group concluded, not use the occasion to advocate for his or her own position.

When a number of groups complete the same exercise, their reports can overlap a great deal and become repetitious and boring. I've used two approaches to address this problem. One approach is to write the exercise instructions so that the groups are told to present some kind of summary information, such as "present the three ideas you believe are most important" instead of their entire list of options.

The other approach is for the meeting leader to act as a kind of master of ceremonies, drawing out the report from the group. For example, instead of having each group present its list of the three items, which will inevitably be repetitive, the meeting leader might say: "I'm going to ask each group around the room to report one idea. Then I'll check back to see if any group has additional ideas that weren't covered by at least one of the groups." Or the meeting leader might say, "Group C believes the answer to the question is . . . Let me see the hands of other groups that felt the same way. Let me see the hands of groups that disagreed. Please give us your reasons for disagreeing." In other words, all the information is reported, but the information is elicited in a way that reduces repetition and overlap.

Structured Small Group Processes

As might be expected, the person or group designing a large group/small group meeting usually spends considerable time making sure that the activity in which small groups engage will produce the best results. Over the years, professional meeting facilitators and people in the group process field have developed numerous techniques or processes for helping groups accomplish specific tasks. You can enhance the effectiveness of your public meetings by using these processes as part of your instructions to small groups. There are literally hundreds of these processes in the group dynamics, organization development, and meeting leadership literature (Gordon, 2004a, 2004b). I describe the techniques that I use most frequently, in alphabetical order.

Backcasting. Backcasting is a technique developed by Matt and Gail Taylor of MGTaylor to get groups to think unconventionally (Creighton and Adams, 1998). Backcasting is the opposite of forecasting. When forecasting, you start in the present and seek to predict the future. With backcasting, you are told what has occurred in the future and your job is to identify a program or series of events that could produce that outcome. For example, the instructions might be, "It is 2010, and the State of California has reduced per person energy use by 40 percent. How did it do that?" Because the amount of change predicted is dramatic, groups have to think creatively to come up with scenarios that could produce the desired outcome.

Brainstorming. Brainstorming is a technique for increasing the number and creativity of ideas developed in a group. In brainstorming, everyone in the group is encouraged to come up with as many ideas as possible, including unconventional ideas. Usually these ideas are recorded on a flip chart or white board. No evaluation is permitted until everybody is completely out of ideas. Brainstorming provides a psychologically safe climate in which people feel free to participate without fear of being judged, and this helps groups break out of the obvious solutions and push for more creative ones. It also greatly increases the number of solutions generated.

While brainstorming may effectively generate a large number of ideas or alternatives in a hurry, other techniques must be used for evaluation. There are also more advanced versions of brainstorming in which additional techniques are employed, using various types of analogies, to increase group creativity. A particularly effective one is to have a group address a problem by asking, "If I could solve this problem any way I wanted, ignoring scientific reality (such as the laws of gravity or economics), the way I would solve this problem is . . . " Although the "way out" ideas that result may defy physical reality, this discussion often leads to a way to produce the same result while coping with reality.

"Dot Democracy." Groups can often generate ideas much faster than they evaluate them. At times during a meeting, there is a need for a quick way of prioritizing options or reducing the number of options being considered. One way is to conduct a straw vote using colored dots. A straw vote is an advisory vote that isn't binding on the group but quickly identifies which items enjoy the greatest support.

Once ideas have been generated (possibly using brainstorming techniques) and recorded on flip chart paper, the group discusses the items just enough to consolidate similar items. Without consolidation, the votes for those items may be watered down, with votes spread among similar items.

People are given a strip of colored dots, typically five to six dots. They are instructed that they can allocate those dots any way they want to. For example, they can give one or two dots each to several items or expend them all on one item. Normally a few items get most of the votes. Then the group can focus attention on these few items rather than the entire list of options.

Jerome Delli Priscoli and Lorenz Aggens, colleagues in the public participation field, have used this technique repeatedly in international forums where the technique has become known as "dot democracy." They have added a feature of color coding the dots so that people from different parts of the world or from different kinds of stakeholders use different colors. For example, representatives of environmental groups might use one color of dots, representatives of government agencies another, representatives of the private sector another, and so on. This allows the group to draw conclusions not only about total votes but also to identify areas of agreement and disagreement among the stakeholders.

Meeting participants can use dots as a way of expressing opinions on scales, not just lists. For example, in water forums, there is substantial debate about the value of building large-scale dams in the developing world. The meeting leader might create a scale to test participants' reactions to some proposition, such as that in Figure 9.1.

Participants record their reaction to the proposition by placing the colored dots at the point on the scale corresponding to their feelings about the proposition. Again, this provides an opportunity to identify those policies with which most people agree and those policies on which opinion remains divided.

Nominal Group Process

Nominal group process is a technique to help groups generate and prioritize a large number of ideas. It has also been successfully used for consensus formation. The process is based on research suggesting that people generate more ideas working by themselves but in the presence of others.

The procedure for nominal group process is as follows:

1. Opening presentation. After an initial presentation describing the process, the audience is broken into small groups of six to nine participants.
2. Discussion leader and recorder. Each group is assigned a discussion leader and a recorder.
3. Introductions. The discussion leader introduces himself or herself, and invites everyone in the group to do the same.

FIGURE 9.1. EXAMPLE OF SCALE USED WITH DOT DEMOCRACY ACTIVITY.

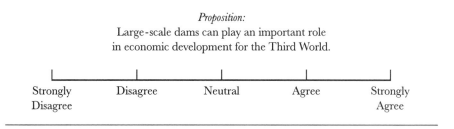

Proposition:
Large-scale dams can play an important role
in economic development for the Third World.

| Strongly Disagree | Disagree | Neutral | Agree | Strongly Agree |

4. Posing the question. The discussion leader presents the question to be answered. It will be carefully worded in order to draw out the specific information desired. The question will be written at the top of a flip chart sheet.

5. Generating ideas. Participants are provided with paper and asked to write down all the answers they can think of to the questions posed.

6. Recording ideas. Each person is asked in turn to report one idea verbally. The idea is summarized by the recorder as accurately as possible. The discussion leader keeps going around the room, one idea per person, until the group is out of ideas. Anyone can say "pass" without giving up a turn on the next round. The process continues until everyone is passing. Participants are not limited to the ideas they have written down but can share new ideas that have been triggered by others' ideas.

7. Discussion. Time is allowed for clarifying the ideas that have been written down and consolidating similar ideas using different wording.

8. Selecting favored ideas. Each person picks the ideas that he or she thinks are best and writes them down on index cards, one idea per card.

9. Ranking favored ideas. Participants arrange their cards in preferential order, with the ones they like the most at the top. Then they assign points to each card, with their top card getting the most points, on down. For example, if the instructions were to select five ideas, the top idea will get five points, the next idea will get four points, and so on.

10. Scoring. The participants call off the items they selected and the points they assigned to each. The points are then tallied, and the recorder creates a list showing the rankings for the top five to ten ideas, depending on where a natural break occurs between high scores and low scores.

11. Discussion of results. The participants may want to discuss the results. Depending on the time remaining in the meeting, this discussion may be brief or lengthy.

12. Reminder of subsequent analysis. Participants should be reminded that staff will conduct a detailed analysis of all items, not just the ones receiving high ranking. Depending on the decision-making process, they should also be reminded that further analysis could result in a considerable change in the ranking of items.

Yellow Stickies

One way for small groups to both generate and organize ideas is by using adhesive pads of yellow sticky notes, slips of paper with enough sticky glue on the back to allow posting on walls. When possible, use three- by five-inch yellow stickies rather than the typical size used in offices. This allows people to write their ideas large enough, using marking pens rather than pen or pencil, so that the whole group can read them when they are posted on the wall.

Have participants generate their ideas, using a brainstorming approach and writing one idea per sticky. Once the brainstorming period is over, participants post their stickies on the wall. Then have the small groups organize their ideas by moving the stickies around so that related ideas are posted next to each other on the wall.

The advantage of this approach is that it eliminates the need for recording ideas on a flip chart, and it is easier to organize ideas when they can be easily moved and clumped together on the wall.

Ranking Processes

There are many occasions in meetings when it is useful to get participants to rank items. For example, participants might be asked to put alternatives in rank order. This was done in the nominal group process technique. If there were five alternatives, the alternative rated highest received five votes, the next highest four votes, and so on.

One problem with this approach, particularly if you try to develop statistics summarizing group responses, is that it assumes that the distance between alternatives is exactly equal. Often this is not the case. Instead, people may have strong preferences for some items and make little distinction among others. These differences can be portrayed best in scales. An individual using a scale might indicate the relative ranking of alternatives in the way shown in Figure 9.2.

In this example, the person doing the ranking not only prefers A to B, but believes that A is much more desirable than B, but B is only slightly more desirable than C. As shown in Figure 9.3, the distance between alternatives A and B is much greater than the distance between alternatives B and C.

Another way to generate rankings that allow participants to show the distance between alternatives is to tell participants they have 100 points (or $100) to allocate among the alternatives—for example, "You have 100 points. Allocate the 100 points among the criteria to show which criteria you think are most important

FIGURE 9.2. RANKING OF
ALTERNATIVES A THROUGH E USING A SCALE.

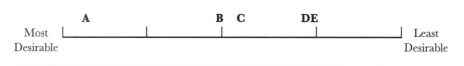

FIGURE 9.3. DISTANCE OF RANKING OF ALTERNATIVES.

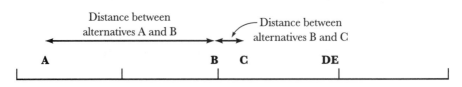

and how important they are. You can allocate the points any way you want. For example, you can decide to allocate 60 points to criterion A, 10 points to criterion B, and 30 points to criterion C."

This technique is easier to understand than using scales. From experience, people have to ask fewer questions about how to complete an assignment using the 100 points than they do using scales, even though the results provide the same information.

Scenario Building

Many times, decisions are being made in response to predictions about future demand for a resource or commodity. For example, water storage facilities are built in response to predictions of future water demand. Power plants are built to respond to predicted energy use. Arguments between stakeholder groups are often based on different assumptions about what the future will be like and the demands created by those different futures. For example, utility companies may propose to build a transmission line to carry electricity from a power plant to an area it believes needs more power. But environmental groups may argue that in the future, energy conservation will reduce the demand for electricity and, in addition, less centralized generation may bring the electricity closer to areas needing electricity, thereby reducing the need for long transmission lines.

One way to develop scenarios for this topic is to ask participants to identify trends or events that would have the greatest impact on future energy use. After discussion, rank those trends or events in order of significance. From the top items on the list, develop a series of themes, for example, "Decentralized energy sources such as fuel cells are available at local shopping centers," or "Competition from the developing world causes values to change, with less emphasis on the environment and more on production." Obviously some themes will contradict the others, and that's the idea. You want to develop a list of themes that bracket all the likely possibilities. Then ask participants to develop a more detailed word picture of what would happen or what actions should be taken, given each theme.

Scenario building is a way of making assumptions about the future explicit. For example, some years ago, a utility company hired me to work with a citizen advisory group to develop a set of alternative futures scenarios for its service area. The company had developed a draft strategy for the future, and it wanted to test how well this strategy held up in each of a set of possible scenarios. The advisory committee came up with a "green" scenario (emphasis on energy conservation and decentralized generation), a "current trends" scenario, a "fuel cell" scenario, and a "deregulated industry" scenario. It has now been more than twenty years since this exercise and it is ironic to note that the scenarios the company thought at the time were unrealistic have actually proven to be the most realistic.

SWOT

SWOT stands for *S*trengths, *W*eaknesses, *O*pportunities, and *T*hreats. Groups are asked to analyze these factors as they affect a specific program or organization. This technique is frequently used in strategic planning workshops. It provides a relatively simple structure for people to identify assumptions and discuss the need for strategic changes in a program or organization.

Wall Charts and Process Guides

A few years ago, my organization operated an interactive meeting center (called a skunkworks) for the U.S. Department of Labor (Creighton and Adams 1998). At times we had more teams conducting strategic planning workshops than we had budget to provide facilitators, so we created a large wall-sized chart that showed all the steps in a strategic planning process. All the teams had to do was fill in the blanks. A bit to our surprise, teams found the charts provided sufficient structure that they had successful planning meetings without any facilitators. The process wisdom that a facilitator might have offered was built into the process shown in the wall chart.

Since then, I have frequently used wall charts (I call them process templates) in both internal and public meetings. Once a workshop activity has been developed, it can be portrayed graphically on the wall chart, and once again all the small groups have to do is fill in the blanks. This visual approach has received a good response from the public, and I find that groups are clearer about what is expected of them.

I later discovered that David Sibbett of Grove Consultants International (www.Grove.com) has worked with this concept for a number of years, calling his wall-sized charts "graphic guides." Sibbett had developed an entire library of graphic guides for different purposes. Figure 9.4 shows a graphic guide developed by Sibbett for strategic planning and Figure 9.5 one for analyzing the structure of an industry.

FIGURE 9.4. JOURNEY VISION GRAPHIC GUIDE.

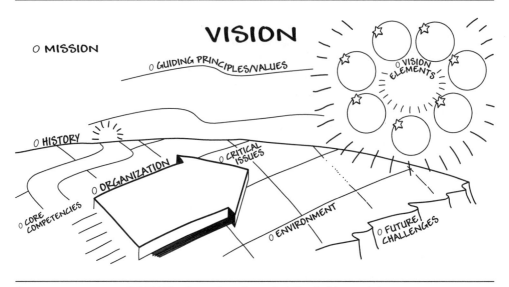

Source: www.grove.com © 1996 The Grove Consultants, Intl. Used with permission.

FIGURE 9.5. INDUSTRY VISION GRAPHIC GUIDE.

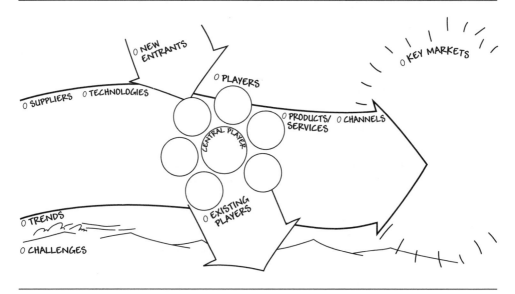

Source: www.grove.com © 1996 The Grove Consultants, Intl. Used with permission.

What a Large Group/Small Group Meeting Looks Like

Here is an example of how the techniques described in this chapter were combined to produce large meetings that were still highly interactive.

CORPS OF ENGINEERS LISTENING SESSIONS

The U.S. Army Corps of Engineers has managed aspects of U.S. water resources for many years, particularly pertaining to flood control and navigation. In 2001, it identified six "water challenges" facing the nation. It hoped that the discussion of these issues could lead to a consensus on actions that needed to be taken to address these challenges. So it scheduled a nationwide series of "listening sessions" to determine what water-related issues were being experienced around the country and how people thought those issues should be addressed. Based on these workshops, the Corps of Engineers would produce a report to distribute to Congress and other influential stakeholders.

The Corps of Engineers planned listening sessions in fourteen U.S. cities, plus two final "nationwide" meetings, one in California and one in Washington, D.C. It anticipated that attendance could be as high as several hundred in some cities, so the meeting design had to be able to accommodate large groups. The Corps of Engineers also wanted to use the same meeting format in each city, so that the outcomes of the meeting would be comparable and could be compiled into a meaningful nationwide report.

The Corps of Engineers quickly concluded that despite the potential size of the audience, it wanted a highly interactive format, not prepared speeches. The goal was to get each participant involved in the discussion and information-sharing process. Participants were encouraged to submit written statements for the meeting record and for inclusion in the regional listening session report. The Corps of Engineers also wanted to limit discussion regarding existing or pending projects. The concern was that people would get so focused on local controversies that they wouldn't engage in long-term thinking.

Based on these considerations, the team designing and conducting the meetings (which included me, who served as the leader for most of the meetings) concluded that it needed to use a variation on the large group/small group format, with smaller groups completing assignments and then reporting back to the larger group.

In each city, the meeting room was set up banquet style: all participants sat at round tables that accommodated eight to ten people.

Each meeting began with a brief introduction by the Corps of Engineers outlining the purpose of the workshop and discussing the six water resources challenges it had identified: aging infrastructure, environmental restoration, emergency response, the marine transportation system, flood control, and smart growth.

Then the meeting was turned over to the facilitator, who explained the format of the workshop and described the first activity. Basically the instructions for the first activity were as follows: "You'll be working in small groups comprising the people at your table. [People sitting at tables with less than a full complement of people were invited to move to other tables.] Introduce yourselves to each other. Then take five to ten minutes to individually write down the water challenges that face your region on the adhesive note pads (yellow stickies) on the table, one idea per sticky. Do this silently, without discussion. Then go around the table, with each person presenting one challenge that he or she feels is important and explaining to the group why. These ideas will be recorded on the flip chart by your recorder. Keep going around the room until everyone is out of ideas. As a group, develop a list of important challenges that you want presented to the entire group. Select a spokesperson to present your report. Save your stickies, as they will be collected and recorded."

Once the group completed this assignment, the entire audience was reassembled (because they were already sitting at banquet tables, this just meant that participants only needed to turn around and stop talking). To cut down on the repetitiousness of lengthy reports from each group, the facilitator asked for one challenge from each group, moving around the room. Each idea was recorded in a computer and projected on the screen, using a digital projector. Once every group had reported at least one challenge, they were asked to report any additional items from their group as long as it didn't repeat an item already on the screen.

At the same time this was going on, other staff were writing down the ideas from the screen onto flip chart paper, one sheet per idea. These sheets were posted on the wall.

Just before a break, the audience was asked to post any stickies with ideas or information that amplified or clarified topics on the appropriate flip chart sheet. In addition, each person was given six dots and told to distribute them on the challenges shown on the flip charts any way he or she wanted. During the break, the audience voted, using the colored dots, for the challenges they thought were most important.

After the break, the facilitator announced the scores received for each topic. Typically five to seven topics received a number of dots, and then there was a relatively sharp drop-off in votes received. The facilitator announced the challenges that would be discussed during the afternoon, based on the voting, and designated a table for each challenge. Participants were asked to move to the table assigned to the challenge they wanted to discuss. Each table was asked to develop a plan for what should be done to address the challenge. Participants were told to assume they had the power they needed to develop solutions for the identified challenges. Groups were also asked to discuss which parts of the plan should be carried out by the federal government, state and local government, local associations, or the private sector. Each group selected a spokesperson to report their plan to the whole audience. The participants had the option of moving around from challenge to challenge if they had more than one topic they wanted to discuss. A Corps of Engineers member was assigned the task of taking notes at each of the group discussion areas.

The whole audience reassembled and heard the plans developed at the tables. The meeting concluded with a quick presentation from the Corps of Engineers on how the information from the listening session would be used and what the next steps would be. Ultimately more than eleven hundred people participated in these listening sessions.

This series of meetings used many of the techniques described in this chapter. People were assigned to tables based on a number on their name tag. During the first small group assignment, the group used the silent generation technique from the nominal group process to generate ideas; each developed ideas individually before sharing the ideas with others in their small group. Participants also made use of yellow stickies to record their ideas, and these stickies were collected later and tallied by the Corps of Engineers as well as being used to amplify the topics discussed in the second small group session. During the reports in the large group session, all the ideas reported from the small groups were visually recorded using a digital projector so the entire group could see the ideas as they were suggested by the small groups. The facilitator did not ask for complete reports from each group, which could have been repetitive, but asked for at least one idea per group, then recycled back through the groups to pick up any ideas not identified during the first round. The participants used "dot democracy" to indicate which topics they thought deserved further discussion. During the second small group session, they could move to the group in which they had the greatest interest and (borrowing an idea from the Open Space technique), participants could move around from group to group based on their own interest and sense of timing.

This particular meeting format required both significant staff support and coordination of complex logistics. One of the challenges was that the arrangements for logistics had to be handled by Corps of Engineers staff in fourteen cities. So part of the challenge in making this series of meetings a success was to communicate effectively with support staff in each of the fourteen cities who obtained the meeting rooms and much of the equipment (such as numerous flip charts), since the facilitator and other meeting staff could carry only the most critical equipment from city to city.

References

Aggens, L. "The Samoan Circle: A Small Group Process for Discussing Controversial Subjects." In J. L. Creighton, J. Delli Priscoli, and C. M. Dunning, *Public Involvement Techniques: A Reader of Ten Years Experience at the Institute for Water Resources*. Alexandria, Va.: Institute for Water Resources, 1983. (Rev. ed. 1998.) [www.iwr.usace.army.mil/iwr/pdf/pifirst.pdf].

Creighton, J., and Adams, J.W.R. *CyberMeeting*. New York: AMACON, 1998.

Gordon, J. (ed.). *Structured Experiences: Learning Activities for Intact Teams and Workgroups*. San Francisco: Jossey-Bass/Pfeiffer, 2004a.

Gordon, J. (ed.). *Structured Experiences: Learning Activities for Personal Development*. San Francisco: Jossey-Bass/Pfeiffer, 2004b.

CHAPTER TEN

FACILITATING PUBLIC MEETINGS

At least half of the work involved in conducting an effective public meeting is done before the meeting starts. How a meeting is structured is a significant determinant of its success. But while a poorly designed meeting can handicap the most skilled of meeting leaders, how the meeting is led matters a great deal. An ineffectual leader can make the meeting seem like a waste of time, while an autocratic leader can create resentment and antagonism toward the agency sponsoring the meeting. This chapter describes facilitation, a style of meeting leadership that has proven to be highly effective in conducting public meetings.

In meetings, how a meeting is run—the process of the meeting—tells the participants whether they are being treated with respect, whether their opinions matter, and what their relative relationship is to each other.

When there's a controversy, people often fight over the meeting format or procedures as a way of defining their relationship or gaining an advantage. They may fight for leadership of a meeting, disagree over how the meeting is to be run, argue over what should be included on the agenda, or strive for dominance during the meeting.

Inside an agency, an organizational leader has management controls that put limits on these struggles. But things are different in public meetings. People don't have to be nice to you. Some groups see breaking up a meeting as a success. Struggles for power and control are more open and more challenging to the meeting leader. As a result, leading a controversial public meeting can challenge even the most experienced meeting leader. This chapter contains suggestions for increasing the chances of success.

General Principles of Meeting Leadership

There are several basic principles to effective meeting leadership.

People Accept Meeting Leadership That Is in Their Interest

To accomplish anything in a meeting, there must be some structure. Limits need to be set on topics. Procedures must be established for recognition of speakers. People can see that they won't get a chance to speak if time limits are not observed. As long as the leader provides this structure in a manner that the participants consider equitable and reasonable, it is in their interest to cooperate.

When the audience feels the leader has been fair and reasonable, the leader, if challenged, will usually be supported by the rest of the audience. But if the structure is not considered equitable or reasonable, the leader's power is diminished and is subject to challenge.

Lead the Process, Not the Content

The meeting leader's job is to ensure a fair and efficient process. The audience understands the need for this process, so participants grant the meeting leader limited authority as long as they are convinced that the meeting leader is exercising his or her authority on behalf of a good meeting. But the minute a meeting leader assumes the role of an advocate or comments on the content of the meeting, the audience will see the leader's action as on behalf of a particular outcome, not just a good meeting. Once this occurs, the authority of the meeting leader is undermined.

Avoid Power Symbols

Some agency representatives show up for meetings in full-dress military uniforms, carrying flags, and with a large entourage. Other show up with a large number of experts and thousands of dollars of displays or costly maps and graphics. These are symbols of power. The message to the public, whether intended or not, is that the agency is more powerful and has infinitely more resources than the public.

This breeds resentment and antagonism that shows up in challenges to the meeting leader, unwillingness to follow meeting procedures, and antagonistic language.

The U.S. Forest Service is a quasi-uniformed service. Rangers working in the field wear uniforms to give them authority when dealing with people using National Forest lands. But uniforms are not mandatory when they are not in the field, and people who work inside Forest Service offices often do not wear uniforms.

The Forest Service decided to conduct research on whether meetings went better when meeting leaders wore uniforms or civilian clothes. They found that meeting leaders wearing uniforms were far more likely to be challenged and met with hostility than meeting leaders in civilian clothes. In other words, power symbols evoke some of the control problems they are designed to prevent.

An effective leader is able to provide structure yet is flexible enough to change formalistic meeting rules when appropriate, accept comments from the audience even though they may be emotionally laden, and convey enthusiasm, sincerity, and commitment for the public participation process.

Who Should Lead a Public Meeting

In many agencies the tradition has been that the highest-ranking official ("the boss") leads the meeting. This has some advantages. The public likes to know that its comments are being heard by someone high up in the agency, a true decision maker. In addition, many top executives have good presence in front of an audience.

But it also has strong disadvantages. It is always harder for a top official to appear neutral. The boss will inevitably be associated in people's minds with the policies and actions of the agency. He or she may, under pressure, get defensive about past actions or programs, make comments that show a bias toward a particular outcome even though the purpose of the meetings is to evaluate those options, or make commitments that should not be offered under the stress of leading a meeting. Also, antagonistic groups are more likely to try to use an attack against a high-ranking official as a way of undermining the agency's position.

My recommendation is that the highest-ranking official be present and open the meeting, give a brief welcome, and then turn the meeting over to another person, who leads the meeting from that point on. This makes it very clear that management is at the meeting to hear the public's comments, but that the meeting leader's role is to establish and maintain a structure that works in everybody's interests and meeting leadership is not just a role bestowed by virtue of rank.

If the top manager is particularly skilled at leading meetings, these skills may compensate for the risks of having the top manager up in front of the meeting. But senior managers sometimes have a grandiose image of their meeting leadership skills, since it may be hard for their subordinates to provide negative feedback.

Some people in your agency may have been trained in meeting leadership or have acquired skills over the years. These people can be considered possible meeting leaders. But because they are from the agency, they may be perceived as running the meeting for the benefit of the agency, not the public. This is particularly likely to be the case when there is substantial controversy. No matter how skilled a meeting leader and no matter how fair and balanced this person acts, the perception that the meeting leader is there to protect the agency's interest, not the interests of the participants, may be difficult to overcome.

Under these conditions, it may be wise to hire an external facilitator, someone who is skilled in meeting leadership but is less likely to be viewed as acting for the agency. The idea is to remove process issues, such as how the meeting is run, as a source of dispute by delegating them to a third party who is impartial about the substantive outcome and who will act on behalf of all the participants.

The Facilitator's Role

A facilitator is a trained specialist who helps people design effective meetings and then acts as the meeting leader. A facilitator may be influential in making decisions about how a meeting is run but does not have the authority to make substantive decisions for the group. Typically a facilitator will consult with participants about major process decisions, such as significant changes in an agenda or revised meeting procedures.

A facilitator uses a style of meeting leadership that is less directive than the kind of leadership associated with chairing a meeting. Some people, when chairing a meeting, make rulings, determine procedures, declare people out of order, and so forth. A facilitator proposes, suggests, invites, and then consults with the participants.

This is not because a facilitator is a weak leader. Facilitation often takes far more skill than being a traditional chair of a meeting, and a facilitator may exercise considerable control over the meeting. The key point is that the facilitator is concerned that everybody feels included and accepted. If the meeting leadership is too heavy-handed or authoritarian, participants can become upset or resentful or may conclude that the facilitator is biased against them. The facilitator's role is to create a climate of mutual respect and psychological safety that makes it possible for people to consider creative new solutions and move from preconceived positions.

Facilitator Behaviors

Facilitators engage in certain characteristic behaviors designed to provide sufficient structure so the meeting accomplishes its goals and bring about a positive atmosphere for collaboration.

Help Keep the Meeting on Track and Focused

Facilitators are skilled at pointing out when the discussion has drifted or at restating the purpose of an activity. Facilitators also play the "traffic cop" role of regulating how long people speak or putting limits on behavior such as accusations or emotional tirades. Often this is done by working with the participants to establish ground rules that everybody feels are fair. When a facilitator intervenes, everybody understands that the intervention is on behalf of an effective meeting, not because of prejudice or bias.

Clarify and Accept Communication

Until we feel our concerns have been understood and accepted, many of us keep saying them over and over again in new and different ways, often with accelerating intensity that's likely to produce a counterreaction. For this reason, one of a facilitator's primary tasks is to be sure that everybody feels listened to and understood. The facilitator may do this by providing a verbal summary of what was said, relating one participant's ideas to another's, inviting expansion of a comment, or asking clarifying questions. Sometimes a facilitator writes a summary of comments on a flip chart or is assisted by another staff person, called a recorder, who will keep a summary of comments on the flip chart. A facilitator might also point out when a participant's contribution was cut off and invite him or her to complete the idea.

Accept and Acknowledge Feelings

During public meetings, people are often upset or angry. Telling them not to feel that way simply reinforces and strengthens those feelings. In some meetings, it is necessary to let everybody ventilate their feelings before it is possible to begin talking about solutions. The facilitator can structure a situation in which it is safe to express feelings, without those feelings causing a permanent breech in communication between the parties. The facilitator will make sure these feelings are acknowledged so that they don't continue to build in intensity.

State a Problem in a Constructive Way

People often express their opinions in such a way that it seems as if they are fixing blame or accusing the agency or other stakeholders of unacceptable, dishonest, or even illegal actions. This causes people to counter with blame and accusations of their own, making the conflict escalate. A facilitator can help by restating comments so they do not blame any party or so they define the problem without implying there is only one possible solution.

Suggest a Procedure or Problem-Solving Approach

During a meeting, a facilitator may suggest a procedure, such as brainstorming or a structured sequence of problem-solving steps, to help the group work more effectively. Or a facilitator may help break an impasse by suggesting alternative ways of addressing the issue or suggest a break.

Summarize and Clarify Direction

Participants may be so involved with the subject being discussed that they lose track of the overall picture. A facilitator may restate the purpose of the meeting or clarify its direction (for example, "We've completed the first two issues; now we're ready to start talking about alternatives").

Test for Consensus

In meetings where some level of agreement is sought, one of the important responsibilities of a facilitator is to sense when participants are coming to agreement and verify that agreement has been reached by stating the potential basis for agreement and checking to see whether it has support from the participants. Since the facilitator doesn't make decisions for the group, this takes the form of: "It sounds as if you are in agreement that. . . . Is that acceptable?" Once an agreement is reached, it should be written on the flip chart by either the facilitator or recorder.

Because a facilitator needs to remain neutral on the outcome of the meeting and wants to create a climate for collaborative problem solving, there are also certain behaviors he or she should avoid:

- Judging or criticizing the ideas of participants
- Using the role of facilitator to push his or her own ideas
- Making significant procedural decisions without consulting the participants
- Taking up the group's time with lengthy comments

The Facilitator's Knowledge of the Subject Matter

Can someone who doesn't know your business run your meeting? It's helpful but not mandatory that the facilitator know about the organizations involved and the subjects of discussion. As a minimum, the facilitator needs to know enough to be able to follow the discussion. Since agencies and organizations often use numerous acronyms and technical jargon, this can be an important issue. But if the facilitator is too directly involved in the subject matter, he or she may have opinions about the issue that make it hard to remain neutral, or may be seen by some of the parties as biased or partial toward a particular point of view or organization.

Resources

Kaner, S., and others. *Facilitator's Guide to Participatory Decision Making.* Gabriola Island, B.C., Canada: New Society Publishers, 1996.

Schuman, S. P. (ed.). *IAF Handbook of Group Facilitation: Best Practices from the Leading Organization in Facilitation.* San Francisco: Jossey-Bass, 2005.

Schwarz, R. *The Skilled Facilitator.* San Francisco: Jossey-Bass, 2002.

CHAPTER ELEVEN

DETERMINING MEETING LOGISTICS

When meeting logistics are handled well, they support and reinforce the meeting design. When they aren't handled well, they can undercut even the best meeting design. This chapter describes some of the key logistics that require attention.

Seating Arrangements

One of the first considerations in selecting a meeting place is whether the facility can accommodate the desired meeting format and seating arrangements. For example, there's little possibility of holding an interactive workshop in a meeting room with auditorium seating bolted to the floor.

Seating arrangements are a direct reflection of the type of meeting to be held and the relationship among participants. If you seat agency staff at the front of the room, with the audience in rows, this establishes a relationship in which all participants talk to the meeting leaders at the front of the room rather than to each other (see Figure 11.1). This is appropriate when all you want to do is give information to the public, but it does not foster interaction among participants.

You can increase the potential for interaction if the seating is semicircular (see Figure 11.2) rather than in rows. This arrangement allows some eye contact with others in the audience, which encourages interaction.

FIGURE 11.1. AUDITORIUM-STYLE SEATING.

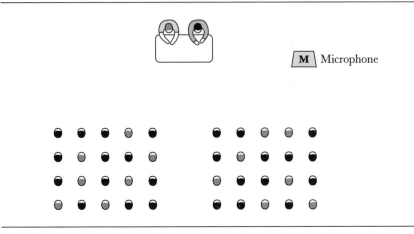

FIGURE 11.2. SEMICIRCULAR SEATING.

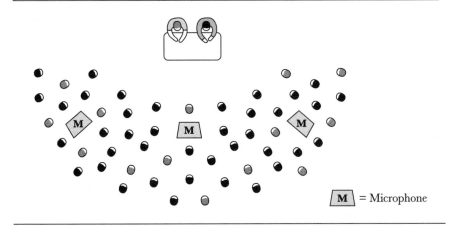

The ideal arrangement for interaction or consensus forming and negotiation is a circle. Not only does a circular arrangement permit eye contact among all participants, it also removes any head of the table, so everyone is equal in status. Figure 11.3 illustrates several circular seating arrangements.

One large group approximation of a circular arrangement is shown in Figure 11.4. Three rows of chairs organized around a fifteen-foot square will accommodate one hundred people.

FIGURE 11.3. CIRCULAR SEATING ARRANGEMENTS.

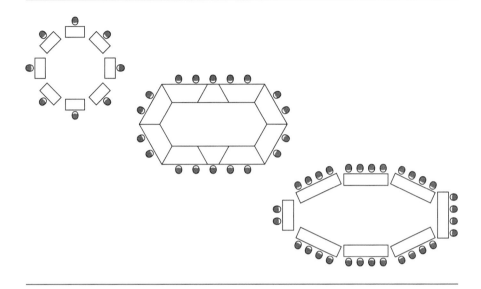

FIGURE 11.4. LARGE GROUP CIRCULAR SEATING.

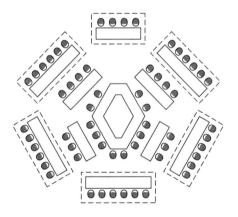

Typical banquet seating, as shown in Figure 11.5, is a natural arrangement for a large group/small group meeting. People can turn to hear the opening presentation, then turn back to the people at their tables as the group with whom they will communicate. This means that the way you assign people to tables will determine the mix of opinions at those tables.

If the meeting is held in a cafeteria, gymnasium, or other large multipurpose room, it is possible to have two meeting setups: half the room is devoted to chairs in rows for the large group portion of the meeting, and the other half of the room is set around small tables for the small group discussion (see Figure 11.6).

Time and Place of Meetings

Meetings should be held at a time and place convenient to the public, with the convenience of staff a secondary consideration. Usually this means that meetings

FIGURE 11.5. BANQUET SEATING.

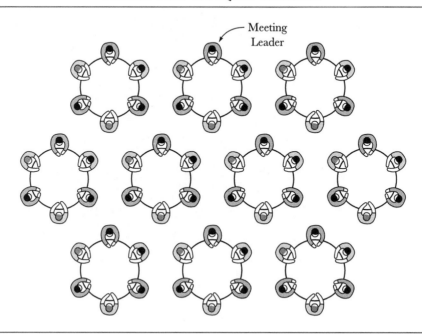

FIGURE 11.6. LARGE GROUP/SMALL GROUP SEATING ARRANGEMENT.

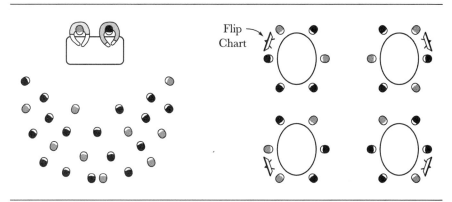

will be held in the evenings, although meetings attended primarily by representatives of governmental entities may be more convenient during the day.

Depending on the circumstances, there may be times when it is more appropriate to meet away from agency facilities, on neutral ground.

Additional Logistics Factors

Among other factors to consider in selecting a meeting place are these:

- Location of the facility (central or outlying)
- Public transportation access
- Space for parking
- Safety of the area
- Access for disabled participants

Exhibit 11.1 displays some key tasks to accomplish in setting up a meeting.

EXHIBIT 11.1. MEETING PREPARATION CHECKLIST.

Providing information to public[a]	• Define what information the public will need to participate in the meeting • Get agreement on what information products you will need to provide this information, such as newsletters and facts sheets • Write text of information products • Get approvals of text • Design the layout of the publication • Print the publication • Distribute the publication to elected officials/policymakers in advance • Mail/distribute the publication to potential participants
Identify date, time, and place for meetings	• Agree on communities where meetings need to be held • Agree on the best time for the convenience of the target audience • Agree on the dates for the meetings • Identify potential meeting rooms • Confirm seating requirements and table arrangements for proposed meeting format • Confirm which of the meeting rooms are appropriate for the planned meeting format, including access to public transportation (if likely to be needed), security, and familiarity to audience • Secure meeting rooms • Communicate seating arrangements to meeting place or identify staff who will arrive early and set up the room • Review all the arrangements regarding keys and access to the room and emergency numbers in case of problems
Meeting design	• Identify meeting design team • If external facilitator to be used, select and make contracting arrangements • Get agreement on meeting type, for example, public comment, workshop, open house • Prepare any instructions needed for meeting activities • Identify staff resources required, for example, small group facilitators, recorders, administrative staff • Conduct premeeting training for facilitators and recorders
Developing presentations	• Identify what topics need to be covered and key points • Identify presenters • Identify what graphics are needed, for example PowerPoint presentation, posters • Identify who will develop presentations

EXHIBIT 11.1. MEETING PREPARATION CHECKLIST, Cont'd.

	• Develop any meeting handouts, for example, copies of presentations
	• Conduct dry runs of all presentations
Premeeting publicity	• Get agreement on how meetings will be publicized, for example, newsletter, mail, paid advertising, press release, elected official briefings
	• Prepare text of any publicity materials
	• Design the layout of publicity materials
	• Distribute publicity materials
	• Conduct any premeeting briefings required
Meeting sign-in	• Develop sign-in sheets
	• Identify meeting handouts
	• Identify name tags needed (including color or numerical coding if used for assignment to small groups)
	• Identify administrative staff required
	• Bring or arrange for sign-in table, chairs, table for meeting handouts
Signing	• Determine the number and kinds of signs needed to lead people to meeting rooms (including determining whether signs need to be in more than one language, or specify handicapped entrances)
	• Prepare signs
	• Identify who will put signs up prior to meeting
Refreshments	• Determine whether refreshments will be needed
	• Determine whether to bring or buy refreshments
	• Determine any equipment needed, such as a coffeemaker, trays
	• Identify who is responsible to get refreshment and equipment to meeting room
Equipment	• Determine equipment needed: for example, microphones, overhead projector or digital projector, screen, power cords, easels and flip chart paper, pens, tape
	• Identify who is responsible for getting equipment to meeting
Leaving meeting rooms	• Clarify what cleanup of meeting room is required
	• Identify person responsible for final lockup

[a]Getting information products ready, particularly obtaining approvals of text and layout, is the most time-consuming part of preparing for a meeting and requires the greatest lead time.

PART FIVE

GENERAL-PURPOSE TOOLS

While much of a public participation practitioners' tool kit is taken up with public meeting techniques, there are other techniques that are used so frequently that they must be given a prominent place in the practitioner's tool kit.

To continue the tool kit analogy, a hammer is a general-purpose tool (you use it for a wide variety of tasks), while a five-eighths-inch lug wrench is a specialized tool, because it works only with five-eighths-inch lugs. Each of the tools described in the chapters in Part Five is a general-purpose tool, serving a number of purposes.

The first two techniques in this part are advisory groups (Chapter Twelve) and conducting interviews (Chapter Thirteen). They are described in considerable detail because they are used almost as frequently as public meetings and deserve this attention.

The other topics discussed in Part Five are what might be called cross-cutting topics. Virtually every public participation program requires working with the media (Chapter Fourteen) and analyzing public comment (Chapter Fifteen). The question of how to evaluate the success of public participation programs (Chapter Sixteen) is another topic that cuts across all types of public participation programs. Each of these topics involves specific techniques and approaches that are discussed in these chapters.

Finally, many agencies rely on consultants to help them design or conduct public participation processes. Agencies often do not have the internal expertise to conduct some aspects of public participation programs, or they require the assistance of a neutral party for credibility. Chapter Seventeen describes the various kinds of consultants and how to use them effectively.

CHAPTER TWELVE

WORKING WITH ADVISORY GROUPS

Many agencies set up advisory groups consisting of people representing various interests, points of view, or fields of expertise to advise the organization on its programs or proposed actions. This chapter provides guidelines for how to establish and manage an advisory group.

Why to Use an Advisory Group

Advisory groups can be effective for a number of reasons:

- They provide a cross sampling of public views and concerns.
- Members of the group have a chance to become informed about the issues before coming to conclusions and have a better understanding of the consequences of decisions. As a result, their counsel to the organization combines a citizen's perspective with a more complete understanding of the situation.
- Because personal relationships are developed in the group, members develop a deeper understanding of the concerns of the other interests and establish relationships that serve as a moderating influence on more extreme views.
- Advisory groups can serve as a communication link back to the constituencies they represent, and advisory groups may be able to reach a consensus among conflicting groups.

Principles for Establishing Advisory Groups

There are several general principles that should be observed in establishing advisory groups:

• An advisory group must represent the full range of interests and values in the community of people interested in the decisions being made. An advisory group that represents only interests that have traditionally supported your organization's policy is misleading and undermines the credibility of the entire public participation effort. To be effective, the group must provide representation for all interests who see themselves as affected by the proposed action.

• The group's role in decision making must be clearly defined. Confusion about the role of the advisory group, coupled with the natural desire on the part of the members to exercise maximum influence on the outcome, can be a source of problems. This problem can be avoided, or at least minimized, if there is a candid discussion of the group's role in decision making at the outset. Develop a written mandate that carefully outlines exactly what is expected of the group.

• Normally the life of the advisory group, or at least the terms of the group's members, should be limited. The longer a group exists, the more likely it is to become simply a new elite. Advisory committees that go on for years have a tendency to outlive their usefulness, so both the group's continuing usefulness and the members' tenure should be monitored. Most public participation comes on issues that have a direct effect on groups or individuals. Once those issues are resolved, the original participants lose interest in attending meetings. This situation can be resolved through regular change in representation. If you want advice on a single important issue, consider setting up a task force (instead of a standing advisory committee) that completes that one important task and then dissolves.

• Efforts should be made to ensure that members of the advisory group maintain regular communication with the constituencies they are supposed to represent. Group members should inform their constituencies through briefings, organizational newsletters, public meetings, or occasional interviews or discussion with other leaders from their constituency. This will ensure that the membership reflects the views of the constituency and that the constituency is educated along with the advisory group members. Consider asking each advisory group member to develop a constituency representation plan outlining how he or she will communicate with his or her constituency.

• Responsible managers from your organization should interact with the advisory group, so the group feels that it is being heard by people with genuine authority and so managers hear public concerns firsthand.

• Organizational staff must speak the public's language when working with advisory groups. This is essential, but it is no simple task. It requires the ability to simplify technical language and jargon without appearing to be patronizing.

• An organization must be prepared to provide considerable staff time and logistical support to the advisory group. Advisory groups may also want direct technical assistance from outside consultants to ensure a fully impartial evaluation.

Some organizations set up advisory groups that have relatively informal membership. Regular invitations are sent to a number of people and those who show up are the membership for that meeting. No votes are taken. People simply express opinions about the subjects being discussed. Other advisory groups have an established membership, well-defined procedures, and rules about attendance of alternate members.

In an informal advisory group, the need to resolve questions of membership will be a low priority, since membership will be changing constantly. But in a formal advisory group, it is crucial to use a technique for selecting members that ensures that the group is representative of all the interests.

Methods for Selecting Advisory Group Members

There are five basic methods for selecting advisory group members:

1. Members are selected by your organization with an effort to balance the different interests. This is by far the most frequently used technique. But on controversial issues, this approach runs the risk that the public will believe the organization has established the group to support its own position. The danger that the public will see the membership as biased can be reduced if affected interest groups and agencies are consulted prior to selecting the members and the selections clearly reflect this consultation process.

2. The selection of the advisory group is turned over to a third party or group. Depending on how localized the issue is, the selection process could be turned over to a local elected body, a community leader or politician, a public participation consultant, or a small group representing the major interests, who in turn select other members.

3. The agency determines the interests it wishes to have represented and allows the groups to select their own representatives. This can create problems for volunteer groups, which sometimes have difficulty coordinating among themselves to select a representative. However, it eliminates the risk of being seen as stacking the deck.

4. Use any of the previous three methods, and augment the membership with volunteers. This allows the different interests to adjust the membership of the group by obtaining volunteers from their ranks. If the advisory group will vote on issues, though, this method permits the various groups to stack the deck by adding a large number of additional volunteers.

5. Determine membership by a popular election. This last method has been used in only a few cases where there was some existing structure for selecting representatives, such as neighborhood councils.

Procedural Issues

A number of procedural issues normally have to be settled with groups that will be working together for some time. An advisory group may choose to devote its first meetings to agreeing on procedures (although protracted debate on procedures can seriously undermine enthusiasm). It may be advisable to prepare and circulate a draft of proposed guidelines for revision and adoption by the advisory group before they meet for the first time. The draft is often based on telephone consultations or interviews with incoming members. Resolving issues such as those described next in the first few meetings can prevent hard feelings later.

Voting

Probably the most important procedural decision is whether subsequent decisions will be made by voting. Most people in the United States are used to voting on issues and assume automatically that this is the right way to make decisions. However, there are several reasons that voting is usually not the best way for advisory groups to make a decision. First, despite efforts to make the group broadly representative, there is no guarantee that representation of interests on the advisory group is proportionate to those interests among the public at large. A majority vote may merely reflect an imbalance in the composition of a group rather than a view of the majority of the public.

A split vote simply means there is a continuing disagreement, which could have been determined without an advisory group. If the objective is to work toward a politically acceptable outcome, a badly divided group serves little purpose. Only if there is some degree of consensus is the advisory group likely to have much impact on either the public at large or agency decision makers.

An alternative to voting is to obtain a sense of the meeting. The meeting leader listens carefully until there appears to be a consensus, states this as his or her "sense of the meeting," and checks to see if it is acceptable to the group. This approach requires a good sense of timing, the ability to summarize effectively, and a credible leader.

If it is impossible to reach agreement on the sense of a meeting, the meeting leader asks the group how to resolve the controversy. One possibility is to keep talking. Another is to vote, possibly requiring a supermajority, such as two-thirds or three-fourths of the membership. Another is to have majority and minority reports. Still another is to obtain agreement on procedures for resolving the key factual issues that prevent resolution. Finally, it may be best to drop consideration of an issue until the next meeting, giving members a chance to think about the issue more.

Attendance

Some groups wish to establish minimum attendance requirements for membership. For example, a member who is absent more than a certain number of times might be dropped from the group.

Alternates

Whether members can send alternates to participate in meetings can be an important issue if the group has decided to make decisions by a majority vote. But if voting rights are not involved, then sending alternates is one way to keep everybody informed. If alternates are not kept informed of what occurred at previous meetings, however, it is very frustrating to the regular members.

Participation of Observers

A ground rule may be needed concerning observers. Are they welcome at advisory group meetings? If so, at what point in the meeting? Some advisory groups set aside a time during which the audience may address the committee, but they do not permit nonmembers to speak at other times.

Subcommittees

It may be necessary to establish subcommittees to accomplish specific work tasks. The responsibilities and authorities of any subcommittees should be clearly defined.

Confidentiality of Materials

If the group will be reviewing documents that need to remain confidential or may undergo substantial modification before being made public, rules may be required to govern their confidentiality. Many experienced public participation practitioners assume that anything turned over to advisory groups, regardless of requests for confidentiality, is a public document.

Constituencies

Specific mechanisms may need to be set up to ensure regular communication with constituencies being represented by group members.

Communication with the Public

It's desirable to keep the advisory group process open and visible to the interested public, so that when the group finally develops recommendations, they are credible to the public. The advisory group might conduct periodic meetings at key points in the process to present the work it has done to date and get reactions to that work. Newsletters and interim reports are also means of keeping the public informed.

Communication with the Media

Many unfortunate situations have occurred when individual advisory group members have gone to the media presenting a distorted or one-sided picture of what was happening in the group. Many advisory groups adopt a rule that only the chair of the group is permitted to represent the advisory group to the media; all other members are to withhold comment. Even the chairperson is expected to consult with the entire group about what should be said, and should always represent the thinking of the entire group, not just his or her own opinion.

Parliamentary Procedure

Formal parliamentary procedure, such as Robert's Rules of Order, assumes there will be an adversarial relationship between the participants and also assumes that issues will be resolved by voting rather than by consensus. For this reason, it is advisable to minimize the use of formal meeting procedures. If the group leader has the trust of the group, it is usually possible to get work done more readily without the use of complicated meeting procedures.

Group Member Expenses

Whether travel expenses and other costs related to participation in the group will be borne by the organization or by individual members should be settled at the beginning. In the event they will be borne by the organization, the rules for expense reimbursement should be clearly defined. Group members are sensitive to any perception of being "bought" by the organization. But it isn't reasonable to expect members to contribute their time as well as travel, lodging, or meal costs. Some groups may be so sensitive to the perception of being "bought" that they may decline to accept travel money.

Scheduling Meetings

One of the issues that haunt every advisory group is whether to have regular group meetings or schedule them as needed. If meetings are called only when needed, it is difficult to notify members of each meeting and there are often scheduling conflicts. Yet there is no surer way to discourage interest and participation in an advisory group than to hold regular meetings that are unproductive or seem to have no purpose.

Staffing

Advisory groups often raise questions that require considerable study or follow-through. One important question that needs to be answered early is the level of staff support provided to the group and for what purposes.

Minutes

Organizational staff are normally responsible for keeping the record of group meetings, but if there is a history of suspicion or mistrust, the group may want to assume this responsibility. At a minimum, advisory group members will want the opportunity to review any minutes carefully before approving them.

External Consultants

If advisory group members are suspicious of organizational staff, there may be requests for external consultants who will assist the group in reviewing technical plans or reports. External consultants are sometimes more credible, no matter what the expertise of the staff is.

Steering Committee

It's often necessary to make decisions between meetings on issues like the agenda for the next meeting, the experts who should make presentations, or whether a meeting should be cancelled. It isn't practical to try to contact everybody in the advisory group to make these kinds of decisions. The group may be comfortable having a chairperson elected from the group make these decisions. In other cases, the group may prefer to establish a steering committee, with two or three members representing major viewpoints in the group. In this way, no major interest feels its needs were not considered when decisions were made.

CHAPTER THIRTEEN

CONDUCTING INTERVIEWS

People often provide much more information in an interview than they will in a public forum. For this reason, interviewing is another general-purpose tool useful in many different kinds of public participation programs.

Why to Use Interviews

Interviews are extremely useful when you want in-depth information from stakeholders, particularly the kind of detailed information it would be difficult for people to share during public forums. I like to begin every public participation process with a round of interviews of a cross-section of people likely to be involved in the process. If the decision-making process will extend over many months, I like to repeat these interviews toward the end of each major stage of the process. Although interviews can't substitute for more public forms of participation, they often provide information that can't be obtained any other way, including their subjective evaluations of how the public participation process is proceeding.

Interviewing doesn't allow scientific sampling, but it can provide highly detailed and valuable qualitative information. By the time you've interviewed fifteen to twenty community leaders, you probably know enough about the situation to know each person's role in the controversy.

The problem with interviews is that they are time-consuming, and it is possible to interview only a limited number of people. An interview that lasts for thirty to forty-five minutes may take a total of two to three hours of staff time to set up the interview appointment, plan the interview, drive to the interview, conduct it, work up the notes into a summary report, and transcribe the interviews for the files. The costs of interviewing can be reduced if interviewing is done by telephone, but some of the relationship-building benefits of this personal contact are lost.

Interviewing only a small number of people can be appropriate if the information needed is the opinions of the organized interests or community leaders. But it is not possible to know for sure that the people talked to are representative of all the interests in the community or what the proportion of viewpoints is in the larger community. The emphasis in informal interviewing is on qualitative, not quantitative, information. It is not appropriate to claim any quantitative validity for the information received through informal interviews for two reasons: sampling bias and interviewer effect.

Sampling bias means that by targeting the groups and individuals to be interviewed rather than making a random selection, a bias has been introduced into the sample. It may be a very useful bias—a bias toward the people who have the kind of information needed—but it precludes making any quantitative statements about what the public feels, since it may be an unrepresentative sample of the public.

Interviewer effect refers to the fact that when questions are asked in different ways or by different people, different information is elicited. As a result, the way a question is asked one time may produce different information than apparently the same question asked a different way another time. The response that is given to one staff member may be different than to the same question asked by another staff member. This is why the wording of questions is carefully designed and pretested when conducting a poll or survey. Even if the same topics are covered in the course of a series of informal interviews, the wording is slightly different each time and the context in which the topic comes up is different, thus producing an interviewer effect that removes any possibility of quantitative validity.

Guidelines for Conducting Interviews

Here are some general guidelines for conducting interviews:

Clarifying the Purpose

The first rather obvious step in conducting interviews is to clarify exactly what is to be learned from the interviews. When the first call is made to set up an appointment, the question that will be asked is, "What is the purpose of the interview?"

Not only do you need to provide a clear, succinct answer to get people to agree to be interviewed, you need clarity about the purpose of the interview in order to know who needs to be interviewed. Although interviews do permit unstructured discussion, they should not be disorganized fishing expeditions, or people will be offended.

Selecting the People to Be Interviewed

Even when no pretense is made of taking a scientific sample, the credibility of a public participation program requires that an effort be made to include all major points of view. Otherwise, major groups that have been left out will assume the assessment is biased. If there are ten environmental groups, it is not necessary to interview all ten. However, representatives of enough groups should be interviewed to be sure that you understand the differences among them, as well as their political dynamics.

Some groups may act as an umbrella for others. It is sometimes a good idea to call those you don't intend to interview and ask, "If I visit with [an organization] to discuss this issue, do you think I will cover most of the concerns your organization has on this issue?" If not, you can respond to any remaining points by telephone. This is a cost-effective use of the interest group leaders' time as well as the organization's. The interest groups usually appreciate it. The informal network that exists among nongovernmental organizations will enable you to learn of other organizations that should be interviewed; they may call you if they feel left out. This informal network will also help communicate the results of your interview rapidly, although this is a good reason to have a written description of the results, so information is passed along accurately.

It is normal practice to arrange an appointment for the interview. Fortunately, there is a subtle flattery involved in asking for an interview (the implication is that their views are very important or they are very wise), so most people will willingly set up an interview. They will, however, want to know the purpose of the interview, how the information will be used (including its confidentiality), who or what kinds of people are being interviewed, and how long the interview will take.

If possible, it is best if the person who will conduct the interview sets up the appointment, since this gives a chance to establish some initial rapport. But since this is a time-consuming process, it is often done by someone else. If this is the case, be sure that the person setting up the interviews is thoroughly acquainted with the purposes and uses of the interview. Also be sure that the person allows time for traveling from interview to interview and about thirty minutes after each interview to fill in notes while the interview is fresh.

If the appointment has been set up several days or more in advance by someone other than the interviewer, the interviewer may want to call the day before to confirm the appointment. This reassures both the interviewer and the person being interviewed that their time will not be wasted, and it may begin to build rapport.

Ideally, the interviewee should be met at a place and time he or she determines—for example, at a citizen group's office.

Interview Length

Normally, leaders of active groups, interests, or agencies are willing to give thirty to sixty minutes to an interview. Anything longer will depend on how interested the person being interviewed is in the topic. Anything shorter will be so rushed, particularly since some time is invariably lost getting in and out of their offices or homes, that many of the benefits of informal interviews will be lost. Some experienced interviewers have found, though, that even if people will schedule for only a short time, if they are interested in the topic, that time will usually be permitted to expand. But if limited interview time has been scheduled and the person being interviewed is clearly restive, don't just assume it is acceptable to extend the interview beyond the agreed-upon time limits.

Asking Questions

One effective way of conducting interviews is to use an informal structured approach, in which the key topics are identified beforehand and used as a guide in conducting the interview, although the order in which questions are addressed may change. If you are using more than one interviewer, though, you may want to use a structured format, in order to have some degree of consistency.

When several interviewers are used, there should be frequent meetings so that they can compare notes on issues, interview structure, questions, and interview techniques. Often interviewers change their approach over time, and it is important to maintain consistency.

There are two general rules to observe in how questions are posed:

• *Don't ask leading questions.* When a leading question is asked, for example, "Don't you think that Project X is needed?" it's clear that the answer the questioner wants is yes. The question is structured in such a way that it leads to the desired answer. Research shows that people who do not have strong opinions are likely to allow themselves to be led. The desired answer will be obtained, but it will be worthless as a predictor of people's position on the issue. Those who already have a strong opinion are likely to be insulted by leading questions and will draw the conclusion that the interviews are biased.

• *Ask open-ended questions.* If the question asked is, "Do you believe Project X is needed?" the answer is likely to be yes or no. Obviously, such an answer is only minimally helpful when in-depth information is needed about what the key issues are or how important they are. It is better to ask open-ended questions—those that cannot be answered yes or no. Examples are, "What do you think future requirements will be?" or, "What do you think are the pros and cons of Project X?" or, "How can issue Y best be resolved?" These questions encourage more complete answers and also permit people being interviewed to address topics or raise issues important to them. Follow up on some points with, "What leads you to say this?" (Phrasing it this way gets better results than asking, "Why?") Also, verbally summarizing what you've heard will encourage people to open up and expand on their answers.

Taking Notes

It is important when conducting an interview to establish a comfortable relationship with the interviewee. This is difficult to do if you are poring over notes, maintaining little or no eye contact, and struggling to keep up with the individual. Some interviewers prefer to take brief notes and use a tape recorder as a backup to fill in the notes later. This is particularly good if there is premium on having the person's exact words, as there would be for a journalist. However, some people feel intimidated by a tape recorder or may be more cautious about what they say for fear the tape will get into someone else's hands. An alternative technique is to keep brief notes of the interview, stressing only the most significant points, and then go to a quiet place immediately after each interview and fill in the notes from memory. The original notes serve as reminders of other notes that need to be written down.

Confidentiality

In return for getting candid information, the interviewer must usually make a commitment about the confidentiality of the information. Normally the commitment would be that only people within the organization who are working directly on the project or study will have access to the summaries from individual interviews. If there is a need, and there usually is in public participation programs, for an overall summary of the interviews that will be distributed to a larger audience, then the report must be written in a way that protects the identity of individuals who provided sensitive information. Any time the information will be made available to people other than the interviewer, the interviewer has a responsibility to inform the person of this at the beginning of the session.

Sharing Information

Almost invariably as an interview ends, the interviewee will ask questions like, "How did Group Z feel about this?" or, "What have other people you've interviewed felt about . . . ?" These questions immediately raise all the problems for the interviewer of confidentiality, leading, or bias. Yet there is a simple reciprocity to these questions that is hard to ignore: this person has just given some information and is now asking for some in return. Obviously this is a judgment call, but within the limits of confidentiality, most interviewers do respond with some general statement similar to those that would be contained in the summary of the interviews that will be made public. The important point is to be prepared for the possibility of such questions, so that confidentiality isn't inadvertently violated if the interviewer is taken by surprise.

Interviews have some limitations as a technique. They aren't transparent (others can't see what went on), don't result in deliberation between stakeholders, and are time-consuming. But you can learn information from interviewing that you cannot learn any other way. They also help you build personal rapport with the people you are interviewing. Interviewing should occupy a significant place in your tool kit of techniques.

CHAPTER FOURTEEN

WORKING WITH THE MEDIA

M any of the public information techniques described in previous chapters
involve working with the media. This chapter discusses the challenges of
working with the media in the context of a public participation program.

The Role of Media Relations in a Public Participation Program

In virtually all public participation programs, you will seek media attention in
order to get information to the general public. Most agencies want to show the
public that the agency is working diligently to address important issues on behalf
of the public.

There are additional obligations for communicating through the media in the
context of a public participation program. "The public" in public participation
is always something less than the broad general public. This can be justified only
if people have a choice to participate. If they don't know about the issue, don't
know about the possible impacts of the decision on their lives, and don't know
they have an opportunity to participate, then they are effectively excluded from
the process. Newsletters, fact sheets, and other publications help broaden the out-
reach to a broader public. But short of paid advertising, which is too expensive
for most purposes, the primary mechanism for reaching out to a broader public
is through news stories in local newspapers, television, and other media.

One component of any public participation plan should be how (and when) to communicate to the public through the media. During the course of a public participation program, you might send out news releases, appear on talk shows, arrange for feature stories, and possibly buy advertising space (particularly to announce meetings or other participation events).

The nature of your relationship with the media depends both on the amount of controversy surrounding the issue being addressed in your public participation program and the media environment in which you work. If your issue is relatively uncontroversial, you will need to seek out media coverage, and you may find it difficult to get the media to pay attention to your program. If the issue is somewhat controversial or otherwise newsworthy, reporters will be attending public meetings and calling you to get reactions to statements made by various groups, and they may even do investigative reporting if they believe the public is not getting the full story. If the issue is highly visible, you may be deluged with media attention.

If your activities take place in a small community, the public participation program may be the most exciting thing that has come along in a long time. As a result, you are likely to get ample coverage in local media, although the media available may be somewhat limited. Some rural communities have difficulty getting attention from broadcast media, for example, because major radio and television stations are likely to be located in the nearest large city, and it may be difficult to get them to turn to an issue in a smaller community.

If you live in a major city (New York, London, or Montreal, for example), you may have great difficulty in getting major broadcast media to pay attention. You'll be just one of many stories competing for attention. By the time your story becomes sufficiently controversial that it catches the attention of larger media, you may end up not appreciating their attention, because they will likely focus largely on the controversy, not the substance of the decision being made.

If you are in a location where it is difficult to get publicity, you will need to plan for ways to involve media that will pay attention, such as weekly local newspapers or programs on broadcast media that focus on events in smaller communities. You also need to work on presenting your issue in a way that sparks positive media attention by humanizing the story, making clear what the impacts are to the community, and presenting the story in such a way that the media understand the implications.

Understanding the Media

Sometimes the media seem like your best friend, helping you get the word out, educating the public, and applauding your efforts. Other times they seem to be enemies, whipping up the opposition, questioning your credibility, distorting (from your perspective, at least) the facts, and so on. You can't get along with them, and you can't get along without them.

Here are a few general observations to help you understand why the media act the way they do.

Newsworthiness

The media are constantly under pressure to provide information that is newsworthy and captures attention. This is why, if you send out a news release, the title and the first few sentences must announce that the topic is important and of interest to their audiences. To arrange for a feature story, you may have to pitch the importance of the story by finding a human interest angle to get attention. Newsworthiness sells papers, wins ratings wars, and holds the audience's attention.

The harsh reality is that if everything is just fine, it's not newsworthy. Contrast the human interest in a story titled, "Edwards County Is Well Managed," versus a story titled, "County Government a Hotbed of Corruption." The second title has much more human interest. The media do not concentrate on the negative just to be mean, but because it's newsworthy. If human beings ever find the fact that everything's going well as stimulating and exciting as the news that everything is going to Hades in a hand basket, the media will be happy to run positive stories. But for the moment, good news usually isn't newsworthy.

This means that a well-run public meeting, with everyone in agreement, is likely to get limited coverage. But if even a few people express discontent, that is likely to be the focus of the story. News stories, like a good novel, need a certain amount of tension or conflict to be interesting, so reporters concentrate on conflicts. Also, politics is more newsworthy than fact. If two local politicians get into an argument, it's the fact they are arguing that's newsworthy, not the technical merits of their positions.

Balance

Different professions have different definitions of what is truth. Scientists search for "facts"; judges search for "justice" or at least "legality"; politicians search for "equity." Journalists search for "balance," which means that all major positions are fairly and adequately presented, and no one position is given undue emphasis.

In practice, a balanced story can be quite maddening. You may have just completed $5 million worth of studies, using the world's preeminent scientists, but the local leader of the neighborhood coalition against something-or-other may get absolutely equal time to make assertions you believe have no basis in fact. Yet the journalist may believe he or she has done a good job in reporting the story: all major points of view have been presented, there's no bias toward one position or the other, and it's balanced.

Limited Time and Expertise

One reason reporters settle for balance rather than trying to discern who's right (over and above the fact they don't believe that deciding who is right is their job) is that typically they don't have the time to explore a story deeply enough to make such a judgment. This problem has gotten worse in recent years. A number of news organizations have made significant cutbacks in the number of their reporters, so fewer reporters have to cover the same news and more quickly.

Many local reporters cover several stories a day, on very different topics, and under strict time limits. One story may involve unemployment, another an environmental crisis, another a major traffic accident, and still another a new cancer treatment. The range of stories and the time pressures the reporter faces make it impossible for this person to be expert in all the fields he or she covers. In addition, there is typically high turnover in local reporters. Young and ambitious reporters are simply putting in time until they land a better-paying job in a major news market. Only in major news organizations are there likely to be reporters who can stay with a specialty, such as environmental stories, sufficiently to develop genuine expertise.

As a result, reporters begin to rely on sources they can call on to give them a brief summary of what's going on in a field. Leaders of local interest groups are often excellent sources for getting a quick story on a particular topic. In fact, if they've been credible in the past, reporters occasionally take short-cuts and don't determine whether the information being presented at the moment is factual. Under time pressures, as long as it is attributable to a source, they may go with the story without checking facts further. They shouldn't, but because of time constraints, it happens.

Everybody Has an Axe to Grind

Everybody likes to see themselves as acting on behalf of the interests of what they believe to be good and fair. As a result, people feel put upon when reporters ask questions that seem to imply that everything is being done for self-interest.

Many reporters do become very cynical over time, suspicious that inspirational rhetoric may well be masking personal interest. It's also true that people often do have a self-interest. Elected officials are well aware that how they are presented in the media can affect the next election. Managers want their agency to be presented as efficient and competent. Staff members want to be viewed as effectively implementing agency policies. Your agency may be doing things that make it an actor in the political process, not a neutral.

Much of the time, self-interest is a small part of the motivation. But having been burned by others in the past, reporters are particularly careful not to be taken advantage of and are probably actually relieved if they are clear on any self-interest that may be involved.

Part of this suspicion is implicit in the reporter's job. They view themselves as the first line of defense in protecting the public from being taken by anyone. As a result, they don't automatically grant you a mantle of virtue and respectability that protects you from scrutiny.

The Public Affairs Officer

Most agencies have professional public affairs or public information staff. Typically this person is designated as the principal point of contact between the agency and the media and is the spokesperson for the agency. Most agencies recognize the need for some control over who speaks to the media, because having multiple people represent an agency can lead to conflicting communications and confuse the public.

In some cases, the people conducting a public participation program work with the public affairs officer (or office) on a regular basis. But in other cases, the public participation team will need to develop a relationship with the public affairs officer.

Ideally, the public affairs officer should be a member of the team that plans the public participation program. The entire team, including the public affairs officer, needs to understand how and where communicating through the media fits into the plan.

It may take some focused communication to develop a good relationship with your public affairs officer. One issue you need to discuss early on is the difference between public relations and public information in the context of a public participation program. Some public affairs officers see their role as making the agency look as good as possible under virtually all circumstances. They see their role as something akin to a spokesperson for a political campaign, always using the media to the advantage of the candidate (or, in this case, the agency).

This is not what you need in a public participation program. In fact, if the public feels that they are getting spin from your agency, they will become very suspicious of your public participation program, no matter how hard you are working to present objective information.

In the context of a public participation program, public information is providing the public the information they need to participate wisely in a decision.

This means that the public information program cannot be slanted to favor the alternative supported by people within the agency, and important information cannot be left out because it doesn't make the agency look good.

Credibility is a valuable commodity, and the best way to protect it is to tell the whole truth, as best you can, in a way that helps the public prepare to participate. With some public affairs officers, this is second nature. They will be preaching this gospel to you. With others, this approach seems naive, uninformed, and almost unprofessional. You may need to have extended discussions with this kind of public affairs officer, and you may even have to draw management into the discussion to ensure a coherent orientation.

Remember that the public affairs officer in your agency has much to bring to the table. First, public affairs officers know (or should know) the media outlets, and in many cases they know the reporters personally. They should be able to pitch a story to get a reporter's interest. They should have writing skills that can translate complex technical information into an understandable story with some human interest. They should have experience conducting interviews and handling challenging questions. If members of the public participation team are going to be handling media interviews or appearing on talk shows, they may be able to conduct training to improve your skills or arrange for training through professional organizations.

Guidelines for Working with the Media

Here are a few guidelines for working with the media:

Maximum Disclosure, Minimum Delay

An agency public affairs officer with whom I work occasionally says that her approach to working with the media can be summed up in the short phrase: "Maximum Disclosure, Minimum Delay." In other words, give full and complete information, and get it to the media in a timely manner.

This public affairs officer, who is the head of public affairs for a major federal agency, believes that full disclosure is good not just for public participation but also for her agency. This doesn't mean that she doesn't work hard to improve the manner in which staff of her agency communicate to the media, but that the overriding philosophy is to provide complete and objective information.

Credibility takes a long time to build and can be destroyed in a flash. Once it is destroyed, it takes much more effort to rebuild. People who try to manage the media by presenting only part of the information or by misleading reporters end up not being believed on anything.

In the long run, the only policy that works with the media is to be open, honest, and frank. Don't leave out important facts, even if they can be used against your agency. Unless they can count on you personally as being completely candid, the media will challenge everything you say.

The other key issue is responsiveness. Because the media work under tight deadlines, they need responses in a timely manner. If a citizen claims that your agency has committed some horrific act and a reporter calls you, return the call promptly. Otherwise the citizen's claim will be featured in the story, along with words to the effect that "no one at the agency was available for comment on the allegations." Unfortunately, this phrase does not communicate to the public, "I phoned the agency, but missed the key person there and she couldn't get back to me before my deadline, so I wrote the story with the information I had available." Instead, what it conveys to the public is, "People at this agency are avoiding the issues, which means this claim is probably true." Treat requests for information from reporters as extremely high priorities. If you don't, the reporter may make it one for you.

Respect Their Professional Obligations

On occasion, your professional obligations and the media's converge. This is often the case when it comes to informing the public. But occasionally their professional obligations require that they challenge and question you or the facts you present. They expect you to understand that they have professional obligations that are different from yours, and at times this may seem to put you in an adversarial relationship. They assume you know this and won't take it personally.

Explore Mutual Interests

Occasionally, your interest in getting information out to the public will dovetail with the media's interest in providing timely information on important issues. You may be able to arrange for special inserts, dedicated Op-Ed pages, major feature stories, and extensive news coverage that can help you get information to the public—and, incidentally, help sell newspapers or boost ratings.

Present Information in an Interesting Manner

There is a difference between providing spin on a story and presenting it in a manner that is interesting to the public. "Spin" means you manipulate the story to give a one-sided point of view. But an objective story that is boring or confusing may be equally useless in informing the public.

So when you prepare information, such as a press release, for the media, write like a journalist. Try some of the devices that journalists use to make their stories interesting. Use attention-grabbing headlines. Put the newsworthy parts of the story at the beginning and the exposition afterward. Put some of the exposition in quotations from agency officials (after you discuss this with them). Focus the story as much as possible on the impact on the local community.

One of the biggest barriers agencies face in communicating with the public is technical jargon. The biggest sources of jargon are the many technical terms the public doesn't understand, the use of abbreviations, and the use of unfamiliar units of measurement of annotation, for example, 3×10^{-9}. Even if you use terms with which the public is more or less familiar, if there are too many concepts or terms the listener or reader only sort of understands in too short a space of time, the reader or listener is likely to experience jargon fog. The problem is that by the time people stop to think about what one term means, they've lost the train of thought.

Professional Support for Public Information Activities

Most technical people do not have the skills to write materials for the public. They may have written scores of technical reports, but that does not equate to writing in simple, understandable language. My advice is that you assume that just about when you think a technical document is complete, you now have the draft from which a professional writer can begin work. Put another way, assume that all news releases, newsletters, fact sheets, executive summaries, and other documents initially prepared by technical people but intended for the public will need to be rewritten by people with skills in communicating with the public. This isn't an insult to technical people. Writing for the public is just a different skill set. There are technical people who have acquired this skill set, but they are few in number. The odds of one of them being in your team is not high.

Someone on your public participation team needs to have experience and skill in writing for the public. This might be the public affairs officer or a consultant, but get someone who can take technical documents and turn them into something the public (including the media) can understand.

Similarly, most agencies are not very good at graphics. The layout of materials put out by many agencies is stodgy and boring. The essential qualities in any publication for the public are friendliness and accessibility, just the opposite of the institutional look. You may have the resources within the agency to develop graphics that are fresh and interesting. There may be people in your graphics group who are begging for an opportunity to do something new and different. But sometimes agency graphic artists have internalized the institutional look to the point that they have great difficulty providing anything different. In that case, you need outside graphics support. Either way, you may need to convince management that if it wants to reach the public, it has to make an effort to make its publications attractive and interesting.

Using the Internet

Much of the buzz in the public affairs field today is about creative ways to use the Internet. More than one-third of the U.S. population now gets its news solely from the Internet instead of radio, television, or newspapers. (Of course, a high percentage of the news on the Internet consists of summaries of news from print or broadcast media.)

But increasingly, people in corporate public affairs roles are talking about communicating with the public through bulletin boards (Web pages where people with a particular interest can communicate about that topic) and blogs (personal e-mail journals that report on personal experiences). This is a new enough area that I have little to offer in the way of advice on how to use these forms of communication more effectively. But it is worth your time to tune in to bulletin boards or listservs that focus on topics related to your public participation program and then consider how to use these media to reach audiences you cannot reach through conventional media.

◆ ◆ ◆

There are many useful books and guides on working with the media. Just remember that the key requirement for communicating through the media as part of a public participation program is your ability to convey objective information in a manner that is simple, understandable, interesting, and timely.

CHAPTER FIFTEEN

ANALYZING PUBLIC COMMENT

Once a public participation program is underway, the agency will begin to accumulate large numbers of comments from the public, interest groups, and government agencies. This chapter discusses how to analyze that information and summarize the information in a manner that can have an impact on decision making.

Let's assume you've done an excellent job of getting the public involved, and you have a mass of information. Now the questions become: How do you go about summarizing what may amount to hundreds or even thousands of comments? How do you determine the relative importance of the comments for the decision makers?

One thing you should not do is simply tally comments as being *for* a proposed action or *against* the proposed action. This kind of summary is unfair to both the public and management trying to interpret what the public said. A carefully argued four-page letter and a one-sentence postcard don't deserve equal weight. Management needs to understand the reasoning behind people's positions, not just their final conclusions.

Nevertheless, it is unrealistic to expect management to laboriously wade through transcripts and hundreds of letters. Public participation programs conducted by some U.S. federal agencies have generated as many as twenty thousand comments or letters to analyze. This makes it impossible for management to be personally involved in reading the comments or letters, so techniques have been developed that provide managers with adequate understanding of the nature of the public's comments, even when the number of comments is very large.

The Difference Between Analysis and Evaluation

It is essential to understand the difference between analyzing public comment and evaluating it. The purpose of an *analysis* is to summarize and display public comment in such a way that maximum information is available to decision makers (and the public) about what was said. To the extent possible, analysis should display public comment without interjecting interpretation or judgment.

Evaluation of public comment takes place after analysis and includes judgment and weighting, or assigning relative value. This is the task of the decision maker, who may have to evaluate the relative importance, for example, of 315 handwritten letters versus 400 names on a petition. The decision maker may also have to weigh the importance of comments from people or groups that are directly and significantly affected by the decisions with the concerns of groups whose position is more philosophical. Obviously evaluation is an essential element of decision making. Analysis is the process of getting the information ready so that evaluation can occur.

Analysis Tools

The primary analytical tool used to summarize large numbers of public comments is content analysis. This is a research tool used in sociology, journalism, and political science to analyze the actual content (arguments, facts, logic) contained in newspaper articles, letters, and so forth. Content analysis has been used, for example, to conduct research comparing the relative frequency of certain topics in letters to the editor as a means of identifying public priorities.

Originally content analysis was performed by analysts who reviewed each comment carefully and several times, hand-coding the comments so that information could be extracted, stored, and summarized in quantitative form. Now, comments can be scanned into a computer in digital form. Then computers can read the comments, develop statistical summaries, and pull up comments in particular categories whenever needed.

But before the computers can do their work, they need to be told what to look for. So it is still worthwhile to understand the basic logic of content analysis. Also, if the number of comments you received isn't large, you may find yourself doing the process by hand anyway.

First, you need to understand what information you want to derive from your comments. Start by considering what information the decision maker will want or need from the public comments in order to make a decision. For example, the decision maker might say, "I need to know all the arguments pro and con for each alternative we're evaluating, including the frequency of those arguments." In other words, she wants to know not only the reasons that people support or oppose each alternative but how many people mentioned each argument.

But your decision maker may go further. She may say, "I don't just want to know about people's logic, I also want to know the emotional tone of their letters. So I want to be able to read some of the comments in selected categories. I might ask you, for example, to show me all the comments from people who opposed the burning-off of vegetation [or some other proposed action] because of health concerns." This means that you not only have to store and count information in categories, you also need to be able to print out these comments by category so the decision maker can read them.

Therefore, you need to accomplish two goals with your summary of the comment: (1) produce tallies of the number of people who make particular arguments, and (2) capture and store the actual language of the public, by category, to give the decision maker a sense of the intensity of the language used or how well thought out the arguments are.

To accomplish this, follow the basic steps in content analysis:

1. Give each letter or comment an identification number. Then code every letter or comment by organizational affiliation, geographical location, and type of comment (for example, letter, comment in public meeting, petition)—for example:

1–499	*Comment*	*Identification Number*
500 Series	*Organizational Affiliation*	
501	Business	
502	Environmental	
503	Government	
600 Series	*Geographic Location*	
601	City	
602	County	
603	Region	

700 Series	*Type of Comment*
701	Letter
702	E-Mail
703	Comment in public meeting
704	Petition or form letter

2. Identify the management questions you want answered (for example, How do people from a particular area feel in comparison to people from other areas? What are the reasons people favor or oppose each alternative?).

3. Scan the comments into a computer or make multiple copies of the comments.

4. Read a sample of the comments to determine the basic categories of information contained in them and make sure that the comments do not address issues that you have not considered, in which case new questions will need to be formulated.

5. If you are doing the analysis by hand, design a codebook and summary form. (For an example of a codebook, the U.S. Forest Service's is posted at http://www.fs.fed.us/emc/cat/includes/tgcont.pdf.) The codebook contains instructions, definitions, and examples of how information should be coded. It is designed to record tallies in enough categories to be able to answer the decision maker's questions. The summary form will be used to record all the codes appropriate for each letter of comment. The codebook would capture information such as:

800 Series	*Alternative Supported*
801	Alternative A
802	Alternative B
803	Alternative C

900 Series	*Reasons for Support*
901	Lowest cost
902	Fewest impacts on endangered species
903	Jobs in local economy

If you are doing the analysis by computer, the same basic thought process applies, but you need to work with a computer expert to be able to tell the computer what categories should be considered.

6. If you are doing the analysis by hand, read the entire comment or letter for its overall meaning. Then reread the comment, underlining all portions that

fit in the defined code categories. If you are using a computer and the comments are digitized, the computer can do this analysis.

7. Go back through the comment or letter again, assigning the appropriate codes to each underlined (or highlighted) comment. When you are done, complete a summary form listing all the code numbers that apply to that particular comment. Even if you have been reviewing the comments by hand, you may want to use a computerized summary form so that the computer can do the tallies. The summary form should include the codes that identify the content of the comment and the identification number for that comment. The identification number is needed for two reasons: it leads the decision maker back to the entire letter if the comment is of particular interest, and it allows the comments in that file to be analyzed by origin or affiliation.

8. If you are completing the process by hand, have a second analyst review the coded comment to ensure that the comment or letter has been analyzed objectively. Any differences in opinion on how the comment should be coded can be resolved by discussion between the two analysts. If the computer is doing the work, do the quality assurance tests that computer people do to ensure the accuracy of the analysis.

9. Store a complete copy of the marked-up comment or letter either physically or in the computer. This copy should be kept in a master file as documentation so that the public or management can always be shown how the analysis was done.

10. If you are working by hand, use the multiple copies you made earlier. Cut up the comment so that you can store the coded portions of the comment in files for each category. Obviously this is the step where it would be helpful to have everything scanned into the computer. Even if you didn't have software that could do the analysis, you could at least copy and paste each comment into an appropriate computer file.

11. Prepare a report that answers the management questions you developed in step 2.

12. Accompany statistical displays with a narrative summary—for example, "A majority (61 percent) of interest groups indicate support of the proposed action for these three reasons . . . " Many people, and this includes decision makers as well as the general public, are intimidated by statistical analyses and will understand the material only in narrative form. It is essential, however, that the narrative simply summarizes the analysis rather than evaluates the comments.

Analyzing Public Comment for Underlying Values

Content analysis focuses on the content (arguments, facts, logic) of the comment or letter. Another important dimension of public comment is the values or underlying political philosophies expressed in the comment. Values are the yardsticks by which we judge things to be right or wrong, moral or immoral, fair or unfair, and so forth. While the content of people's views on a topic often changes in response to new information or dialogue with other groups, basic values positions are relatively permanent. As a result, values are often a better long-term predictor of people's eventual positions than content.

The difficulty with analyzing values is that they are often implied rather than stated explicitly. This makes it more difficult to do an objective analysis, because the analyst must surmise the values rather than deal with explicit material. In addition, some letters will clearly contain only content, so it is impossible to record them in a values analysis. This can lead to charges of ignoring some letters or comments. Thus, the results of any values analysis can usually be reported only in qualitative terms, not quantitatively.

There are several indicators of implied values:

Values-laden language: "corporate rip-offs," "energy pigs."

Predictions of dire consequences: "A working man won't be able to live in this town."

Characterizations of opponents: "hippie freaks," "yes men," or "rip-off artists."

Quoting venerable sources: Quotations from the Bible, the Bill of Rights, or leading thinkers or writers.

By looking for these indicators, an analyst is often able to come up with a reasonable assessment of people's values and beliefs based on a spoken or written comment. One of the best checks to ensure objectivity is to undertake a second analysis without knowledge of the results of the first. Any differences in interpretation can be worked out by discussion between the analysts.

Values comments can be coded in the same way as content, with values categories set up in just the same way as content categories. Given the limitations of values analysis, it would be more appropriate to store actual comments from the public in each category rather than to tally the number of responses in each category. In this way, management could be given the flavor of the values expressed, without any misleading claims to a statistically valid analysis.

Visual Summaries

Most people, including decision makers, understand material better when they see it displayed visually. The simplest kind of visual displays are pie charts and graphs such as those found as part of standard office software packages. For example, the graph in Figure 15.1 shows responses to a question about a possible prescribed burn, burning-off vegetation using a carefully controlled fire, part of the cleanup program at a former army base.

Still another way to display information is to create a visual portrayal of how concepts are linked together. Figure 15.2 is a concept map, once again related to the use of prescribed burns.

Maps such as these help people see the overall picture and connections between ideas that are not immediately obvious from purely statistical analyses. Concept maps can also reflect statistics. A concept map could show how often a particular argument is mentioned by varying the size of the shapes (for example, an argument that is mentioned frequently could be portrayed in a much larger circle than one mentioned infrequently).

Evaluation of Public Comments

All of the work described in this chapter is designed to analyze the comment in a manner that is both objective and pulls out as much information as possible that could be useful to the decision maker. Now the burden is on the decision maker to evaluate the comment. The decision maker has a tough job. He or she may have to decide how important hundreds or even thousands of signatures on a petition are compared to lengthy letters. Moreover, this is not a vote. What does it mean that a majority of comments came from people opposed to an action? Just because you received hundreds of letters doesn't make this equivalent to a vote

FIGURE 15.1. BAR CHART.

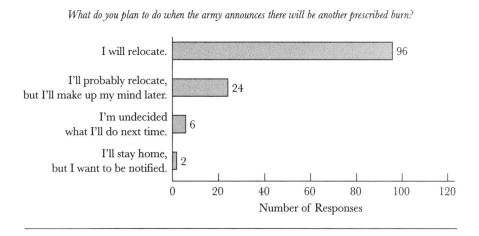

What do you plan to do when the army announces there will be another prescribed burn?

FIGURE 15.2. CONCEPT MAPPING.

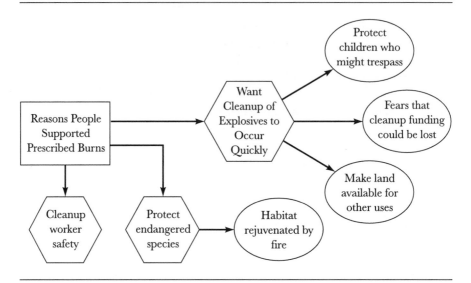

by the thousands or millions of people who may be affected by the decision. The decision maker will also always need to make the decision within legal and budgetary constraints, and within an overall political context.

Reporting Information to the Public

Here are several things I've learned about preparing reports that summarize public comment:

• *Give the public quick feedback.* The public's sense of timeliness is to get a summary in two or three weeks (one week is even better). But agencies sometimes take months. By the time the summary arrives, the issue no longer has the emotional relevance it did when the comment was submitted. Agencies may not be ready to say much in two or three weeks about their response to public comment. But it is perfectly acceptable to send out a report that summarizes the comments received but makes no effort to say "this is what we're going to do," except to specify a time frame for when that response will occur.

• *Once you've decided how to respond, make sure the summary communicates how public comment affected your decision making.* If I'm a citizen participating in your decision-making process, the real payoff—and the incentive to keep participating—is to see that my participation has made a difference. So whenever possible, show how public comment influenced decisions, for example, "Based on the comments we received, we added a third alternative that relies primarily on energy conservation."

• *If you can't do what the people ask you to do, acknowledge their comments, and then respond to them directly.* There will be occasions when it is impossible to respond to all the people who comment on your proposed actions, and sometimes even a majority of the people who comment. You must comply with laws, financial realities, and other parameters. If that is the case, take the issue on directly. Start by acknowledging what the comments were, and then provide a clear explanation of why you cannot respond—for example: "A number of people recommended that we use energy conservation as an alternative to constructing a transmission line. While energy conservation can reduce the growth of demand for electric power, conservation will not solve the problem of delivering electricity to local areas requiring substantial new energy supplies in the immediate future." In this way, people know that you considered their comments, even if you were not able to do what they asked.

CHAPTER SIXTEEN

EVALUATING PUBLIC PARTICIPATION

Public participation, like everything else, improves when you evaluate how you're doing and make necessary changes. How can you tell whether a public participation program is a success or what changes should be made to improve future programs? This chapter discusses the challenging subject of evaluating public participation programs.

Being Clear on Your Criteria for Success

The first crucial step is to be clear on what you mean by *successful* or *effective*. For example, if your agency presents a proposed action to the public for review and is met with a resounding, "We don't like it!" is the public participation effort a success or a failure? If your criterion for success was to ascertain public opinion, it has been a huge success. You now have a clear sense of how the public feels about the proposal. But if your criterion was to get public support for the program, the program has been a disaster.

This same problem of differing criteria holds true for the participants in a public participation program. One group may feel that the public participation was a huge success because "it was fair, everybody got listened to, and nobody can say they didn't have a chance to participate." Another group may think the program was a failure because they were not able to persuade most other citizens to their point of view.

The big difference between these two groups is that the first group is applying *process criteria* and the second group is applying *outcome criteria*. This is an important distinction. Your public participation program may meet all of its process goals yet be soundly criticized because it didn't result in the decision someone or some group wanted.

It's not unreasonable to hope that your public participation program will be perceived as adequate, fair, open, visible, and credible—all process criteria. If you don't meet these criteria, improvements need to be made. But if you evaluate your success in public participation by always achieving a consensus, your mental health is likely to be unsettled. No one can produce that outcome every time, because no one has the ability to force agreement until the public is ready to agree. You may have provided the best opportunity the public will ever have to collaborate on a consensus decision. But if the public isn't ready, it isn't ready. Issues take time to mature to the point that people are willing to work together. That time could be years from now.

Evaluating Your Overall Program

The manner in which you approach evaluation depends in part on whether you are trying to evaluate an entire public participation process, which may have involved a number of public participation activities spread over months or even several years, or you are trying to evaluate your last round of workshops.

Here are three approaches to evaluating entire public participation programs. Each has been used by leading experts on evaluation.

Evaluation Based on Stakeholder-Generated Objectives and Measures

This approach was developed by Judy B. Rosener, from the University of California, Irvine (1983a). There are two premises underlying this approach: (1) public participation goals and objectives need to be spelled out at the beginning of the process, and (2) different stakeholders will have different objectives and measures.

The first step is to conduct a preprocess interview with representatives of key stakeholders. The purpose of this interview is to define goals, objectives, and criteria for measuring goal achievement. An example is shown in Table 16.1, although this shows only one goal each for an agency official and an environmentalist.

TABLE 16.1. STAKEHOLDERS' GOALS AND OBJECTIVES.

Stakeholder	Goal	Objectives	Criteria for Measuring Goal Achievement
Agency official	Create a positive image of the agency.	Provide a mechanism for positive interaction with agency personnel and affected citizens.	Indication of positive interaction between agency personnel and participants.
Environmentalist	Protect the interior wetlands on Sanibel Island.	Develop conditions that are restrictive enough to protect the wetlands	General permit conditions that are acceptable to environmentalists.

The second step is to have participants complete questionnaires following each workshop or major activity. Some criteria can also be measured by evaluator observation during public participation activities.

When the process is concluded, there is one more round of postprocess interviews to determine how well the program satisfied each group's criteria. The final evaluation report displays the levels of satisfaction for each stakeholder.

Rosener argues that this approach to evaluation is not only workable, but provides added benefits by getting stakeholders to clarify their goals, objectives, and measures at the beginning of the process. This, she believes, improves the quality and focus of their participation.

Evaluation Based on Best Practices

A team of British researchers, headed by Lynn Frewer and Gene Marsh, has conducted extensive research on evaluation of public participation for the U.K. Department of Health and Safety Executive, with a goal of developing a set of validated methodological tools to help people running participation programs to evaluate their effectiveness (Frewer, Row, Marsh, and Reynolds, 2001).

They have developed a tool kit based on an analysis of best practices gleaned from public participation literature (see Exhibit 16.1). In other words, the focus of this evaluation is based on how the public participation process is conducted. They believe their research shows that if these best practices are observed, it will result in satisfaction for all concerned.

The actual process for evaluating how well these best practices criteria are met is through the use of questionnaires. The team has developed three measurement instruments (a short questionnaire, a long questionnaire, and a spread-

EXHIBIT 16.1. BEST PRACTICES CRITERIA.

Criteria	Definition
Acceptance criteria	
Representativeness	The participants in the exercise should comprise a broadly representative sample of the affected populace.
Independence	The participation process should be conducted in an independent (unbiased) way.
Early involvement	The participants should be involved as early as possible in the process, as soon as value judgments become salient or relevant.
Influence	The output of the procedure should have a genuine impact on policy.
Transparency	The process should be transparent so that the relevant population can see what is going on and how decisions are being made.
Process criteria	
Resource accessibility	Participants should have access to the appropriate resources to enable them to successfully fulfill their brief.
Task definition	The nature and scope of the participation task should be clearly defined.
Structured decision making	The participation exercise should use or provide appropriate mechanisms for structuring and displaying the decision making.
Cost-effectiveness	The process should in some sense be cost-effective from the point of view of the sponsors.

Source: Frewer, Row, Marsh, and Reynolds (2001). Reproduced with permission.

sheet to help with the analysis), which can be distributed by e-mail. Each evaluation criterion is assessed against a number of different measures.

Evaluation Based on Social Goals

Thomas C. Beierle and Jerry Cayford (2002), from Resources for the Future, a major Washington, D.C., think tank, propose an evaluation approach that focuses on the desired outcomes—what they call the "social goals"—of public participation. They identify five "social goals":

Goal 1. Incorporating public values into decisions

Goal 2. Improving the substantive quality of decisions

Goal 3. Resolving conflict among competing interests

Goal 4. Building trust in institutions

Goal 5. Educating and informing the public

Beierle developed a methodology to evaluate the performance of a citizen advisory group at a former army base, now in the process of being cleaned up and transferred to the community, based on these social goals. Subsequently, Beierle and Cayford evaluated 239 public participation cases carefully developing scores for how well each case performed on the five goals.

Evaluating the Evaluation Models

Which of these three approaches is the best depends on the situation. If you are particularly concerned with the reaction of key stakeholder interests to the public participation program, you may want to use the stakeholder-generated goals approach. Also, if you think there is value in having various stakeholders (including the agency) think through carefully what public participation success means in the context of this particular issue, then it is a useful approach. One disadvantage of the approach is the amount of time it takes to do all the front-end interviews. Another disadvantage is having to decide what the evaluation means if you end up with some groups thinking the program was a success and others thinking it was a failure. If, for example, some stakeholders believe the program was a success (the process was good) and other groups think it was a failure (their viewpoint didn't prevail), what conclusions can you draw from this for how to improve your program?

The second approach is the best-practices approach. The list of best practices that Frewer, Row, Marsh, and Reynolds (2001) identify is helpful, although not every criterion applies to the use of every technique. For example, the appropriate time for mediation is likely to be toward the end of the process, not early in it. But I would feel very good, as a public participation practitioner, if a program I designed met all those goals. Also, I would very much want to know if the program did not follow these best practices. Unless there was a compelling reason, such as a particular best practice not being applicable to the technique we chose, I would want to make some changes in future programs.

The problem is that I've conducted public participation processes that met all those goals but were still not considered a success. This usually had something to do with the context in which the program occurred. Sometimes the agency had done a poor job of defining the question it was asking the public. Sometimes it didn't do an adequate job with the engineering or environmental study and had to repeat the process. Other times a political event intervened, and a decision was imposed on the agency. Sometimes the public was so divided and adversarial (either with the agency or between stakeholders) that nothing positive could happen, no matter how well designed the public participation program was. So there are times when I've felt we satisfied all the process goals, and the program was still perceived as a failure.

The advantage of the social goals approach is that there is almost universal acceptance that those are in fact the presumed outcomes of a public participation program. So you don't have to spend a lot of time getting buy-in to those goals.

If a major concern is justifying public participation to upper management, the social goals approach would be most persuasive to them. The social goals approach also incorporates impacts resulting from the context in which the public participation program occurs. But I'm not sure whether the information I get back from a social goals evaluation helps me pinpoint exactly the changes I need to make in the public participation program activities in order to be a success. So if the primary reason for conducting the evaluation is to identify needed improvements in the program, the social goals approach may not be that effective.

Although each of the three approaches uses different standards by which to measure the success of a public participation approach, the methodologies for measuring success really come down to three basic techniques: (1) interviews, whether preprogram, postprogram, or both, (2) questionnaires, or (3) observation by a trained neutral party.

Evaluating Specific Public Participation Activities

There will be many situations where what you want to do is evaluate specific public participation activities. Instead of evaluating your entire public participation program, for example, you may want reactions to your last round of workshops.

The admonishment to be clear on your criteria for success applies whether you're doing a full-fledged (and possibly expensive) evaluation program or you simply want a quick impression of how a specific activity went. Either way, you need to define what constitutes success, and you may want to be sure that management buys into those criteria, so that they assess the program the same way you do.

Here are a few techniques for getting a quick assessment of the success of your public participation activities.

Hand-In Response Forms

One way to increase the number of comments you receive during public meetings and workshops is to give participants a hand-in response form on which they can write comments. Many people who choose not to speak will complete these forms. The questions do not have to be limited to the topic under discussion. Put a few questions on the form such as: "How do you evaluate [using a scale] the manner in which the meeting was run?" "What changes do you suggest?" "What other information would you like to receive?" "What other public participation activities would you like to see?" This will give you a quick read on public reaction to the meeting and may also provide an early warning of any problems.

Mail-In Response Form for Newsletters

Another way to increase the number of people commenting is to include a response form in your newsletters. Design it so it can be folded over and mailed. You can ask questions about the newsletter itself or about other public participation activities to give you a quick assessment of how you're doing.

Interviews

If I am conducting a public participation program that spans several years, I normally schedule a round of interviews at the front end of the process, the conclusion of each major stage, and the end of the process. Because I am a practitioner rather than a researcher, I am interested in almost anything I can learn that can help me understand how groups are viewing the process. Often this is subjective material that is very difficult to quantify from a research perspective. Also, I learn information about how the entire decision-making process is viewed, with the public participation process only a part of that.

People can make comments in interviews about what is happening within their own groups and how they perceive actions of the various groups that they cannot say out loud in public forums. Often this kind of information is exactly what you need to do a better job, but it doesn't always result in quantitative research.

Advisory Committee Review

If you have established an advisory committee, consult with it when you plan public participation activities, but also occasionally ask, "How are we doing with our public participation program?" Not only will group members have their own impressions, they'll probably know what other opinion leaders in the community are thinking.

Focus Group Review

Some of my clients, particularly corporate clients, use focus groups to help them evaluate their publications. They take draft versions of their publications to the focus group before distributing them to the public. Focus groups have been helpful in identifying information that was seen as biased and have also identified important questions that were not addressed in the publications.

Checkpoint Meetings

When you design a public participation program, build in some checkpoints at which you assess whether you need more public participation activities than originally planned, fewer activities, different activities, or something else. No one, no matter how expert, can entirely anticipate the level of public interest or controversy that will be generated by an issue. Checkpoint meetings provide a scheduled opportunity for the planning group to get together again and reassess. Because they're a scheduled part of the program, you don't have to have a major crisis on your hands before you get together and talk. These meetings also provide opportunities for different parts of the agency to discuss perceptions about how the program is being run. It's not unusual for various parts of your agency to argue for different approaches based on different assessments of public reaction. Sometimes these differences can be resolved only by agreeing to a particular approach until the next checkpoint. Then the decision about how to proceed from there can be based on actual experience of how the public responded.

Postmortems

It's helpful to meet to assess what worked well and what went wrong after each public participation program. The entire purpose of these sessions should be future oriented: What did this experience teach us that we want to do differently in the future? Blame fixing should be avoided. Who messed up in the past is not nearly as important as how you're going to do well in the future.

Polls

From time to time organizations or agencies conduct polls to assess public attitudes. The next time your agency does a poll, include a few questions about recent public participation programs to see how they were received (or whether people even knew about them).

◆ ◆ ◆

A major advantage of doing a good evaluation program is that it requires you to have a thorough discussion upfront about what constitutes success. Public participation practitioners often carry around an almost unconscious set of criteria in their head, something very similar to the best practices list discussed above. But this does not mean that others involved in the project, particularly agency management, either understand or share the values that underlie the practitioner's personal list of criteria. By discussing how you are going to evaluate your program, you also initiate a process to get commitment and buy-in for what you are doing. You'll often learn important lessons from the evaluation that are essential for improving your practice of public participation.

References

Beierle, T., and Cayford, J. *Democracy in Practice: Public Participation in Environmental Decisions.* Washington, D.C.: Resources for the Future, 2002.

Frewer, L., Row, G., Marsh, R., and Reynolds, C. *Summary Project Report: Public Participation Methods: Evolving and Operationalizing an Evaluation Framework.* Norwich, U.K.: Department of Health and Health and Safety Executive, Institute of Food Research, 2001. [www.dh.gov.uk/assetRoot/04/07/61/92/04076192.pdf].

Rosener, J. B. "The Sanibel Evaluation: What Was Learned?" In J. L. Creighton, J. Delli Priscoli, and C. M. Dunning (eds.), *Public Involvement Techniques: A Reader of Ten Years Experience at the Institute for Water Resources.* Alexandria, Va.: Institute for Water Resources, 1983a. (Rev. ed. 1998.)

Rosener, J. B. "User-Oriented Evaluation: A New Way to View Citizen Participation." In G. Daneke, M. W. Garcia, and J. Delli Priscoli (eds.), *Public Involvement and Social Impact Assessment.* Boulder, Colo.: Westview Press, 1983b.

CHAPTER SEVENTEEN

USING PUBLIC PARTICIPATION CONSULTANTS

Consultants can play a useful role in helping to design and implement a public participation program. This chapter describes the different kinds of consultants and the different roles they can play.

Types of Consultants

The first step is to be clear on what kind of consultant you are looking for. There are different roles that a consultant can play.

Facilitation

A facilitator is a neutral party brought in to help design and conduct meetings. Facilitators have been trained in meeting leadership, and it is their job to ensure that everybody gets listened to and to keep the meeting on track. The facilitator is given a leadership role in conducting the meetings, but has no authority when it comes to the substance of decisions. Because he or she has no position regarding the content of the meeting, participants can be assured that the meeting is being run fairly, without advantage to any group or position.

Even if people on staff are skilled at facilitation, there may still be times when a neutral facilitator is needed. When there is controversy, the agency may be viewed as one of the actors rather than a neutral party. Under those conditions, a staff person may not be accepted as a credible neutral, no matter how skilled he or she is in facilitation.

Process Design and Management

An experienced public participation consultant can help you design a public participation program. He or she may have extensive experience with a wide range of public participation techniques and may help you select which techniques are useful in your situation.

Keep in mind the lessons discussed in other chapters. If a consultant simply prescribes a public participation plan, it is likely to be accepted by some without much thought but resisted by others because "it wasn't invented here." Have the consultant help your team develop the plan, so that the team feels emotional ownership for the plan rather than just accept a consultant's plan.

Program Implementation

Some organizations do not have internal staff with the skills or experience to implement a full-scale public participation program, or they need additional staff to implement the program. These organizations may want to retain a full-service firm that will implement services in addition to facilitation and process design—for example:

- Writing newsletters or fact sheets
- Preparing layouts of newsletters or fact sheets
- Developing and maintaining mailing lists
- Preparing summaries of public comment
- Preparing and sending mailings
- Maintaining the Web site for the public participation program
- Setting up meeting rooms and arranging meeting logistics
- Scheduling briefings or interviews
- Scheduling media interviews, talk shows, or editorial board interviews

A number of public participation consultants can offer some or all of these services. The one concern with contracting for much or all of the implementation of a public participation program is the danger that organizational decision makers will become detached from the process and will be insulated from day-to-day contact with the public.

Even if you hire a full-service firm, be sure to keep the internal team involved in developing the public participation plan, playing an active role in all meetings and workshops, and participating in periodic reviews and checkpoint meetings so they remain emotionally involved in the program. Effective public participation is not just a task on a checklist that needs to be completed. It is an integrated part of the decision making process.

Pointers for Using Consultants

Consultants come in all sizes and shapes, with very different levels of experience. Daily rates also differ considerably. In theory, these rates reflect different levels of expertise, but this is not always the case.

The first question to ask is which of the three consultant uses you need: meeting facilitation, process design, or program implementation. There are far more qualified meeting facilitators than there are people with extensive experience in process design. Many of those helping out with program implementation will be at an administrative or even clerical level. You don't need, and you can't afford, people with years of experience designing and conducting public participation programs to put out mailings or set up interviews.

You also need to consider the level of authority that a consultant must have. If you need a consultant who is perceived as a heavyweight in order for management to feel comfortable with the process or to bridge differences between parts of your organization, then you may need someone with a great deal more experience and reputation than if you primarily need someone who is good at program implementation.

There are times when hiring a consultant has value because this person can say things to management and be an authority in a way that internal staff cannot. If this is a function you need the consultant to play, share this with the consultant and know your consultant well. Some consultants are comfortable with raising questions with management and some are not.

You also need to consider the level of innovation that is required. If you expect your program to be rather simple and straightforward, you may not need someone with years of experience. If you are designing a program that is extremely controversial or highly innovative or cutting edge, then you may want someone with considerable experience, and you particularly want someone with some passion for the kind of innovation you require.

One place to start a search for a consultant is the International Association for Public Participation. This association, made up of public participation practitioners and people interested in public participation, maintains membership rosters that include descriptions of people's experience and specialties (www.iap2.org).

Once you have selected a consultant, don't put this person in the position of speaking for your agency. The public participation consultant may be an advocate for the participation process but should not be an advocate for organizational policy. When it comes to policies, the agency should always be represented by its own staff. This protects it from having consultants make commitments they have no authority to make, and it protects consultants from losing their subject matter neutrality.

PART SIX

PUBLIC PARTICIPATION IN ACTION

Throughout this book, I have emphasized that there is no one-size-fits-all public participation program. Each program should be designed in response to the specific needs of the issue, the situation, and the stakeholders.

Chapter Eighteen describes three public participation programs that represent three very different kinds of public participation. The Salt River Project case centered entirely around a task force, albeit a task force with obligations to reach out to the broader public. The Central Arizona Water Control Study was a large-scale public participation program, in which many (indeed, almost all) of the techniques described in previous chapters are employed. The Hewlett Packard case was a small-scale neighborhood project, although it had the potential to become a much more controversial issue.

I introduce each case with a discussion of the main issues that concerned me as I was involved in program design. Each case ends with a brief description of the outcome of the program.

CHAPTER EIGHTEEN

PUBLIC PARTICIPATION CASES

The three cases in this chapter provide a sense of what a public participation program is like, from beginning to end. These also illustrate very different types of public participation.

Salt River Project Task Force

The client, a large electric utility from the greater Phoenix, Arizona, area, approached us having already decided that it wanted to set up a citizen task force composed of representatives of all customer classes. After initial discussions with the company, it became clear that a task force was a giant step for this company, and using other techniques that involved more people from the community was not an option.

There were four major considerations during the design of this process:

• The company's credibility was very low due to a variety of prior circumstances and events. If the company selected the task force itself, the task force was likely to be seen as simply a tool of the company, and task force recommendations would have little credibility.

• One of the main issues with any task force or advisory committee is whether the members can deliver their constituency—that is, when the process is over, will the various stakeholders represented on the task force perceive themselves as having been fully represented, or will they simply dismiss the conclusions of the task force as being decided by a small group that represents nobody but themselves?

• People who chose to be part of the task force needed a basic education in running an electric utility before they could participate intelligently in some of the complex issues they would be considering. But with the company's low credibility, anything the company told them was far more likely to be considered indoctrination rather than education.

• The company's management wanted to have company staff interact directly with task force members, believing this was the way staff would build skills working with the public. This meant they did not want to use outside consultants to advise the task force on rate structures and other technical issues. We accepted this constraint, although at one point we reached an impasse and had to get company management to reverse this policy.

As you will see, the process of selecting the participants was a rather elaborate, and expensive, process involving, among other things, personal interviews of 110 candidates for membership on the task force. This paid off. There was little criticism of the task force membership.

We also worked diligently to build connections from the task force back to the community. One of our primary considerations when selecting task force members was that they had some mechanism, and a willingness to make the effort, to communicate with the members of the customer class they supposedly represented. Each task force member prepared a constituency representation plan, discussing how he or she would communicate with the constituency he or she was supposed to represent. The task force as a whole conducted public meetings to get comments on their draft recommendations before those recommendations were sent on to the company's board of directors.

Case Description

The Salt River Project (SRP) is a publicly owned electric utility that supplies water and electricity to major parts of the suburban area near Phoenix. SRP's service area includes Scottsdale, Tempe, and other communities.

During the period when this public participation process occurred, SRP was going through a difficult time politically. Its credibility was very low. At the same time, federal law required SRP (and all other utilities nationally) to review a number of policies on which rates were based. The purpose of this review was to ensure that policies encouraged energy conservation rather than increased energy use.

SRP management feared that without some level of consensus among concerned stakeholders, this policy review, particularly given SRP's low credibility at the moment, would turn into a political nightmare. SRP decided that it wanted to establish a citizen task force to review these policies and make recommendations to the board. It contacted my public participation firm to help design and implement the program.

The consultants and management first agreed on a list of the classes of customers who needed to be represented, such as single-family residential, apartment dwellers, apartment owners, industry, low-income residential, senior citizen residential, and commercial. SRP then included an announcement in its monthly bill stuffer that it was setting up the task force and invited people to apply to represent different customer groups. From the beginning, people were told that an important criterion would be members' ability to communicate with the constituency they were supposed to represent. The bill stuffer also announced that the task force would be publishing a newsletter and asked customers to indicate whether they wanted to receive the newsletter. More than ten thousand people said they wanted to receive the newsletter.

One hundred ten people applied to be on the task force. This was considerably more than expected, so the consultants worked with management to develop a list of criteria. Then the public participation consultants interviewed each candidate individually and developed ratings for each applicant, within the class of customers the applicant proposed to represent. The consultants reported back to management and, working with management, developed a list of task force members representative of all the classes of SRP customers.

The first few meetings of the task force consisted of training on how a utility company works. Because SRP's credibility was low, these classes were taught by professors from local universities or other independent consultants. One of the public participation consultants served as facilitator of the task force until the task force selected a chair, and the chair attended some facilitation training.

From the beginning, the task force agreed to work on a consensus basis. The logic was that if the task force made decisions by a majority vote, that would communicate to the board of directors that stakeholders were divided. But if they could make recommendations by consensus, the board would have to take the recommendations seriously.

The consensus rule was put to an early test. The first policy under consideration had to do with providing electricity to people who could not afford it. Most of the people on the task force argued that SRP was not a welfare agency and shouldn't have to support people who couldn't pay. But one individual, representing low-income people, claimed that electricity was a basic need, and there had to be some way of providing for people who could not afford it. As the afternoon wore on and as the facilitator used up much of her credibility insisting on the consensus rule, one person finally said in frustration, "Look, I'd be happy to donate myself to provide electricity for these people. I just don't think it's the responsibility of the electric company." This comment inspired another task force member to come up with the idea of a check-off box on everybody's bill that would allow SRP to add one dollar to their bill each month to go into a fund set aside to provide electricity for low-income people. Ultimately this idea was adopted by the SRP board and proved to be a huge success. In fact, the concept has been adopted by nearly half of the utilities in the United States.

Another crisis arose when the task force wanted to test out some new concepts for designing rates. SRP staff responsible for rates argued that SRP's revenue needs could not be met using the new policies, and a stalemate ensued. Ultimately the public participation consultants went to the SRP general manager and asked him to provide funds for an independent rates consultant. The consultant was given the assignment of trying to design a rate structure using the premises proposed by the task force while still meeting SRP's revenue requirements. Several weeks later, the consultant came back with a recommendation that met both goals. SRP's rates staff adopted the consultant's proposal and submitted the new structure to the board of directors, which ultimately approved it.

One of the key qualifications for selection of task force members was the ability to communicate with the class of customers they were supposed to be representing. Each task force member was asked to prepare a constituency consultation plan, which they then discussed with the public participation consultant. A member of the task force also became the editor of the newsletter describing the task force's activities that was sent to ten thousand SRP customers. As the task force got close to finalizing its recommendations, it also conducted several public meetings during which it discussed proposed recommendations with the public.

Ultimately the task force completed a review of the thirteen policies and standards that had to be reviewed under federal law. Under SRP procedures, there was then a series of formal public hearings, followed by a decision by the board.

Case Outcome

Because the task force made unanimous recommendations, with representatives of all major customer classes agreeing to the recommendations, its recommendations had great credibility and political force. All of the recommendations were adopted by SRP's board of director, with a few minor changes.

The U.S. Department of Energy, the federal agency overseeing the policy review, was so pleased that it asked SRP to prepare a summary of the process, which the Energy Department then distributed to other utilities as an example.

Central Arizona Water Control Study

This was a massive study and a massive public participation process that spread over three years. The public participation program alone cost approximately $1 million (in 1980 dollars). I was responsible for overall design of the public participation program and oversaw its implementation. But there was also a full-time public participation person (Martha Rozelle, now one of the leading lights in the field) responsible for day-to-day implementation, with considerable staff support from others. At the time, this was one of the largest public participation programs ever, with both public information and public participation activities targeted at the greater Phoenix, Arizona, area (a huge geographical area).

This was an extremely high-visibility study. The assistant secretary of the Department of Interior and the governor were directly involved. There was substantial polarization in the community. Downtown business interests and agriculture were lined up in support of Orme Dam. Environmentalists and the Fort McDowell Indians (a portion of their reservation would be flooded if the dam were built) were just as opposed. In fact, during the first round of workshops, environmentalists handed out leaflets describing how to manipulate the workshop to produce the result they desired.

Because this was a multiyear planning study, one of the main design considerations was to ensure that the public participation activities were well integrated into the planning process. The goal was to be sure that when we reached key decision points, we had not only the needed environmental and engineering data but also a real sense of community attitudes.

Case Description

In 1968, the U.S. Congress passed legislation authorizing the Central Arizona Project, one feature of which was a dam, to be known as Orme Dam, at the confluence of the Salt and Verde rivers near Phoenix. The purpose of the dam was to provide irrigation water and flood protection to the Phoenix metropolitan area. Stiff opposition to the dam emerged. One reason was that the reservoir behind the proposed dam would flood out fifteen thousand acres of the Fort McDowell Indian Community, located near the confluence of the two rivers. In addition, the reservoir would have flooded out bald eagle nesting sites, and the upstream portion of the Verde River is very sensitive environmentally. In more recent years, one portion has been designated a Wild River, and another portion has been designated a Scenic River, designations designed to protect the river from future development.

In 1977, President Carter placed Orme Dam on a list of western water projects he wanted deauthorized. However, in an eighteen-month period in 1978–1979, there were three major floods in the Phoenix area and a resulting political outcry for construction of Orme Dam. The Carter administration continued to be opposed to the dam but, in the face of the political heat, agreed to a compromise directing the U.S. Bureau of Reclamation and U.S. Army Corps of Engineers to conduct a study of all the alternatives, including the dam. The study was known as the Central Arizona Water Control Study (CAWCS).

This was a major study, with funding at a level of approximately $10 million. Management of the study was shared by the two agencies, since the Bureau of Reclamation is responsible for development of irrigation water supplies and the Army Corps of Engineers is responsible for flood control. The governor, Bruce Babbitt (later secretary of the interior), also had a seat at the table, but he was usually represented by the director of the Arizona Department of Water Resources. The bureau and Corps of Engineers retained a large environmental-engineering firm to conduct the studies and prepare the environmental documentation. The public participation team was part of this contract.

Before the study team was selected, the governor appointed an advisory committee representing all the stakeholders, including water users, environmental groups, the Fort McDowell Indian community, and downtown business interests. Because the governor was involved in setting up the committee, the members of the committee were political heavyweights, including the mayor of Phoenix and the president of Arizona Public Service, the electric utility in Phoenix. When he was setting up the committee, the governor announced that if the committee could agree on a preferred alternative, he would adopt that option as his own and advocate it to the federal government.

Once established, the advisory committee met approximately monthly over the life of the study. Because everything about the study was controversial, meetings were planned by a steering group that included the chairman of the committee (appointed by the governor), the director of the Arizona Department of Water Resources, project managers from the Bureau of Reclamation and Corps of Engineers, the consultant study director, and the public participation staff.

There was considerable controversy around the study methodologies, particularly those for evaluating wildlife habitats and assessing social impacts on Indian tribes. The study established a technical advisory group consisting of technical experts from federal, state, and local agencies to resolve issues about methodology. If issues could not be resolved at that level, there was a policy group consisting of the local senior managers of the Bureau of Reclamation and Corps of Engineers, and the director of the Arizona Department of Water Resources.

Throughout the three years of the study, the study team published a series of periodic newsletters providing background information and updates on the studies and the alternatives under consideration. The study mailing list grew to more than five thousand people who received the newsletters on a regular basis.

There were three major rounds of workshops during the study, with workshops held in six or seven communities during each round. The first round of workshops discussed the project purposes and involved the public in identifying criteria for selecting and evaluating alternatives. The second round evaluated a number of elements (separate actions that could be part of plans). The final round evaluated alternative plans. Each round of workshops was announced with paid advertisements in newspapers and on the radio. Study leaders were also interviewed on talk shows. Many of the workshops were attended by several hundred people.

During the first round of workshops, it became clear that there was little trust between the study team and environmental groups. In fact, after attending the first night of the first round of workshops, environmentalists prepared a handout on how to manipulate the workshop activities to produce the result the environmentalists desired. This led to the recognition that direct meetings were needed between the study staff, agency project managers, and environmental managers. Several subsequent sessions led to improved trust by and with environmental groups.

As the selection of alternative drew closer, one member of the public participation team spearheaded the use of multiattribute utility analysis (see Chapter Seven) to assist in understanding the underlying values of the stakeholders, and a consultant was retained to assist with this process. Initially a list was developed of the key attributes by which alternatives could be evaluated. These were visualized as branches and twigs. A branch might be "economics." Twigs might be benefit-cost ratio, total cost amortized, or local economic benefits. An "environmental" branch might have twigs such as endangered species habitat, game species habitat, water quality, and air quality.

Study staff were asked to rank the alternatives for each twig. That is, they ranked the alternatives based on attributes such as benefit-cost ratio, net present value, acres of natural habitat affected, and many others.

Public participation staff then met with homogeneous groups. For example, environmental groups were invited to one meeting, agriculture to another, and downtown business interests to another. During these meetings, these groups were asked to rank the branches, that is, how important cost should be in comparison to environment compared to flood control or other major branches. Public participation staff then analyzed the values systems of the stakeholders and compared those values with how well the alternatives performed in reaching those values.

At the second round of meetings, the public participation staff reported back on how well the alternatives satisfied the values priorities each group had identified in its first meeting. This produced some surprises. It turned out that Orme Dam, strongly supported by agriculture and downtown business interests, didn't satisfy the values expressed by those groups as well as another alternative that involved two smaller dams, one on the Verde River and one on the Aqua Fria River, located northwest of Phoenix. More surprising, this alternative also performed best for the values expressed by environmental groups.

This information ultimately proved to be important in softening the rigid positions taken by some of the stakeholders. Over the years, the fight over Orme Dam had become a power struggle, a fight over who is in charge. When provided information showing that stakeholders could meet their own interests and values best by picking another alternative entirely, people began to rethink their positions.

Case Outcome

Because the governor had committed to adopt the position taken by the Governor's Advisory Committee, the final meeting of the committee was pivotal in reaching a decision. During that meeting, the committee voted twenty-three to one to adopt the two-dam solution on the Verde and Aqua Fria rivers. The one holdout was the leader of an environmental group who continued to be unhappy with a dam affecting the Verde River.

The agencies and the governor adopted the two-dam solution. However, a later lawsuit by the environmental group that opposed the dam on the Verde River was settled when the agencies agreed to proceed only with the dam on the Aqua Fria River. This dam, known as the New Waddell Dam, has now been built and is in operation. It could be the last major dam built in the United States for a generation.

Subsequently a doctoral candidate conducted an analysis of four public participation programs conducted by the Bureau of Reclamation, including the CAWCS study as one of the cases (Linda Loveless, personal communication). The public rated the CAWCS public participation process as the only one of the four where they felt their participation had made a difference and it was frequently described as the kind of public participation that should be conducted by federal agencies.

Hewlett Packard Office Building

Hewlett Packard (HP) wanted to build a new office building on the site of a former factory that had been empty for two years. Ordinarily that would seem to be a relatively uncontroversial project. But this project had considerable potential for controversy.

First, the project was in Palo Alto, California, where most major projects are controversial. Palo Alto is the home of Stanford University and the birthplace of Silicon Valley. There is a significant intellectual community, and issues about development within the community are often infused with strident ideological fervor; controversies over local development have been described as a blood sport. Property values are extremely high. Homes often cost far more than an average person can afford, and home owners protect the value of their homes zealously. There is also an avid activist community whose primary and continuing concern is to advocate the need to include new affordable housing as part of virtually all new projects within the city.

The project was surrounded on two sides by single-family residences, directly across the street. These residents were being asked to accept a large office building in their neighborhood. Two years earlier, the City of Palo Alto had conducted a planning workshop in which participants proposed that the site serve multiple purposes, not just an office building, including affordable housing. City planners did not want to make decisions that seemed to undercut their own planning workshop, and HP managers did not want company management to be dealing with a major political controversy in the community where management lived.

During the first meetings with the HP staff, I found that they had a number of very different reasons for proceeding with the project. I pointed out that HP needed to be able to give the community a clear statement of need and observed that there were conflicting explanations for why the project was needed.

I also argued that despite HP's excellent reputation in the community, the project was not certain to receive approval. If the project became entangled in the many issues being raised by activist groups, such as demands for affordable housing, there could be significant delays; the project might even become untenable. If HP wanted to get its permits, it would need to work directly with neighbors to resolve as many of their concerns as possible. If the neighbors felt their concerns were not being addressed, they might form a coalition with activists to oppose the project. HP's goal should be to ensure that neighbors felt their needs were best met by working cooperatively with the company. That would require a far more active public participation process than the company normally used when siting such projects.

HP believed my observations were valid but was not able to provide a quick answer. Instead there was a period of several months during which HP management revisited these questions. Ultimately they committed to a significant public participation program with neighbors. In fact, they were prepared to mount a larger public participation program than the project ultimately required.

One of my major goals in designing the program was to ensure that HP established a relationship with the immediate neighbors before the issue became a communitywide issue. I was concerned that if the project got caught up in the continuing planning wars in Palo Alto, we would soon have activists speaking for the residents rather than the residents speaking for themselves.

Under these circumstances, I recommended techniques that used one-on-one communication with each neighboring household or business rather than techniques involving a large number of people, such as large public meetings. Calling on individual homes is staff intensive, but it often saves considerable wear-and-tear in the long run. I have found this approach to be very effective, particularly in cases involving perception of risk.

Case Description

The site at 395 Page Mill Road is a large area that was the location of HP's first factory, the first building the company occupied after it moved from the now-famous Palo Alto garage in which it was founded in 1936. (HP is considered to be the progenitor of Silicon Valley.) The factory, while historic, was an unattractive and utilitarian building that aroused little impulse for preservation. In addition to the original building were five or six newer buildings on the site in which manufacturing operations continued until around 1995, when manufacturing operations were moved from Palo Alto. For two years, the site had been vacant, surrounded by a large security fence. Nearby residents had not had to experience traffic or noise from the site for several years.

The site is bounded on two sides by a residential neighborhood. Although the homes are modest by Palo Alto standards, they would have a purchase price in the vicinity of $700,000 to $900,000 (in 2005). This is a neighborhood in transition. At one time it was sprinkled with auto repair shops, auto body shops, a print shop, and other small-scale industrial uses. Some of these operations still remain, and a few former shops have been converted to live-work space for artists. The third side of the site remains commercial, with a frozen food packaging plant and a Mercedes dealer the nearest businesses. The fourth side of the site is bounded by Page Mill Road, a major four-lane thoroughfare. Across Page Mill is a luxury office building and a high-density apartment complex.

Within the past few years, there had been a major controversy in this neighborhood when a firm was given a permit to open a giant retail computer and electronics store in an old warehouse two blocks away from the HP site. Neighbors felt the retail store attracted traffic and detracted from the residential nature of the neighborhood. Nevertheless, HP is a highly respected and valued organization within the community.

HP staff met with the city's planning director. He informed them that city staff were not opposed to the project, and, in fact, an office building would be consistent with current planning regulations. However, he pointed out that two years before, the City Planning Department had held a community workshop in which community activists and residents had participated in generating ideas for development of the neighborhood in which the 395 Page Mill site was located. The general conclusion of the participants was that the site should contain a mix of office, retail, and residential uses that fit with the scale and character of the surrounding area. Specifically, the suggestion was made that single-family residences be placed at the edge of the site nearest existing residential neighbors to provide a buffer between the residences and commercial uses. Participants also suggested that new roads be built to bisect the site. These land use policies were cited in a draft comprehensive plan that was under public review. The planning director suggested HP would be wise to recognize that these issues were bound to come up and would need to be addressed.

Above all, the planning director asked that HP "bring him a winner," a project that enjoyed community support, particularly in the light of other controversial projects in which the city was embroiled. He suggested that HP work with neighbors and community leaders and resolve as many issues as possible before bringing its application to the city. He also suggested public participation consultants who could assist HP in developing such a program. HP interviewed these consultants, and I was selected.

The public participation program was planned by a team that included HP's real estate manager, the project manager for potential construction, the architectural firm that would design the building, media relations staff, an attorney, and me. We took a number of steps to work with its neighbors and the community.

Communications Brochure. The team prepared a communications brochure of everything that was known about the site: the site's history as a manufacturing center, a summary of the community workshop that had occurred two years before, HP's conceptual plans for the site (at the "bubble diagram" stage), and HP's desire to solicit community feedback. After door-to-door visits to neighbors, this brochure was mailed to all residents within a three-hundred-foot radius, a number of neighborhood associations, city planning staff, city council members, Architectural Review Board members and other influential city leaders.

Visits to Neighbors. HP prepared a one-page announcement of a community meeting to be held at the site. HP staff and the public participation consultant walked to every home in the immediate neighborhood inviting people to the meeting and leaving it on their doorstep if they were not home. Later HP staff called on all the businesses in the area and mailed the meeting announcement to everybody within a three-hundred-foot radius.

First Neighborhood Meeting. The first community meeting was held at the 395 Page Mill site on a Saturday morning. Approximately twenty-five people were in attendance, all neighbors. As one would expect in Palo Alto, the meeting was very active, even challenging. The major concerns of neighbors were to minimize any traffic impact on the neighborhood; keep all entrances and exits on major streets away from the residences; increase the amount of landscape buffer, particularly where people looking down the street will see the site; avoid a monolithic look ("Don't build a fortress"); and take into account the view down the streets toward the site. Other concerns were site security and protecting the neighborhood from light and noise.

There was a discussion of the earlier city planning workshop on which the city was basing its thinking about possible zoning changes to the site. Only one of the neighbors in attendance had participated in the city's planning workshop two years earlier. Several people were aware of it but viewed the plans developed during that workshop as unrealistic and undesirable for their area.

Meeting with Neighborhood Association Leaders. HP contacted leaders of the three major neighborhood associations in the area and had a separate meeting with them on the same day as the first workshop.

Modifications to Site Plan. HP reviewed the comments from the public meeting. It had no objections to moving the entrances and exits so long as it did not interfere with traffic on Page Mill Road. It met with the city traffic engineer, who had no objections to the changed entrances. So HP worked with its traffic consultant and architects to identify new entrances and exits to the site. HP also concluded that buildings should be located toward the corner of the site away from the neighbors and decided that two or three connected smaller buildings would have less visual impact than a very large single building. The company also decided that it could add more landscaping, concentrating it in places that would be viewed by neighbors looking down the street at the site.

HP reviewed its plans with City Planning Department staff. In these discussions, HP identified the option of not creating as many parking spaces as would be required by city regulations so long as the land was available for parking if it proved to be needed later. This allowed it to increase the amount of landscape buffer significantly, with the understanding that some of that land (on the inside of the buffer) might need to be converted to parking in the future.

City staff raised the issue of housing on the site. HP said that it had no interest in developing housing on the site, and felt that the neighborhood was so transitional that a small area of high-density housing might well be stranded by future development in the neighborhood. But it agreed to raise the issue with neighbors to assess their attitude toward additional housing on the sides of the site nearest existing residences.

Second Invitation and Mailing. HP prepared a second mailing that summarized its understanding of what the neighbors had told it, outlined its response to these concerns, and invited people to a second community meeting. These materials were also sent to city staff and Architectural Review Board members.

Second Neighborhood Meeting. At this meeting, HP staff presented the design changes they proposed based on comments at the first meeting. The neighbors were very pleased that the traffic entrances and exits were removed from streets near residences and pleased as well with the enlarged landscape buffer. HP presented several plans for positioning of buildings on the sites. Most of the neighbors preferred a site plan that minimized the views of the building from residences. On the issue of housing, the neighbors were quite emphatic that they preferred a significant landscape buffer to additional housing. The city traffic engineer, who was in attendance, said they he would relay these sentiments back to Planning Department staff. Subsequently, the city did not push the issue.

Selection of the Site Plan. HP reviewed the comments from the neighborhood meeting and chose the site plan that the neighbors preferred. It then had its architects begin working on the architectural options for the building and on a more detailed landscaping plan.

Third Mailing. HP sent a third mailing to neighbors announcing which site plan had been selected and inviting them to attend a final neighborhood meeting to discuss the exterior design of the building. These materials were also sent to city staff and Architectural Review Board members.

Third Neighborhood Meeting. The third meeting was held in one of the neighbors' home. By this time, the number of attendees had dropped to about eight, but those who attended said the lower attendance was because most of the neighbors were satisfied that HP had responded to their concerns. The comments focused on two exterior design options for the building. Both options seemed generally acceptable to the neighbors.

Case Outcome

HP developed final plans for development of the site and submitted them to the city's Architectural Review Board. These plans included all the commitments the company made to the neighbors.

The Architectural Review Board in Palo Alto consists of five appointed members who are concerned with the architectural character of buildings built in the city, as well as their relationship to the site and surrounding uses. Several of the board members are architects, with strong opinions about both design and planning issues. So long as the project remained relatively uncontroversial, the Architectural Review Board would be the decision maker. If it became controversial, the City Council could decide to review the board's decision, at which point the project would likely become a community-wide controversy. The city was responsible for notifying neighbors and community leaders about the Architectural Review Board hearing.

The HP team was holding its breath. Everything had gone well until now, with HP able to respond to the concerns of neighbors. But had its assessment of neighbors' response been unduly positive? One positive sign was that the major community newspaper ran a story with the headline, "Residents Pleased with HP's Page Mill Plans." The newspaper story quoted a local resident, an activist on development issues, who said, "They bent over backwards to address people's concerns. I gave them my thoughts, and each time they were responsive."

The members of the Architectural Review Board made minor comments about the building design, most of which HP's architects found useful and were able to incorporate into subsequent design drawings. Mostly the Architectural Review Board members commented favorably on HP's efforts to work with the public.

When the time came for public comments, no one from the neighborhood spoke out, nor did any representatives of activist groups. HP chose to interpret this positively, but it seemed a bit anticlimactic after all the hard work.

It was too good to be true. Several weeks later, the City Planning Department called HP and told them that a mistake had been made: the announcement of the Architectural Review Board meeting had not been sent to neighbors and other interested parties, as required. The only way to fulfill legal requirements was to hold the meeting again, after proper notification to neighbors and other interested people.

The second time, four or five neighbors did show up. HP went through its presentation again (which by now included some of the suggestions made during the previous Architectural Review Board meeting). When the time for public comment came, the neighbors did speak out—in favor of the project. The project was unanimously approved by the Architectural Review Board. This time the HP team's sigh of relief was both genuine and lasting.

HP successfully sited and built a 215,000-square-foot office complex across the street from residential neighbors, in a community where development issues are highly charged. Construction of the building is finished. Late in 1999, HP had spun off several of its divisions, including its scientific instrumentation division, to create Agilent Technologies. The newly completed 395 Page Mill office building now serves as the international headquarters offices of Agilent Technologies.

CONCLUSION

Designing and conducting public participation programs is a curious blend of the idealistic and the pragmatic. On the one hand, practitioners are inspired by the sense that they are on the cutting edge of democracy, literally creating new forms of democratic practice. On the other hand, this is always being done in the context of limited budgets, tight schedules, organizational constraints, scientific uncertainty, and political pressures.

Although agencies frequently mouth platitudes about participation, some of the best public participation I have seen has come from agencies that were in some pain, when their credibility was lowest, and they had to take action or face extinction. On these occasions, they wisely chose to open their windows and doors to allow the public to participate in agency decision making, letting the fresh breeze of differing opinions flow in. The result was that these agencies were revitalized and soon enjoyed higher support than ever before. But some of these agencies forgot the lesson, and with the cushion of public goodwill, they began to shut the windows and doors and soon were in pain again.

An old cynic once said, "I trust people when their platitudes and their self-interest say the same thing." I am a firm believer that the values of democracy and the self-interest of agencies do coincide. Public participation can produce better decisions. It can result in greater public acceptance so that programs that might have been blocked by controversy can proceed with public support.

This does not mean that decisions can be made more quickly and more cheaply than they would be by top-down decision making. In my experience, it is a practical reality that participatory decision making takes longer and costs more than command-and-control decision making. But in pluralistic democracies, command decisions rarely stand the test of time. Many agencies have announced decisions and even invested millions of dollars, never to be able to implement their plans due to public opposition.

The real cost of a decision is not how long and how costly it is to reach the decision, but how long it takes and how much it costs to solve the problem. By that measure, public participation is a winner. If you consider the total costs of the project or program, from its inception to satisfactory implementation, public participation usually saves time and money.

This doesn't mean that there aren't some public participation programs that are unsuccessful in getting resolution. Public participation is a bit like a safety program. The measure of success is the number of accidents (or polarized public controversies) prevented. The circumstances that cause accidents, and unsuccessful public participation, are not always in your control. When there is an accident, the remedy is not to dismantle the program but to improve it.

Saving money and time is not the only measure of success. Agencies also have an obligation to build and sustain a strong civic society. Our recent experience watching the efforts of former Soviet bloc countries to establish democracy has been instructive. Although we tend to think of elections as being the essence of democracy, in many of these countries the institutions of voting were established first, but the underpinnings of a strong civil society were not yet there to support full-fledged democracy.

The people who make up our communities and societies possess knowledge and skills that make our democracies work. But that knowledge and skill can atrophy through disuse. Public participation is a way to exercise the skills we need to sustain democratic society and build the base of knowledge that we need not just for the immediate decision, but for many decisions into the future.

I have endeavored in this book to maintain an appropriate balance between the idealistic thrust of participatory theory and the realities I have experienced in more than thirty years of implementing public participation programs. If you are too idealistic, your program may fail in such a way that it not only discredits you but also discredits public participation within your agency. But if you are totally pragmatic, forgetting the democratic impetus beneath the mechanics, you are likely to find yourself burned out, engaged in mundane activities that do not provide the intrinsic meaning you need to stay enthusiastic about what you are doing.

The best balance between idealism and pragmatism, I have found, lies in certain basic themes that have been emphasized throughout this book:

- Make sure your public participation program is an integral part of the decision-making process, not something external to the deliberations that actually result in the decision.
- Use a systematic thought process when you design a public participation program to ensure that you have a clear rationale for the activities you choose to implement.
- Match your public participation program to the specific circumstances of the issue and audience. Don't use cookie-cutter public participation.
- Emphasize interactive approaches in preference to formalized procedures and speechmaking.
- Feel free to innovate, developing new techniques as needed for your situation. This is how the field grew and how it can continue to grow.

Public participation remains a craft, not a science. I don't think it will ever be different. It partakes too much of the messy emotional stuff of intense human interaction, struggles for power, and strongly held beliefs about what is good for our societies. If you plan to design and conduct public participation programs, you will need to develop your craft. I hope this book has been a helpful start, or if you are already experienced at the craft, that it has provided new approaches or ways of addressing problems. I look forward to your contribution to the field.

AN EXAMPLE:
SUNNY GLEN LANDFILL SITING
PUBLIC PARTICIPATION PLAN

This is a public participation plan for the siting of a solid waste landfill for the City of Sunny Glen, California, and unincorporated areas surrounding the town.

Background

In 1999, the California Department of Health Services ordered Sunny Glen to close its existing landfill because seepage from the landfill was causing groundwater contamination. In response, Sunny Glen executed a three-year contract with its adjoining neighbor, Jamesville, to dispose of wastes in an existing landfill owned and operated by Jamesville. Jamesville has announced that it will not extend the contract unless, by the time the three years is up, a new landfill is under construction in Sunny Glen. Any extension would cover only the period until construction of the new landfill is completed.

Sunny Glen already has a solid waste management plan in place, including curbside separation. Several years ago, there was discussion of building an incinerator to convert trash to energy, but this plan was widely opposed by citizens concerned about air quality. The city council does not believe there is any point in reopening this issue.

The Sunny Glen Department of Public Works is the lead agency for the city for siting the project. Site selection must be approved by the city council and will be reviewed by the Los Diablos County Solid Waste Division and the California State Department of Health Services.

Preliminary Consultation

An interagency group has been established consisting of staff from the Sunny Glen Public Works and Planning Departments; Los Diablos County Solid Waste, Planning, and Environmental Compliance Divisions; California Department of Health Services; and representatives from the engineering and environmental consultants. In addition to overseeing the technical studies, this group will be responsible for planning and conducting the public involvement program.

During the preparation of this plan, the members of this team consulted with individual members of the city council, the League of Women Voters, Neighborhoods Against Garbage (NAG), and the presidents of three neighborhood home owners' associations.

Major Issues

The following major issues were identified during the prior consultation interviews:

- The city's credibility: Because the city has claimed for years that the old facility was safe, its credibility as a source of reliable technical information has been badly damaged.
- Health risk and groundwater contamination: Because the old facility was found to be causing groundwater contamination, neighbors of any landfill will be extremely concerned with both health risks and groundwater contamination resulting from the new landfill.
- Land use compatibility: All neighborhoods will be concerned whether a landfill is compatible with existing and future land uses.
- Stigma: Many citizens view landfills as innately undesirable and threatening to property values and the image of their neighborhood.
- Traffic: Citizens will be concerned about noise, dust, and traffic safety from movement of trucks through neighborhoods to the new landfill. This is often expressed as a concern for children en route to or from school.

- Reduction of waste stream: Several environmental groups may oppose siting of the landfill in an attempt to force greater efforts to reduce the amount of waste generated in the community.

Issues Management Program

The following issues management activities will take place to address the major issues identified:

- The city's credibility: The issue of the city's credibility is best addressed by the openness and visibility of this entire public participation program.
- Health risk and groundwater contamination: The impacts of any facility on groundwater will be a major part of the technical work to be performed during this study. In order to ensure that these studies are perceived as credible, the following steps will be taken:

  The technical advisory committee will be asked to develop the scope of groundwater contamination studies to be performed.

  A draft scope of studies will be reviewed with the citizen advisory committee.

  Members of the technical advisory committee will be included in the panel selecting the engineering consultants who will conduct the groundwater studies.

- Land use compatibility: During stage 1, the members of the citizen advisory committee will be taken on a field trip to visit a modern sanitary landfill. Subsequent trips for neighborhood leaders may be scheduled as needed.
- Stigma: A study will be conducted to assess the impact on property values from siting of comparable facilities in other communities. This study will be concluded by the end of stage 1, before alternative sites have been identified. The design of this study will be discussed with both the citizen and technical advisory committees. If the study shows there are property value effects, alternative forms of mitigation will be identified and analyzed during stage 2.
- Traffic: Traffic studies will be conducted for each alternative site. The scope of study and consultant selection will be reviewed with both the citizen and technical advisory committees.

Level of Interest

With the history of the old landfill and the potential for neighborhoods to become organized in opposition to proposed sites, the level of citizen and group interest is expected to be very high, justifying an extensive public participation program.

Interested Groups

Several neighborhood groups, notably NAG, which organized during the closure of the old landfill, are certain to be quite active. Also, each neighborhood in which a potential site is located is likely to become organized while that site is being considered.

Developers and owners of large parcels of land will be both interested and concerned. Future growth of Sunny Glen depends on solving the solid waste problem. The location of the landfill could also influence which areas of the city are developed in the future.

Environmental groups will be concerned with reducing the waste stream and with groundwater contamination. Environmentalists will also want the site selected to have the fewest environmental impacts.

Because of the potential level of controversy, city council members wish to be kept fully informed of all activities, particularly within their electoral district.

Decision-Making Process

The basic stages in the siting process will be as follows:

Stage	*Completion*
Stage 1: Informing the public about the need for a landfill	December 2004
Stage 2: Identifying alternative sites	April 2005
Stage 3: Evaluating alternative sites	February 2006
Stage 4: Selecting a site	June 2006
Stage 5: Construction planning	January 2007

Public Participation Activities

Below are the specific public participation activities that will be conducted at each stage in the decision-making process:

Stage 1: Informing the Public About the Need for a Landfill

Because of the crisis brought about by the closure of the old landfill, the objective of the first stage of the program will be to make the public fully aware of the siting emergency. A second objective is to gain acceptance that the proposed study methodology and public participation plan are adequate. The public participation activities during this stage include:

1. Prepare and distribute a newspaper insert describing why a new landfill is needed. This insert should be signed by as many influential community leaders as possible.
2. Work with newspapers on feature stories to describe the problem.
3. Prepare a slide show and establish a speakers' bureau to make presentations at civic clubs, home owners' association meetings, and other local gatherings.
4. Have city council, city managers, or other recognized leaders appear on talk shows to discuss the problem.
5. Establish both a citizen advisory group and a technical advisory group (with technical representatives from agencies). Hire a facilitator to manage meetings of both advisory groups.
6. Review the study methodology and public participation plan with both advisory groups.
7. Publish newsletter 1 describing (1) project need, (2) the establishment of the advisory groups, (3) the study methodology, and (4) the public participation plan.

Stage 2: Identifying Alternative Sites

During this stage, a number of technical studies will be conducted to identify potential sites. The two public participation objectives for this stage are to (1) ensure that the public is satisfied that all potential sites have been considered and (2) get agreement on the criteria to be used to evaluate sites. The public participation activities during this stage include:

1. Conduct a series of public workshops during which the public will be asked to (1) propose alternative sites for consideration and (2) review the study methodology and public participation process.
2. Conduct a series of meetings with the advisory groups to get agreement on evaluation criteria.
3. Conduct a series of coffee klatches with home owners' associations to discuss proposed evaluation criteria.
4. Publish newsletter 2, describing proposed evaluation criteria and process and announcing a town meeting.
5. Hold a town meeting to receive final comments on the evaluation criteria.

Stage 3: Evaluating Alternative Sites

This stage involves screening out unacceptable sites and identifying final alternatives. The primary public participation objectives are to (1) ensure that the public is satisfied that the alternatives screened out were screened out for good reason and (2) ensure that the public is fully informed about the remaining alternatives. The activities are:

1. Conduct a series of screening workshops with both advisory groups to screen out clearly unacceptable alternatives.
2. Review screening decisions in a series of meetings with home owners' associations.
3. Publish newspaper insert 2 to describe the alternatives that have been dropped and those remaining. Also announce upcoming public workshops.
4. Use paid advertisements to announce public workshops.
5. Conduct a series of public workshops to review remaining alternatives.
6. Publish newsletter 3 describing public comment on remaining alternatives.

Stage 4: Selecting a Site

During this stage, a preferred alternative will be identified and recommended to the city council. The primary public participation objective is to develop as high a level of consensus as possible on a preferred alternative. The public participation activities will be:

1. Conduct a final evaluation workshop with the technical advisory group.
2. Conduct an evaluation workshop with the citizens' advisory group.
3. Conduct a neighborhood workshop with each of the remaining neighborhoods in which there are alternative sites.
4. Hold a retreat with the citizen advisory group to develop recommendations for a preferred site.
5. Conduct briefings with elected officials to announce the advisory group recommendation.
6. Conduct meetings with neighborhood home owners' associations to explain the advisory committee recommendation.
7. Conduct a series of meetings with the neighborhood in which the proposed site is located to identify mitigation measures.
8. Publish newsletter 4 to announce the advisory group recommendation and final public meeting.
9. Conduct the final public meeting to discuss the advisory group recommendation.

10. Publish newsletter 5 to announce the site selection and describe the review process that the city council will use.
11. The city council holds public hearings, as required by city regulations.
12. The city council makes the decision.
13. Publish newsletter 6, announcing the city council decision.

Stage 5: Construction Planning

During this stage, a detailed construction plan will be developed. The primary public involvement objective will be to finalize the mitigation measures and minimize issues during the construction process. The public participation activities during this stage include:

1. Hold a series of coffee klatches in the neighborhood to discuss how construction will proceed and begin to identify neighborhood issues.
2. Establish a new advisory group consisting primarily of neighbors of the landfill, plus one or two members each from the previous citizen advisory group and technical advisory group to ensure continuity and information transfer.
3. Work with the new advisory group to develop alternative approaches for addressing neighborhood concerns and reducing construction impacts.
4. Prepare a handout describing the alternative approaches for addressing neighborhood concerns and inviting people to a series of neighborhood meetings.
5. Conduct a series of neighborhood meetings to get neighborhood reactions to the alternative approaches for reducing construction impacts.
6. Work with the neighborhood advisory group to evaluate the alternative approaches for reducing construction impacts, and develop a proposed plan.
7. Prepare a handout summarizing the proposed plan, and distribute it along with an invitation to a final round of meetings.
8. Hold a series of neighborhood meetings to review the proposed plan.
9. Produce a brochure describing the plan to minimize construction impacts, and mail it to every home in the neighborhood.

Review Points

Meetings to review this plan will be held at the end of stage 1 (December 2004), stage 2 (April 2005), and stage 3 (February 2006).

INDEX